THE IDEALS GUIDE TO

PRESIDENTIAL HOMES AND LIBRARIES

THE IDEALS GUIDE TO

PRESIDENTIAL HOMES AND LIBRARIES

BY PEGGY SCHAEFER

IDEALS PRESS
NASHVILLE, TENNESSEE

ISBN 0-8249-4302-3

Published by Ideals Press
An imprint of Ideals Publications, a division of Guideposts
535 Metroplex Drive, Suite 250
Nashville, Tennessee 37211
www.idealsbooks.com

10 9 8 7 6 5 4 3 2 1

Publisher: Patricia A. Pingry
Art Director: Eve DeGrie
Designer: Marisa Calvin
Managing Editor: Peggy Schaefer
Copy Editors: Amy Johnson, Lisa Ragan

Historical review of presidential biographies: Dorothy Twohig,
Associate Professor Emeritus, Editor-in-Chief Emeritus, *Papers of
George Washington*, University of Virginia.

Portions of the presidential biographies are taken from *Our Presidents: Their Lives and Stories*, by Nancy J.
Skarmeas, copyright © 2000 by Ideals Publications, a division of Guideposts.

Library of Congress CIP data is on file.

Color separations by Precision Color Graphics, Franklin, Wisconsin.
Printed and bound in the U.S.A. by R. R. Donnelley.

Front cover photograph: The White House, Washington, D.C., photo by G.L. French/H. Armstrong Roberts
Back cover photograph: Monticello, courtesy of Monticello/Thomas Jefferson Foundation, Inc.
Title page photograph: Interior of the Woodrow Wilson House, Washington, D.C., courtesy of the Woodrow Wilson House
Photograph, this page: Monticello, courtesy of Monticello/Thomas Jefferson Foundation, Inc.

<u>Note</u>
Hours, prices, and site details in this guide are subject to change. Please call sites for the
most current information prior to planning your travel.

TABLE OF CONTENTS

INTRODUCTION

A journey through the presidential homes and libraries profiled in this guide offers more than a travel experience—it provides a journey through the history of the United States. Each home reveals details of the lives of those who have led our nation, and each library and museum houses papers and artifacts that document the political decisions that have shaped our government.

Many of the early U.S. presidents were deeply involved in the establishment of the United States as an independent nation. They fought in battles, they contributed to the drafting of the nation's founding principles, and they struggled through the challenges of establishing a viable democratic political system. As time passed, the challenges changed—to providing for the social welfare of the American people, to defending the democratic process at home and abroad, and to ensuring a strong domestic economy—yet the desire to move the country forward remained strong.

In visiting these birthplaces, homes, and libraries, one gains a sense of the personal as well as the political lives of our presidents. A walk through Monticello reveals Jefferson's passion for architecture and innovation. A visit to the Adams National Historical Park offers a glimpse into generations of a family who gave years of public service. Franklin D. Roosevelt's Little White House reverberates with the courage of a man who overcame a great personal challenge to lead the country in a time of national crisis. And a visit to the presidential libraries administered by the National Archives and Records Administration provides the opportunity to access the documents and materials related to the administrations of Herbert Hoover, Dwight D. Eisenhower, and Jimmy Carter, to name a few.

In addition to sites related to specific presidents, this guide features profiles of the White House, the grandest presidential home of all; the Library of Congress, where many of the early presidents' papers are archived; and the National Archives and Records Administration, a source of much of the documentation that chronicles the political history of the United States.

The book is organized by president, with a brief biography of each followed by listings of related homes and libraries that are open to the public. The appendix includes state maps; simply note the state in which a site resides and check the corresponding map in the back. (Specific directions to each site are included in each listing.) Indexes in the back of the book are organized by site name and by location for easy cross-referencing.

From West Coast to East Coast, from frontier cabin to state-of-the-art library, the homes, libraries, and museums described within will enlighten and educate visitors who seek to discover the men who formed, led, and sustained our uniquely successful system of government.

GEORGE WASHINGTON

1732–1799
1st President • 1789–1797

George Washington took his oath of office as first president of the United States on April 30, 1789, in New York City. Washington had proven himself a skilled leader both during the Revolutionary War and in his presiding role over the Constitutional Convention in 1787. The country rewarded him by overwhelmingly electing him to the office of president.

Washington was born in Westmoreland County, Virginia, on February 22, 1732, to Augustine Washington and his wife, Mary Ball Washington. Little is known of Washington's childhood except for the fact that his father died when Washington was still quite young, and he was raised mainly by his mother and his half brother Lawrence. Washington married Martha Dandridge Custis, a wealthy Virginia widow, in 1759. Although they had no children of their own, Washington and Martha raised her two children from her first marriage and, later, two of her son's children.

In June 1775, after the outbreak of the American Revolution, Washington was appointed commander in chief of the Continental army. He found his forces unorganized, poorly disciplined, and often insubordinate. Washington overcame these and many other challenges, however, as he stole across the Delaware River to surprise and defeat the British at Princeton and Trenton, survived a winter at Valley Forge, and finally accepted the surrender of General Cornwallis at Yorktown in 1781. General George Washington emerged from the Revolutionary War the most important and popular man in the country and retired from the military to his estate at Mount Vernon.

Soon Washington left retirement to join the movement to strengthen and reorganize the government as it struggled to operate under the Articles of Confederation. He was the unanimous selection of his fellow delegates to be president of the Constitutional Convention, and his presence was pivotal in the national acceptance of the document on which our democracy was founded.

In his first term, Washington made great strides in establishing a new government, and he created precedents that are still followed today. He was less successful in establishing a government without partisanship. By the end of the term, the Republican (forerunner to today's Democratic party) and Federalist parties were emerging. Washington was unanimously reelected for a second term in 1793, but he declined to run for a third term four years later. He retired with Martha to Mount Vernon in 1797 and died there two years later.

Today, our nation's capital, one state, several colleges and universities, and countless counties, towns, villages, and streets are named after the "Father of Our Country."

THIS GOVERNMENT, THE OFFSPRING OF YOUR OWN CHOICE, uninfluenced and unawed, adopted upon full investigation and mature deliberation, completely free in its principles, in the distribution of its powers, uniting security with energy, and containing within itself a provision for its own amendment, has a just claim to your confidence and support. Respect for its authority, compliance with its laws, acquiescence in its measures, are duties enjoined by the fundamental maxims of true liberty. The basis of our political system is the right of the people to make and alter their constitutions of government. But the constitution which at any time exists till changed by an explicit and authentic act of the whole people is sacredly obligatory upon all. The very idea of the power and right of the people to establish government presupposes the duty of every individual to obey the established government. . . .

–from George Washington's Farewell Address, September 17, 1796

MOUNT VERNON

George Washington Parkway, Mount Vernon, Virginia 22121

PHONE: 703-780-2000

www.mountvernon.org

HOURS: daily

ADMISSION: fee; student, senior, and group discounts

WHEELCHAIR ACCESSIBILITY: grounds—yes; mansion—first floor only

Mount Vernon was home to George Washington for more than forty-five years. Here he made his life with Martha, returned from war, retired from public life, practiced pioneering farming methods, and left an indelible stamp of his personality and private tastes. Today, more than one million people per year visit the estate to find the essence of the man known as the "Father of Our Country."

George Washington inherited the property upon the death of his brother Lawrence's widow in 1761. Over the years, he enlarged the mansion and built up the property from 2,000 acres to nearly 8,000 acres comprising five working farms. When Washington inherited the estate, the house consisted of four rooms and the central passage on the first floor plus three bedrooms on the second. Washington raised the mansion from one-and-a-half stories to two-and-a-half stories and extensively redecorated the interior.

George Washington's Mount Vernon

The house is constructed of pine but is rusticated, an exterior decorative treatment that gives the appearance of stone. Washington rebuilt the outbuildings, lanes, and gardens; the grounds around the mansion reflect both his practical and aesthetic sides. From the north to the south are the dependencies where the work of the plantation took place. Along the east-west axis are the gardens and

Pioneer farmer site at Mount Vernon

pleasure grounds where Washington, his family, and guests enjoyed leisurely strolls. Today, the home has been restored to its appearance in 1799, the last year of George Washington's life, and is situated on 500 acres of land.

Tours of the mansion as well as the grounds are available daily. Grounds tours include a variety of outbuildings, such as stables, coach house, smoke house, kitchen, and more. A number of tour options are possible, including adventure maps for children and self-directed audio tours. Additionally, Mount Vernon hosts a wide array of special events throughout the year. Details can be found on their website.

The estate's curatorial collection consists of some 15,000 items—furniture, glass, textiles, paintings, and sculpture—and is largely displayed in the mansion, its out-

The Washington Tomb

buildings, an online exhibition, and the museum facilities. The objects in this collection include either those used by the Washingtons at Mount Vernon or those representative of items known to have furnished their residence.

The library collection includes books, newspapers, pamphlets, and unpublished materials such as manuscripts, photographs, and archives. The collection provides a continuous history of Mount Vernon from the original land patent in 1674 up to the present day. This non-circulating collection is available to visiting scholars by appointment.

The Mount Vernon Ladies' Association, the oldest historic preservation organization in the United States, owns and maintains Mount Vernon. The mansion and its grounds, programs, and events are supported through the donations of individuals, foundations, and corporations, plus income from gate receipts and gift shop and restaurant revenue. Under the Association's 140-year-long trusteeship, Mount Vernon has been authentically restored to its 1799 appearance.

NEAREST AIRPORT: Washington, D.C.; Baltimore, Maryland; Richmond, Virginia
GENERAL DIRECTIONS: Eight miles south of Alexandria off the George Washington Parkway (called Washington Street in downtown Alexandria).
NEARBY ATTRACTIONS: Nearby Washington, D.C., is home to many historic attractions; among them are the White House, presidential memorials, Stephen Decatur House Museum, Woodrow Wilson House Museum, Ford's Theatre, and the Smithsonian Institution.

George Washington's study

GEORGE WASHINGTON BIRTHPLACE NATIONAL MONUMENT

1732 Popes Creek Road, Washington's Birthplace, Virginia 22443

PHONE: 804-224-1732

www.nps.gov/gewa

HOURS: daily; closed Thanksgiving, Christmas Day, and New Year's Day

ADMISSION: fee; student discounts; park passes

WHEELCHAIR ACCESSIBILITY: yes

George Washington was born at Popes Creek Plantation and lived there for the first three years of his life. He also spent extended periods of time on the plantation with his older stepbrother after the death of his father in 1743. Today's visitors can experience a re-creation of an eighteenth-century colonial plantation.

The 550-acre park includes the Memorial House, plantation outbuildings, and scenic natural landscapes from beaches to open farmland to upland forest. The original house burned to the ground on Christmas Day in 1779 and was never rebuilt. The Memorial House, built in 1932, represents a typical Georgian-style home of the upper class of the period—perhaps a bit finer than the original. It is decorated with period furnishings, including a tea table believed to be original to the Washingtons.

A Colonial-style kitchen house was built on the site of the original in 1930. It is furnished with period furniture, cooking utensils, and equipment. Outside is the

The Memorial House (left) and Colonial kitchen (right) at George Washington Birthplace

colonial herb and flower garden, which includes many of the herbs and flowers commonly found in eighteenth-century Virginia. On the other side of the park, visitors can tour the burial grounds where at least thirty-two burials have been found, including those of Washington's father, grandfather, and great-grandfather. Visitors can view replicas of two original gravestones and five memorial tablets.

A leisurely visit takes one to two hours, and the fourteen-minute film shown at the visitor center is recommended as a starting point. Visitors could spend much longer if they choose to visit the hiking trails, picnic areas, and beach areas. Special events are scheduled nearly every month, including the First Inauguration, Revolutionary War Encampment, Founders' Day, and Christmas at Popes Creek. Call for details and dates.

Interest in preserving and restoring the homesite began in 1858, but it was in 1932 that the park officially opened under the National Park Service. It remains under their control today. The George Washington Birthplace National Memorial Association operates the bookstore in the visitor center. The Association is an outgrowth of the Wakefield National Memorial Association that raised funds to build and furnish the Memorial House, kitchen, and gardens. The Association gave the area to the U.S. government in 1931 to celebrate Washington's 200th birthday. All profits from the bookstore are returned to the park.

NEAREST AIRPORT: Fredericksburg, Virginia

GENERAL DIRECTIONS: Located on the Potomac River and Popes Creek, approximately 38 miles east of Fredericksburg. Accessible via Virginia Route 3 and Route 204.

NEARBY ATTRACTIONS: Stratford Hall (Robert E. Lee's birthplace) and Ferry Farm (George Washington's boyhood home).

GEORGE WASHINGTON'S FERRY FARM

Route 3 East at Ferry Road, Fredericksburg, Virginia 22401

PHONE: 540-373-3381

www.kenmore.org

HOURS: Mid-February through December, daily; closed January through mid-February except to school groups by reservation; closed Thanksgiving, Christmas Eve, Christmas Day, New Year's Eve.

ADMISSION: fee; student discounts

WHEELCHAIR ACCESSIBILITY: yes

George Washington spent much of his early childhood at Ferry Farm, although he made extended visits to Mount Vernon during these years as well. It was at Ferry Farm that he received his formal education, learned his love of horses and fishing, and developed his strength of character. Legend holds that it was here a young Washington cut the cherry tree, then admitted so to his father, saying, "I

Ferry Farm Surveyor's Cottage

cannot tell a lie." Ferry Farm was his inheritance upon the death of his father in 1743, and Washington continued to live there with his mother and siblings.

Although the buildings and landscape visitors see today are relatively new, underground traces of the original farm remain. Archaeologists at Ferry Farm are reconstructing the appearance of the farm as George Washington would have known it by locating and recording these buried remains. In addition to the cellar of the dwelling house, the possible remains of a storehouse and sawpit have been identified. Thousands of artifacts have been found as well, including ceramics, glass, clay tobacco pipes—even personal items such as wig curlers and buttons! Plans include the identification of the Washington family outbuildings and yard features, exploration of the ferry landings, and the reconstruction of a survey of Ferry Farm done by George Washington in 1771. Visitor programs focus on archaeology, the environment, and the Civil War.

Interest in preserving the history of Ferry Farm grew as the bicentennial of Washington's birth drew near in the early 1930s. The National Park Service considered undertaking the project but chose instead to focus on Popes Creek, Washington's birthplace. George Washington's Fredericksburg Foundation operates the farm in conjunction with the Kenmore Plantation, home to George Washington's sister. Ferry Farm has been dedicated a National Historic Landmark.

NEAREST AIRPORT: Fredericksburg, Virginia

GENERAL DIRECTIONS: East of Fredericksburg on State Route 3 in Stafford County. Follow Route 3 East (Business) through old town Fredericksburg and cross the river at Chatham Bridge. After crossing the river, stay on Route 3, turn right at split rail fence into Ferry Farm.

NEARBY ATTRACTIONS: George Washington Birthplace National Monument, Historic Kenmore.

JOHN ADAMS

1735–1826
2nd President • 1797–1801

A stubborn and principled man, John Adams made a name for himself early in his career by defending the British soldiers accused of killing three colonists in the Boston Massacre. Despite his strong colonial sympathies and amid a wave of anti-British hysteria, Adams remained resolute, believing the soldiers had been provoked. By the time the trial ended, Adams was known as an intelligent and skilled lawyer.

John Adams was born in 1735 in the Massachusetts Bay Colony. As a child, he dreamed of becoming a farmer, but his family sent him to Harvard, where he discovered his talent for law. He soon became identified with the patriot cause, and he was sent as a delegate to both the First and Second Continental Congresses. Adams served as a diplomat during and after the Revolutionary War and was one of the negotiators to draft the 1782 Treaty of Paris.

Adams served as vice president under George Washington for both his terms, a position he found frustrating. He is quoted as having told his wife, Abigail, "My country has in its wisdom contrived for me the most insignificant office that ever the invention of man contrived or his imagination conceived." In 1797, Adams won a closely contested presidential race against Thomas Jefferson. Abigail, however, was somewhat reluctant to take on the role of first lady. She was a woman of strong opinions and was used to speaking freely with her husband and her colleagues. As she feared, some criticized her for being too outspoken; but Abigail ignored their remarks, continued to advise her husband, and attended meetings of the House of Representatives.

Adams's administration was one of crisis and conflict. The war between the French and British was causing difficulty for United States shipping on the high seas, and the French refused to negotiate without payment of a large bribe. In what became known as the XYZ Affair, Adams refused payment and Congress appropriated money to build new ships and raise a provisional army. Despite early conflicts at sea, Adams held his ground and averted all-out war. Peace secured, Adams nonetheless faced the disapproval of many at home who felt he had failed to defend the nation's honor. His identification with the Alien and Sedition Acts of 1798 added to Adams's growing unpopularity, and he left office after one term.

John Adams was the first president to live in the White House; upon leaving it, he returned to Quincy, Massachusetts, where he issued political statements and engaged in extensive correspondence with Thomas Jefferson. Adams lived to see one of his two sons, John Quincy Adams, elected president in 1825; but he died the next year on July 4, 1826, the same day, coincidentally, as Jefferson's death.

LET THE PULPIT RESOUND WITH THE DOCTRINES AND SENTIMENTS of religious liberty. Let us hear the danger of thraldom to our consciences from ignorance, extreme poverty, and dependence; in short, from civil and political slavery. Let us see delineated before us the true map of man. Let us hear the dignity of his nature, and the noble rank he holds among the works of God— that consenting to slavery is a sacrilegious breach of trust, as offensive in the sight of God as it is derogatory from our own honor or interest or happiness—and that God Almighty has promulgated from heaven liberty, peace, and goodwill to man!

–from John Adams's article in the *Boston Gazette* in 1765, in response to the Stamp Act

ADAMS NATIONAL HISTORICAL PARK

135 Adams Street, Quincy, Massachusetts 02169

PHONE: 617-770-1175

www.nps.gov/adam

HOURS: mid-April through mid-November, daily; visitor center open year-round

ADMISSION: fee; student discounts; park passes

WHEELCHAIR ACCESSIBILITY: yes, except second floor of Old House

The fourteen-acre Adams National Historical Park commemorates members of the distinguished Adams family who gave years of service to the nation. Foremost among them are John Adams and his son John Quincy Adams, our second and sixth presidents, respectively. The park contains a number of structures, including the birthplaces of John Adams and John Quincy Adams and the Old House. The homes feature original furnishings, decorative arts, and personal possessions of four generations of the Adams family. There is also a visitor center nearby.

The Birthplaces

The John Adams and John Quincy Adams Birthplaces are the oldest presidential birthplaces in the United States. They are located only seventy-five feet apart from each other and are open for tours daily during the park's season. The John Quincy Adams Birthplace is the small farmhouse in which John Adams and his wife, Abigail, began their life and family together. It is here that John Adams launched his legal and political careers, maintaining a law office in the house. In that office, together with Samuel Adams and James Bowdoin, John Adams wrote the Massachusetts Constitution, a document that greatly influenced the U.S. Constitution.

John Adams's Birthplace (left) and John Quincy Adams's Birthplace (right)

JOHN ADAMS

The Old House

In 1787, John Adams arranged for the purchase of the Vassall-Borland house, now known as the Old House, in preparation for his and Abigail's return from Europe. They moved into the house in 1788, and it became the residence of four generations of Adamses from 1788 to 1927. Nearly 78,000 artifacts reside in the house, a tribute to the service of the Adams family. Outside, a tour of the grounds includes a historic orchard, formal gardens, and a carriage house.

John Adams's law office in the John Quincy Adams Birthplace

United Parish Church

The United Parish Church, built in 1828, was partially financed through the generous land donation of John Adams. The crypt beneath the sanctuary is the burial site of John Adams and John Quincy Adams and their first ladies. The church remains an active parish, but tours are possible throughout the day. The church provides its own tour operation with additional donations requested.

All tours begin at the visitor center in the Presidents' Place Galleria with a trolley providing transportation to each of the sites. Guided tours of the houses last approximately two-and-a-half hours, and the last trolley departs at 3 P.M. Tours of the church are offered throughout the day and last approximately twenty minutes. In addition, the visitor center offers site orientation, a bookstore, and the site's only public restroom.

Special events at Adams National Historical Park include reenactments of the Second Continental Congress and the Constitutional Convention as well as a Colonial Day, a Civil War Day, and a Victorian Day. Contact the visitor center for details. This site is a part of the National Park Service.

NEAREST AIRPORT: Boston, Massachusetts
GENERAL DIRECTIONS: Approximately 10 miles from downtown Boston.
From the north: Route 93 South to Route 3 South, exit 18 Washington Street/Quincy Center. From the south: Route 93 North to exit 19 Quincy Center. The park is also accessible by rail—MBTA Red Line Subway or Old Colony Commuter Rail to Quincy Center Station.
NEARBY ATTRACTIONS: Boston National Historical Park in Boston; Abigail Adams Birthplace in Weymouth; the USS *Salem*, the Quincy Homestead, and the Josiah Quincy House, all in Quincy.

THOMAS JEFFERSON

1743–1826
3rd President • 1801–1809

Thomas Jefferson, our third president, was also one of our greatest leaders. He was a man of intelligence and integrity, and a man who passionately believed that government must respect the rights of each individual it governed.

Jefferson was born on April 13, 1743, at Shadwell Plantation in Virginia. He was graduated from the College of William and Mary and then went on to study law. Jefferson married Martha Wayles Skelton in 1772, and together they had three daughters who survived infancy. Martha died during childbirth in 1782; after her death, Jefferson turned all his energy to public life.

A member of the drafting committee of the Continental Congress, Thomas Jefferson, with the exception of minor editing, authored the Declaration of Independence. He succeeded Patrick Henry as governor of Virginia, then went on to succeed Benjamin Franklin as minister to France. He served as secretary of state under George Washington and as vice president under John Adams. In 1800, after an electoral vote tie with Aaron Burr that had to be broken by the House of Representatives, Jefferson was elected president.

He was the first president to be inaugurated in the nation's new capital of Washington, D.C.

In his two terms as president, Jefferson made a deep impact on the emerging nation. He was an outspoken proponent of states' rights, believing that the federal government should focus on foreign policy and leave state and local governments to administer their own matters. He opened exploration into the West, purchasing the Louisiana Territory and then commissioning the Lewis and Clark expedition to the Pacific Northwest. In 1809, Jefferson retired to Monticello, but he often advised his successors, James Madison and James Monroe. He died on July 4, 1826, fifty years after the signing of the Declaration of Independence.

In addition to his political achievements, Thomas Jefferson is remembered as a scientist, an architect, and a philosopher. He founded the University of Virginia, he designed his beloved Monticello, and he invented countless objects that made everyday life easier. And after the burning of the Capitol during the invasion of the British army in 1814, Jefferson offered to sell his library collection to Congress to restart the Library of Congress. The offer was accepted and Jefferson's 6,487-volume collection became the basis for the library.

I BELIEVE THIS, ON CONTRARY, THE STRONGEST GOVERNMENT on earth. I believe it is the only one where every man, at the call of the law, would fly to the standard of the law and would meet invasions of the public order as his personal concern. Sometimes it is said that man cannot be trusted with the government of himself. Can he, then, be trusted with the government of others? Or have we found angels in the form of kings to govern for him? Let history answer this question.

–from Thomas Jefferson's first Inaugural Address, March 4, 1801

MONTICELLO, THE HOME OF
THOMAS JEFFERSON

Virginia Route 53, Charlottesville, Virginia 22902

PHONE: 434-984-9822

www.monticello.org

HOURS: daily; closed Christmas Day

ADMISSION: fee; student and group discounts; local resident discounts

WHEELCHAIR ACCESSIBILITY: yes

In 1768, Thomas Jefferson began building his home atop the "Little Mountain" where he had played as a boy. After returning from his stint as minister to France in 1789 with new ideas about architecture, he set about completely redesigning the house. Today it is a fine example of Roman neoclassicism, incorporating Jefferson's love of classical architecture and his passion for innovation. It is the only house in the United States on the United Nation's World Heritage List of international treasures. In addition to the home, visitors can explore the gardens, the grounds, and the Monticello Visitor Center.

The first design of the house had fourteen rooms; the final structure had forty-three—thirty-three rooms in the house itself, four in the pavilions, and six under the South Terrace. The bricks and nails for the remodeled house were made at Monticello, and most of the structural timber and the stone for the cellars came from Jefferson's land. The window glass came from Europe, and about one-third of today's window

Monticello

glass is original. Approximately 60 percent of the items on display in the house are or may be original to Jefferson. The remainder are period pieces or reproductions.

Most people think of the dome when they think of Monticello. In fact, it is not known how Jefferson used this room, which he sometimes called the "sky-room." Visitors cannot actually enter the Dome Room; however, they can view it through photos in the site's guidebook and a continuously running video at the visitor center. Rooms above the first floor are currently used for offices and are off-limits to visitors as well.

During the busy season, tours of the home are limited to twenty-five people, begin about every five minutes, and are about thirty minutes long. During winter, tours highlight special themes, are smaller in size, and are a bit longer. Tickets are purchased at the Ticket Office adjacent to the main parking area and collected prior to boarding the shuttle bus to the house.

Located about two miles from Monticello on Route 20 South, the Monticello Visitor Center contains an exhibit on Jefferson and Monticello, a museum shop, and a fifty-seat theater. The south end of the Center houses the Charlottesville-Albemarle Convention and Visitors Bureau, the Monticello Learning Center, and the Monticello Education Department.

The Jefferson exhibit serves as an introduction or supplement to a visit to Monticello. The exhibit displays an assortment of nearly 400 artifacts, drawings, and models. It is suggested that visitors plan to tour the house first. The film *Thomas Jefferson: The Pursuit of Liberty* is shown at least twice each day and offers insights into Jefferson's life and career.

In addition to the house and visitor center, specialized tours of the gardens and grounds, as well as of the plantation community, are available during the day (except in winter). Visitors can also take self-guided tours of the grounds, including Jefferson's burial place, using brochures available at distribution boxes on the grounds. Special events are planned year-round; a calendar of events is available by calling the Monticello Public Affairs office at 434-984-9822.

The Thomas Jefferson Foundation has owned and operated Monticello since 1923. The Foundation owns the original 1,000 acres of land, as well as another 1,000 acres of land from portions of Jefferson's adjoining farms. The Foundation receives no ongoing federal or state funds. It relies on ticket and merchandise sales, annual giving, a modest endowment, and gifts and grants for support of daily operations and long-term projects.

NEAREST AIRPORT: Charlottesville or Richmond, Virginia
GENERAL DIRECTIONS: Located on the Thomas Jefferson Parkway (Route 53), about two miles southeast of Charlottesville near the intersection of Route 20 South and I-64.
NEARBY ATTRACTIONS: University of Virginia, Ash Lawn-Highland(home of James Monroe), Montpelier (home of James Madison).

THOMAS JEFFERSON'S POPLAR FOREST ────────

Route 661, Forest, Virginia 24551

PHONE: 434-525-1806

www.poplarforest.org

HOURS: April through November, daily; closed Thanksgiving Day

ADMISSION: fee; student and senior discounts

WHEELCHAIR ACCESSIBILITY: limited (lift construction completion scheduled in 2004)

Poplar Forest is the octagonal, Palladian-style villa that Jefferson designed as a retreat for his use after he retired from the presidency. The plantation was sold soon after Jefferson's death in 1826. A fire in 1845 damaged the house, prompting the owners to remodel. In 1984, the Corporation for Jefferson's Poplar Forest, a nonprofit organization started by a group of area residents, purchased the house and the remaining grounds. Its mission is to restore Poplar Forest to its earlier glory; the task has been an exercise in restoration and archaeology.

Guided tours of the house are available even as work continues on restoration of the interior. The completed exterior restoration earned an Honor Award from the National Trust for Historic Preservation. Tour topics include the design and construction of the retreat, Jefferson's landscape designs, the plantation community, and the rescue and restoration of the property. Outside, visitors can take self-guided tours of the grounds. Visitors can also view the restoration workshop, the

Front view of Poplar Forest

archaeology lab, and cellar exhibits, and see archaeologists and craftspeople at work. Brochures describing the plantation community and landscape design are available in the museum shop.

Poplar Forest hosts a hands-on history tent during the summer. The tent features activities that let visitors get a feel for life in Jefferson's time. Visitors can make a mud brick, write with a quill pen, try on period clothes, or play with clay marbles. There are also simulated archaeological activities for visitors.

NEAREST AIRPORT: Charlottesville or Roanoke, Virginia
GENERAL DIRECTIONS: Take U.S. 221 or U.S. 460 to Route 811. Turn onto Route 661 and entrance is one mile on right.
NEARBY ATTRACTIONS: Appomattox and National D-Day Memorial.

TUCKAHOE PLANTATION

12601 River Road, Richmond, Virginia 23233
PHONE: 804-784-5736
HOURS: by appointment only
ADMISSION: fee; discounts for groups of ten or more
WHEELCHAIR ACCESSIBILITY: no

Tuckahoe Plantation, begun in 1733 and completed by 1740, is the boyhood home of Thomas Jefferson. In addition to the home itself, the plantation includes gardens, outbuildings, and the schoolhouse where Jefferson learned to read and write. The schoolhouse now serves as a gift shop.

Tuckahoe is considered by many historians to have the finest existing example of an early eighteenth-century plantation. It is also said to be the only remaining original early Randolph home still situated on its original site. Among the many features of the home are its magnificent interior paneling and staircases. The plantation is a Registered National Historic Landmark.

Because the plantation is a private home and working farm, it is open by appointment only. Depending upon the group's size and time of visit, visitors should have access to a majority of rooms. Interior tours are guided, while visitors are welcome to roam the grounds. The plantation may be reserved for special occasions such as weddings, and arrangements can be made in advance for hayrides.

NEAREST AIRPORT: Richmond, Virginia
GENERAL DIRECTIONS: The plantation fronts on River Road seven miles west of the Richmond city limits. Enter the country lane through the white pillars about five miles west of the intersection of Parham Road South and River Road or about three miles west of the intersection of Gaskins and River roads.
NEARBY ATTRACTIONS: Wilton House and Monticello.

JAMES MADISON

1751–1836
4th President • 1809–1817

Despite his slight build and soft, unassuming voice, James Madison played a powerful role in the establishment and enforcement of American independence. Along with his wife, Dolley, who earned fame for her heroism during the British siege of Washington during the War of 1812, Madison spent eight years in the White House at a critical time in American history.

Madison was born in 1751 in King George County (now Orange County), Virginia, and grew up at Montpelier, his family's plantation near the Blue Ridge Mountains. He was educated at the College of New Jersey, now known as Princeton. Upon graduation he intended to practice law but became caught up in the revolutionary spirit sweeping the colonies. Madison was a leader in the Virginia Assembly and played a critical role in the framing of the Virginia Declaration of Rights. This experience and his extensive knowledge of government and politics positioned him to play a key role in the Constitutional Convention of 1787.

James Madison became known as the "Father of the Constitution," drafting much of the document, including the Bill of Rights, and pushing hard for its ratification. He went on to a successful career in public service; he represented Virginia in the House of Representatives and served as secretary of state for eight years. In 1808, Madison, the Jeffersonian Republican candidate for president, soundly defeated his Federalist opponent in the national election. He served two terms in the White House and was able to circumvent trade wars with France and territorial disputes with Spain, but the bulk of his energies were consumed by the conflict with Great Britain that culminated in the War of 1812.

At the center of that conflict was the British navy's refusal to respect the rights of American ships at sea. For years British ships had been impressing American sailors and seizing American goods. In 1812, President Madison asked Congress to declare war. The war lasted two years and took a heavy toll, including the burning of the White House. It ended with the main issues unresolved in the signing of the Treaty of Ghent. Nonetheless, domestic industry had flourished in the void created by embargoes on British goods; no longer were Americans dependent upon foreign imports for survival. Although the military objectives of the war fell short, a new American independence was born.

At the completion of Madison's second term, he and his wife left the White House for Montpelier. There, he concentrated on running the plantation but also remained active in Virginia and national politics until his death in 1836.

THE PRESENT SITUATION OF THE WORLD IS INDEED WITHOUT PARALLEL, and that of our own country is full of difficulties. The pressure of these, too, is the more severely felt because they have fallen upon us at a moment when the national prosperity being at a height not before attained, the contrast resulting from the change has been rendered the more striking. . . . It is a precious reflection that the transition from this prosperous condition of our country to the scene which has for some time been distressing us is not chargeable on any unwarrantable views, nor, as I trust, on any involuntary errors in the public councils. Indulging no passions which trespass on the rights or repose of other nations, it has been the true glory of the United States to cultivate peace by observing justice and to entitle themselves to the respect of the nations at war by fulfilling their neutral obligations with the most scrupulous impartiality. If there be candor in the world, the truth of these assertions will not be questioned; posterity will at least do justice to them.

–from James Madison's first Inaugural Address, March 4, 1809

JAMES MADISON'S MONTPELIER

11407 Constitution Highway, Montpelier Station, Virginia 22957

PHONE: 540-672-2728

www.montpelier.org

HOURS: daily; closed Thanksgiving, Christmas Eve, Christmas Day, New Year's Day

ADMISSION: fee; student and senior discounts

WHEELCHAIR ACCESSIBILITY: house and some trails

Montpelier was home to three generations of Madisons, from the time of James Madison's grandfather (1723) until his widow, Dolley, was forced to sell the estate in 1844. It was Madison's lifelong home—from shortly after his birth, intermittently throughout his political career, and as the home to which he retired after his presidency. Madison is buried on the grounds of the estate.

Montpelier is a 2,700-acre estate with more than 130 structures, a formal garden, the Madison family cemetery and a slave cemetery, two race courses, a 200-acre old-growth forest, and active archaeological sites. The jewel of the site is the mansion. Built by James Madison's father in 1760, the home was twice enlarged during Madison's lifetime and was significantly enlarged by subsequent owners in the early twentieth century. Today, the mansion boasts fifty-five rooms, compared to the twelve that made up the core of the building during Madison's time. Most of

Montpelier

the first floor rooms are open to the public, while second floor rooms are available during "Behind-the-Scenes" tours that are offered daily.

In 2001, Montpelier opened two exhibits in the mansion: a re-creation of the Madison dining room—featuring original Madison pieces, period silver, reproduction china, and crystal—and "The Madisons' Style and Taste"—an exhibit of original and period furniture and artwork collected by James and Dolley Madison.

Tours of the mansion and grounds are largely self-guided through use of a hand-held audio system. Guides are also available to provide information and answer questions. Special events are hosted throughout the year, including James's and Dolley's birthday celebrations, the Montpelier Wine Festival, Archaeology Field School, and the Montpelier Hunt Races. Children might enjoy the James Madison Scout Trail, a treasure hunt that guides children through a visit to Montpelier.

Montpelier is a National Trust Historic Site. The Montpelier Foundation, a Virginia-based nonprofit organization, administers and manages the site. The next major project planned by the Foundation is the restoration of the Dolley Madison bedroom wing.

NEAREST AIRPORT: Charlottesville, Virginia

GENERAL DIRECTIONS: Located on Route 20, four miles southwest of Orange, Virginia.

NEARBY ATTRACTIONS: Monticello; Ash Lawn-Highland (home of James Monroe). Nearby Historic Orange is home to a number of Civil War battle sites, antique shops, and award-winning vineyards.

Temple at Montpelier

JAMES MONROE

1758–1831
5th President • 1817–1825

James Monroe took office at a rather peaceful time in history. The battle for independence was won, and the divisive issue of slavery had yet to reach a crisis point. The administration was popularly known as the "Era of Good Feeling," as Monroe and the Jeffersonian Republican party enjoyed the almost unanimous support of the nation.

Born in Westmoreland County, Virginia, in 1758, Monroe was the son of a Virginia planter. He studied at the College of William and Mary in Williamsburg, but he quit his studies to join the Continental army. Monroe studied law under Thomas Jefferson, and the two formed a lifelong friendship. He and his wife, Elizabeth Kortright Monroe, had a son, who died in infancy, and two daughters, one of whom was married in the first wedding ever held at the White House.

Monroe's legacy of public service began long before his election as president. He served as a member of the Continental Congress; United States senator; minister to France, London, and Madrid; governor of Virginia; minister to Great Britain; and secretary of state under James Madison. Monroe easily won two consecutive terms as president.

Monroe's accomplishments in office included the acquisition of

Florida and the definition of the boundaries of Louisiana. Although "good feeling" ruled the day during the early Monroe years, the question of slavery was beginning to demand attention. Like so many of his contemporaries, Monroe believed that slavery, whatever one's moral stand, was protected by the Constitution, and that the nation could survive part slave and part free. He supported the Missouri Compromise of 1820, which drew a line at latitude 36°30' dividing the free North from the slaveholding South. According to the Compromise, Missouri was admitted to the Union as a slave state and Maine as a free state, thus preserving the balance between slave and free states. Days to come would prove the Compromise inadequate and the division it formalized incompatible with the survival of the Union. President Monroe made a more lasting contribution to American history with the Monroe Doctrine, which warned the nations of Europe that the Americas were no longer open to colonization or exploitation. This strong statement entered the United States into world politics and remains at the foundation of American foreign policy almost two hundred years later.

After a lifetime of service, President Monroe retired to Virginia with Elizabeth, who had lived a quiet, private life as first lady. After his wife's death, the former president moved to New York City, where he lived with his daughter and her family until his death in 1831. Monroe was the third of our first five presidents to die on Independence Day.

NEVER DID A GOVERNMENT COMMENCE UNDER AUSPICES SO FAVORABLE, nor ever was success so complete. If we look to the history of other nations, ancient or modern, we find no example of a growth so rapid, so gigantic, of a people so prosperous and happy. In contemplating what we have still to perform, the heart of every citizen must expand with joy when he reflects how near our Government has approached to perfection; that in respect to it we have no essential improvement to make; that the great object is to preserve in it the essential principles and features which characterize it, and that is to be done by preserving the virtue and enlightening the minds of the people; and as a security against foreign dangers to adopt such arrangements as are indispensable to the support of our independence, our rights and liberties. If we persevere in the career in which we have advanced so far and in the path already traced, we can not fail, under the favor of a gracious Providence, to attain the high destiny which seems to await us.

–from James Monroe's first Inaugural Address, March 4, 1817

ASH LAWN-HIGHLAND

1000 James Monroe Parkway, Charlottesville, Virginia 22902

PHONE: 434-293-9539

www.avenue.org/ashlawn

HOURS: daily; closed Thanksgiving, Christmas Day, and New Year's Day

ADMISSION: fee; senior and child discounts

WHEELCHAIR ACCESSIBILITY: yes

Ash Lawn-Highland, or Highland as it was known during the period of James Monroe's residence, was home to the president and his wife, Elizabeth, from 1799 to 1823. The home provides visitors with the opportunity to see a variety of furnishings and decorative items from the eighteenth and nineteenth centuries.

Monroe House

Highland showcases period American and French furnishings, the latter recalling Monroe's ministerial appointments in Europe under presidents Washington and Jefferson. A major renovation program is underway to restore the home's wall and floor finishes to historically correct colors and materials. Portraits of notable family friends grace the drawing room walls, and Old Paris china re-creates a dessert course in the dining room. Throughout Highland, tour guides emphasize original Monroe pieces, including examples of rare White House china.

Monroe bedchamber

Highland was a working plantation. Today, as in Monroe's time, its service yard includes a smokehouse, reconstructed slave quarters, and an icehouse. The yard features ornamental and utilitarian gardens as well as a variety of domestic and game animals.

Special events are scheduled year-round, including Garden Week tours, Virginia Wine Festival, Plantation Days, Summer Music Festival, and Christmas celebrations.

NEAREST AIRPORT: Charlottesville, Virginia

GENERAL DIRECTIONS: Take exit 121 south off I-64 and follow signs.

NEARBY ATTRACTIONS: Monticello, University of Virginia, and Montpelier.

James Monroe Museum and Memorial Library

908 Charles Street, Fredericksburg, Virginia 22401

Phone: 540-654-1043

www.mwc.edu/galleries

Hours: daily; closed Thanksgiving, Christmas Day, New Year's Day

Admission: fee; child, senior, and member discounts

Wheelchair accessibility: limited

Situated on a parcel of land that housed James Monroe's law office for a time, the museum is dedicated to the study and presentation of the social, political, and intellectual influences of Monroe. Prominent among the museum's collection is the Louis XVI secretary that Monroe purchased during his time as minister to France. It is thought that he penned his seventh annual message to Congress on this desk; a portion of that message later became known as the Monroe Doctrine.

James Monroe Museum

Furniture, jewelry, fine arts, weaponry, and other personal items are on display in the museum. The library houses thousands of books, historical papers, drawings, and images and is available for research. The guided tour takes about thirty minutes, but visitors can return to spend more time in the self-guided galleries. A gift shop is on site, and visitors can walk outside through the Memorial Garden, which features a bronze bust of Monroe. Special events take place year-round; a calendar of events is available on the website.

The museum was established by the Monroes' great-granddaughter in the 1920s. In 1964, it was gifted to the Commonwealth of Virginia by the James Monroe Memorial Foundation. It is currently administered by the Rectors and Visitors of Mary Washington College. Fundraising for a sister site, the James Monroe Presidential Center, began in 1998.

Nearest airport: Richmond, Virginia; Washington, D.C.

General directions: Located an hour's drive from Richmond or Washington, D.C. From I-95, take exit 103A to Route 3 East. Follow Business Route 3 past Mary Washington College to Charles Street and turn right.

Nearby attractions: Mary Washington House, Kenmore Plantation and Gardens, George Washington's Ferry Farm, and Chancellorsville Battlefield. Fredericksburg is home to many historic attractions; visit www.fredericks burgva.com for information.

JOHN QUINCY ADAMS

1767–1848
6th President • 1825–1829

A brilliant man with a flair for negotiation, John Quincy Adams, the son of second president John Adams, experienced firsthand the American fight for independence and the founding of the nation. As a boy, Adams traveled extensively overseas, received education from the most respected tutors, and lived a comfortable life of privilege.

Adams was born in the home adjacent to his father's birthplace in Quincy (then called Braintree), Massachusetts, in 1767. As his father before him, Adams attended Harvard College and studied law. Not long after his graduation, his family connections—and his fluency in Dutch—won him appointment by President George Washington as minister to the Netherlands. During his father's administration, young Adams served as minister to Russia. On his return to the United States, Adams won his first elective office, a seat in the Massachusetts State Senate. This led to a seat in the U.S. Senate and, in 1814, appointment to a special delegation sent to negotiate the Treaty of Ghent, which formally ended the War of 1812. As secretary of state under President James Monroe, Adams was extremely involved in the creation of the Monroe Doctrine. Adams ran for president in 1824 and was caught in a tight four-way race in which no candidate secured a majority of electoral votes. The election was decided by the House of Representatives, and Adams prevailed after Henry Clay, one of his rivals, threw his support to Adams.

Adams's single term in the White House was largely uneventful. He was not generally popular, but he was high-minded and knowledgeable. His greatest achievement was a comprehensive program of internal improvements. He was the first president to believe that the Constitution gave the federal government authority and responsibility to build roads and canals, and he did much to extend and modernize both. Adams left his boldest mark on history, however, after his days in the White House when, as a U.S. representative from Massachusetts, he fought courageously against slavery at a time when most public figures were unwilling to do so.

John Quincy Adams died in 1848 in the U.S. Capitol building after suffering a stroke on the floor of the House. He was survived by his wife, Louisa, and one of their three sons. Adams's passing was observed by clergyman and abolitionist Theodore Parker, who recognized the former president's achievement: "The slave has lost a champion who gained new ardor and new strength the longer he fought; America has lost a man who loved her with his heart; religion has lost a supporter; freedom an unfailing friend; and mankind a noble vindicator of our inalienable rights."

TEN YEARS OF PEACE, AT HOME AND ABROAD, have assuaged the animosities of political contention and blended into harmony the most discordant elements of public opinion. There still remains one effort of magnanimity, one sacrifice of prejudice and passion, to be made by the individuals throughout the nation who have heretofore followed the standards of political party. It is that of discarding every element of rancor against each other, of embracing as countrymen and friends, and of yielding to talents and virtue alone that confidence which in times of contention for principle was bestowed only upon those who bore the badge of party communion.

–from John Quincy Adams's Inaugural Address, March 4, 1825

ADAMS NATIONAL HISTORICAL PARK ———

135 Adams Street, Quincy, Massachusetts 02169

PHONE: 617-770-1175

www.nps.gov/adam

HOURS: mid-April through mid-November, daily; visitor center open year-round

ADMISSION: fee; student discounts; park passes

WHEELCHAIR ACCESSIBILITY: yes, except second floor of Old House

The fourteen-acre Adams National Historical Park commemorates members of the distinguished Adams family who gave years of service to the nation. Foremost among them are John Adams and his son John Quincy Adams, our second and sixth presidents, respectively. The park contains a number of structures, including the birthplaces of John Adams and John Quincy Adams and the Old House. The homes feature original furnishings, decorative arts, and personal possessions of four generations of the Adams family. There is also a visitor center nearby.

The Birthplaces

John Quincy Adams was born in the small farmhouse in which John Adams and his wife, Abigail, began their lives together. It is located only about seventy-five feet from the birthplace of his father, and the structures are the oldest presidential

Adams National Historical Park

birthplaces in the country. In addition to being John Quincy Adams's birthplace, the site is also where John Adams launched his legal and political careers in the law office in the house. In that office, together with Samuel Adams and James Bowdoin, John Adams wrote the Massachusetts Constitution, a document that greatly influenced the U.S. Constitution.

The Old House
In 1787, John Adams arranged for the purchase of the Vassall-Borland house, now known as the Old House, in preparation for his and Abigail's return from Europe. They moved into the house in 1788, and later it became the residence of four generations of Adamses, including John Quincy Adams and his wife Louisa. Nearly 78,000 artifacts reside in the house, a tribute to the service of the Adams family. Outside, a tour of the grounds includes a historic orchard, formal gardens, and a carriage house.

United Parish Church
The United Parish Church, built in 1828, was partially financed through the generous land donation of John Adams. The crypt beneath the sanctuary is the burial site of John Adams and John Quincy Adams as well as their first ladies. The church remains an active parish, but tours are possible throughout the day. The church provides its own tour operation with additional donations requested.

All tours begin at the visitor center in the Presidents' Place Galleria with a trolley providing transportation to each of the sites. Guided tours of the houses last approximately two-and-a-half hours, and the last trolley departs at 3 P.M. Tours of the church are offered throughout the day and last approximately twenty minutes. In addition, the visitor center offers site orientation, a bookstore, and the site's only public restroom.

Special events at Adams National Historical Park include reenactments of the Second Continental Congress and the Constitutional Convention as well as a Colonial Day, a Civil War Day, and a Victorian Day. Contact the visitor center for details. This site is a part of the National Park Service.

NEAREST AIRPORT: Boston, Massachusetts
GENERAL DIRECTIONS: Approximately 10 miles from downtown Boston. From the north: Route 93 South to Route 3 South, exit 18 Washington Street/Quincy Center. From the south: Route 93 North to exit 19 Quincy Center. The park is also accessible by rail—MBTA Red Line Subway or Old Colony Commuter Rail to Quincy Center Station.
NEARBY ATTRACTIONS: Boston National Historical Park in Boston; Abigail Adams Birthplace in Weymouth; the USS *Salem*, the Quincy Homestead, and the Josiah Quincy House, all in Quincy.

ANDREW JACKSON

1767–1845
7th President • 1829–1837

Charismatic and combative, Andrew Jackson met the challenge of the presidency as he did everything else in life—head on. In the course of two terms, the power of his will and of his belief in the necessity of a strong, unyielding federal government substantially redefined the office of president.

Jackson's birthplace remains a matter of dispute. Both Union County, North Carolina, and neighboring Lancaster County in South Carolina claim him as a native, and no records exist to prove either state wrong. Jackson's father died before Andrew was born, and his mother when he was only fourteen. As a boy, Jackson received a good, if sporadic, education; legend has it that when the Declaration of Independence was signed, nine-year-old Andrew read it aloud from the newspapers to illiterate family members and neighbors. Jackson joined the colonial army when he was just thirteen and later fought in the War of 1812 and the First Seminole War. His toughness and heroism in battle earned him the nickname "Old Hickory," and he became a national hero with his victory over the British at New Orleans in the War of 1812. Before his election to the presidency in

1828, Jackson served as the first person from Tennessee elected to the House of Representatives; he later served as a U.S. senator from 1797 to 1798.

As president, Jackson stood firmly on the side of a strong central government at a time when the majority of his fellow southerners were fighting hard for states' rights, with the issues of slavery and nullification at the heart of the battle. Jackson used his presidential veto liberally to oppose Congress and all others who did not share his vision. The most controversial of his vetoes was on the re-charter of the Second Bank of the United States. Jackson wanted the bank shut down; he viewed it as representing special interests and therefore unconstitutional. His will prevailed despite the strong disapproval of the Congress.

Tall and lean, with thick, red hair turned gray and a gaunt, striking face, Andrew Jackson had a physical presence to match his temperament. Most of his public life was marked by controversy. His wife, Rachel Donelson Jackson, was still legally married to her first husband when she wed Jackson; and despite the fact that the legal technicalities of the situation were eventually resolved, Mrs. Jackson remained the object of much criticism. Jackson valiantly defended his wife's honor; and in 1806, he challenged one of her critics, Charles Dickinson, to a duel, which ended with Dickinson dead and Jackson badly wounded. Despite the controversy, and despite the fact that Jackson angered as many as he inspired, he was a strong and effective president whose confident use of the authority of his office set a precedent for every president to come.

When he left office, Andrew Jackson returned to the Hermitage, his plantation in Nashville. Rachel Jackson had died in 1828, only months before her husband's inauguration as president. Jackson spent his retirement alone and died in Nashville in 1845.

THE TIME AT WHICH I STAND BEFORE YOU IS FULL OF INTEREST. The eyes of all nations are fixed on our Republic. The event of the existing crisis will be decisive in the opinion of mankind of the practicability of our federal system of government. Great is the stake placed in our hands; great is the responsibility which must rest upon the people of the United States. Let us realize the importance of the attitude in which we stand before the world. Let us exercise forbearance and firmness. Let us extricate our country from the dangers which surround it and learn wisdom from the lessons they inculcate.

–from Andrew Jackson's second Inaugural Address, March 4, 1833

THE HERMITAGE

4580 Rachel's Lane, Nashville, Tennessee 37076
PHONE: 615-889-2941
www.thehermitage.com
HOURS: daily; closed Thanksgiving, Christmas, and third week of January
ADMISSION: fee; student, senior, and family discounts
WHEELCHAIR ACCESSIBILITY: yes, except second floor of mansion

The Hermitage plantation was home to President Andrew Jackson from 1804 until his death in 1845. The plantation's 700 acres are the site of the Hermitage mansion, first built between 1819 and 1821, enlarged in 1831, and rebuilt between 1834 and 1836 after a fire; the First Hermitage, the original log buildings that were home to Rachel and Andrew Jackson from 1804 to 1821; Alfred's Cabin, an original slave cabin; and Tulip Grove mansion, the home of Jackson's nephew Andrew Jackson Donelson and his wife, Emily. The 1836 Hermitage mansion is the most accurately restored early presidential home in the country. In addition, the property includes the garden and tomb where Jackson and his wife are buried; the Hermitage Church, built in 1824 on land donated by Jackson; and a visitor center and museum.

In August of 1804, Andrew Jackson purchased a 425-acre tract of land which he named the Hermitage. He and Rachel moved into the two-story farmhouse, the largest of the complex's buildings. Rachel filled the farmhouse with fine furniture, carpets, and china; and they stayed there for the next seventeen years, until a brick mansion was built on the property in 1821. Surrounding buildings included a log kitchen, barns, smokehouse, distillery, cotton gin, and springhouse.

The Hermitage

ANDREW JACKSON

Following their move into the brick mansion, the Jacksons' original farmhouse was turned into slave quarters and, later, a tenant house after emancipation. Only two of the original buildings remain today: the farmhouse and the kitchen. A major renovation project has been underway in recent years, and among the findings are evidence that the farmhouse was originally a two-story house. During conversion into slave quarters, the first floor was removed and the second story lowered.

In 1819, as his wealth and his reputation grew, Jackson ordered the construction of a brick, Federal-style home on the property. The building was completed in 1821, and the transition was made from the original log farmhouse to this new home. This was the only Hermitage mansion that Rachel would live in. She died in December 1828, shortly before her husband's inauguration as the seventh president of the United States.

Jackson's bedroom

While serving a second term in office, Jackson was notified that the home had been severely damaged by fire. Under the supervision of Jackson's adopted son, Andrew Jackson Jr., the home was rebuilt—this time in the Greek Revival style. This is the home that visitors today will see, and it is furnished with nearly all original pieces. Many of the Jacksons' original possessions, ranging from silver to portraits to books, eyeglasses, and Bible, are on display. Paint colors, fabrics, and carpets have been painstakingly reproduced, and six rooms retain their original 1836 wallpapers. Interpreters in period costume give tours of the mansion and add to the feeling of authenticity.

Visitors to the Hermitage can also stroll the grounds and visit the garden, which was first created in 1819, and the Greek-inspired tomb in which Andrew and Rachel are buried. Outdoor tours of the garden, farm, and archaeology sites are available seasonally; archaeology excavation takes place each summer.

The visitor center includes a museum, gift shop, cafe, and auditorium where a film on Jackson's life is shown. Special events include children's classes and programs such as author lectures. Details are available on the Hermitage website.

The Hermitage is a nonprofit organization and has been managed by the Ladies' Hermitage Association since 1889, when a group of Nashville women convinced the Tennessee State Legislature to deed the house and land for their care and management. The Hermitage is a National Historic Landmark.

NEAREST AIRPORT: Nashville, Tennessee

GENERAL DIRECTIONS: Nashville, I-40 east, exit 221, entrance 4 miles ahead on the right.

NEARBY ATTRACTIONS: Tennessee State Capitol, Tennessee State Museum, Carl Van Vechten Art Gallery at Fisk University, historic downtown Nashville district.

ANDREW JACKSON STATE PARK

196 Andrew Jackson Park Road, Lancaster, South Carolina 29720

PHONE: 803-285-3344

www.discoverSouthCarolina.com

HOURS: daily

ADMISSION: no fee

WHEELCHAIR ACCESSIBILITY: limited

This 360-acre state park was created in 1952 to honor President Andrew Jackson. When Jackson's father died shortly before his birth, Jackson's mother moved to and raised her family in the home of her brother-in-law, James Crawford. While the exact location of Jackson's birth remains in dispute (both Union County, North Carolina, and Lancaster County, South Carolina, claim him as their own), the park does encompass the property that once belonged to James Crawford, and Jackson spent his boyhood here.

Visitors looking to spend time in nature will enjoy the park's offerings: two nature trails, fishing lake, campgrounds, and picnic areas. For those whose interests lie in the historical vein, the park offers a small museum with gift shop and a replica 18th-century schoolhouse. The museum's four rooms tell the story of Jackson's boyhood experiences and reveal colonial life in South Carolina's backcountry. A bronze sculpture of a young Andrew Jackson by famed sculptor Anna Hyatt Huntington is a focal point of the museum grounds. And a marker has been placed by the Daughters of the American Revolution, citing the park as Jackson's birthplace.

Occasional special events take place on the park grounds, including the Andrew Jackson birthday celebration and the Carolina Legends Bluegrass Festival.

The site is operated by the South Carolina State Park Service.

NEAREST AIRPORT: Charlotte, North Carolina

GENERAL DIRECTIONS: Nine miles north of Lancaster on U.S. 521.

NEARBY ATTRACTIONS: Clinton Memorial Cemetery, Old Waxhaw Presbyterian Church, Lancaster and Chester Railway Museum.

MARTIN VAN BUREN

1782–1862
8th President • 1837–1841

Just months after Martin Van Buren's inaugural address, in which he held up the United States as an example of a successful experiment in government, the Panic of 1837 burst the bubble of prosperity the country had been enjoying. The depression deepened over the next four years and became the defining event of Van Buren's presidency.

Born in 1782, Martin Van Buren grew up in poverty on his father's farm in Kinderhook, New York, in a family where the Dutch language was spoken and Dutch customs observed. As a young man, Van Buren married his childhood sweetheart, Hannah Hoes, with whom he had four sons. Educated at local schools, he later studied law and was admitted to the bar in 1803. It was as a young lawyer that Van Buren first became involved in politics. Before his election as president in 1836, he served as a senator from New York, governor of New York, secretary of state, and vice president. He was a skilled politician who knew just what to say and when to say it.

As Van Buren took office as president and the Panic of 1837 was unfolding, the nation's banks refused to convert paper money to silver and gold. Along with this monetary policy, land speculation, risky loans, tight credit, and declining cotton prices abroad combined to create a major depression. The depression lasted until 1843, two years after Van Buren left office, and resulted in a great deal of unpopularity for the man. But Van Buren's administration was not without its political successes. He avoided war with Great Britain in a dispute over the border between Maine and Canada by beginning negotiations that eventually led to the Webster-Ashburton Treaty—a treaty that determined the present-day border. He established the independent treasury system, which required that money owed to the United States be paid in gold or silver rather than paper. Van Buren opposed the annexation of Texas, which he feared would upset the balance between free and slave states and lead the nation closer to civil war.

In retirement, Van Buren came to believe that the complete abolition of slavery was the only answer to the division troubling the Union. Van Buren ran again for the presidency in 1848 as the candidate of the Free-Soil Party with the son of John Quincy Adams as his running mate. The Van Buren-Adams ticket received enough votes to affect the outcome of the election, but its abolitionist message went largely unheeded. Following his defeat, Van Buren retired permanently from public life and lived his remaining years on his estate near his hometown of Kinderhook. He died there in 1862 with the country in the midst of the Civil War.

From a small community we have risen to a people powerful in numbers and in strength; but with our increase has gone hand in hand the progress of just principles. The privileges, civil and religious, of the humblest individual are still sacredly protected at home, and while the valor and fortitude of our people have removed far from us the slightest apprehension of foreign power, they have not yet induced us in a single instance to forget what is right. . . . We have learned by experience a fruitful lesson—that an implicit and undeviating adherence to the principles on which we set out can carry us prosperously onward through all the conflicts of circumstance and vicissitudes inseparable from the lapse of years.

–from Martin Van Buren's Inaugural Address, March 4, 1837

MARTIN VAN BUREN NATIONAL HISTORIC SITE —

1013 Old Post Road, Kinderhook, New York 12106

PHONE: 518-758-9689

www.nps.gov/mava

HOURS: mid-May through October, daily; November
and first week in December, Saturday and Sunday

ADMISSION: fee

WHEELCHAIR ACCESSIBILITY: limited

Martin Van Buren was born in Kinderhook in 1782 and bought the estate he named
Lindenwald in 1839. He lived in the mansion until his death in 1862. Although the
estate, which was a working farm, grew to 226 acres under Van Buren's direction,
the current park site is thirty-eight acres. Much of the surrounding land is conservation land; thus, the park with its mansion and the adjacent lands are reflective of Van
Buren's time.

Lindenwald

Guided tours of
the home are available;
guests can sign up for
the tours at the visitor
center across Old Post
Road. The park hosts a
number of ongoing and
special events through-
out the year, including
children's activities, concerts, and walking tours.
Martin Van Buren
National Historic Site is
on the National Register of Historic Places and is part of the National Park Service.

NEAREST AIRPORT: Albany, New York

GENERAL DIRECTIONS: Exit 12 from I-90 to NY Route 9 south; NY Route 9 to NY
Route 9H, then watch for park sign.

NEARBY ATTRACTIONS: Olana State Historic Site, Lyukas Van Allen House.

THE STEPHEN DECATUR HOUSE MUSEUM ——

748 Jackson Place, NW, Washington, D.C. 20006

PHONE: 202-842-0920

www.decaturhouse.org

HOURS: daily

ADMISSION: no fee

WHEELCHAIR ACCESSIBILITY: yes

The Decatur House was completed in 1818 and is one of only three remaining residential buildings in the country designed by Benjamin Henry Latrobe, who is sometimes called the father of American architecture. The neo-classical structure sits just a block north of the White House and has been home to many of our nation's political leaders in addition to its original owners, Stephen and Susan Decatur. It was home to Martin Van Buren from 1829 to 1831 during his tenure as secretary of state under President Andrew Jackson. Van Buren resigned his office in 1831; six years later he moved into the White House as our eighth president.

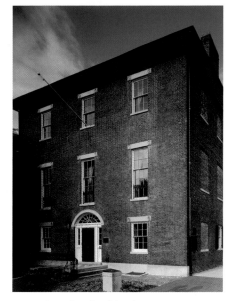

Front façade of Stephen Decatur House

The Decatur House was designed with three specific areas of usage: the service space, used by slaves and servants; the private spaces, used by the families in their daily activities; and the public spaces, used for formal entertaining. Exhibits showcase the lifestyle of the house's nineteenth- and early twentieth-century residents. The museum also features a special exhibition on the slaves and servants who worked in the house; and an extensive collection of more than 12,000 items includes furniture, ceramics, textiles, silver, and art that span nearly 200 years.

Docent-led tours begin every half hour and last thirty to forty-five minutes. Special events are scheduled year-round and include lectures, family programming, and music events.

The Stephen Decatur House Museum is operated by the National Trust for Historic Preservation. The Trust relies on the support of donations and the generosity of its volunteers, interns, and interpreters. The museum is in the midst of a four-million dollar renovation that will result in an expanded 2,000-square-foot gallery, a new entrance, and new interactive exhibits, among other improvements. The museum will remain open during all phases of the renovation.

NEAREST AIRPORT: Washington, D.C.; Baltimore, Maryland
GENERAL DIRECTIONS: The museum is located on the corner of H Street and Jackson Place. Take 17th Street to H Street. By Metro, take the Orange or Blue line to the Farragut West station or take the Red line to the Farragut North station.
NEARBY ATTRACTIONS: Washington, D.C., is home to many historic attractions; among them are the White House, presidential memorials, Woodrow Wilson House, Smithsonian Institution.

WILLIAM HENRY HARRISON

1773–1841
9th President • 1841

———

William Henry Harrison, the son of Benjamin Harrison, who signed the Declaration of Independence, was born to wealth and privilege on Berkeley Plantation in Charles City County, Virginia. His supporters, however, portrayed him as a simple, backwoods frontiersman, in contrast to the upper-class image of his opponent, Martin Van Buren. The campaign was dubbed "The Log Cabin Campaign;" and the American people embraced Harrison's rugged frontier image, thanks in great part to legends of his heroism in the Indian Wars.

As a child, Harrison had dreams of becoming a doctor; he studied classics and history at Hampden-Sydney College and then studied medicine briefly. At the age of eighteen, however, Harrison abandoned his education and joined the army to fight in the Indian Wars in the Northwest Territory. For most of the next fifty years, Harrison remained on the frontier as a professional soldier and a public official.

Harrison's road to the presidency began with an appointment as secretary of the Northwest Territory and his selection as the region's first delegate to the United States House of Representatives. In 1801, he was appointed governor of the Indiana Territory and served twelve years in this role. After another stint in the army during the War of 1812, Harrison again turned to public life, serving as a congressman and senator for the state of Ohio before he made his run for the presidency in 1840. In a campaign of slogans and personalities, Harrison ran as the rugged man of the frontier. His campaign slogan, "Tippecanoe and Tyler, too," was a tribute to his heroism in the Battle of Tippecanoe during the Indian Wars. Harrison won the popular vote by a relatively small majority, but he swept the electoral college by a vote of 234 to 60.

Harrison had the unfortunate distinction of serving the shortest term. During his inauguration ceremony, Harrison caught cold. Within a month, he was dead of pneumonia, leaving his vice president, John Tyler, to assume the office and duties of the president.

William Henry Harrison was the father of ten children, only four of whom lived long enough to see their father elected president. His wife, Anna Tuthill Symmes Harrison, never lived in the White House with her husband. She had been planning to travel to Washington from Ohio in the spring after his inauguration, but he died before she could make the trip.

OUR CONFEDERACY, FELLOW CITIZENS, CAN ONLY BE PRESERVED by the same forbearance. Our citizens must be content with the exercise of the powers with which the Constitution clothes them. The attempt of those of one State to control the domestic institutions of another can only result in feelings of distrust and jealousy, the certain harbingers of disunion, violence, and civil war, and the ultimate destruction of our free institutions. Our Confederacy is perfectly illustrated by the terms and principles governing a common copartnership. There is a fund of power to be exercised under the direction of the joint councils of the allied members, but that which has been reserved by the individual members is intangible by the common Government or the individual members composing it. To attempt it finds no support in the principles of our Constitution.

–from William Henry Harrison's Inaugural Address, March 4, 1841

BERKELEY PLANTATION

12602 Harrison Landing Road, Charles City, Virginia 23030

PHONE: 804-829-6018 or 888-466-6018

www.berkeleyplantation.com

HOURS: open daily; closed Christmas Day

ADMISSION: fee; child, student, senior discounts

WHEELCHAIR ACCESSIBILITY: contact office at 888-466-6018

Berkeley Plantation is not only the birthplace of William Henry Harrison, but it is also birthplace to his father, Benjamin, a signer of the Declaration of Independence. To further support its claim as Virginia's most historic plantation, Berkeley has been identified by historians as the site of the first Thanksgiving. On December 4, 1619, early English settlers came ashore at Berkeley and celebrated the first official Thanksgiving in America.

The early Georgian-style mansion dates back to 1726 and sits atop a hillside overlooking the historic James River. The mansion was built with bricks fired on the plantation. Visitors can tour the first floor and basement of the house, which includes the original window frames, doors, and masonry. The first floor includes the central hall, formal and informal drawing rooms, the dining room, and the gentleman's room. Chinese porcelain, English silver, and Waterford crystal are authentic to the period.

Visits begin with an orientation program and museum exhibit. Costumed guides then lead a tour of the manor house. Grounds tours of outstanding boxwood and flower gardens are self-guided. Special events are scheduled year-round.

Berkeley Plantation

NEAREST AIRPORT: Richmond, Virginia

GENERAL DIRECTIONS: Located 27 miles west of Williamsburg and 22 miles east of Richmond on Virginia Route 5. From downtown Richmond, follow Main Street East (Route 5 East). From the north, take I-95 south to I-295 South and take Exit 22A to Route 5. From the west, take I-64 East to exit 242A (Jamestown/ Route 199) to Route 5.

NEARBY ATTRACTIONS: Westover, Shirley, and Evelynton plantations.

GROUSELAND
WILLIAM HENRY HARRISON MANSION

3 W. Scott Street, Vincennes, Indiana 47591

PHONE: 812-882-2096

HOURS: Monday to Saturday; closed Thanksgiving, Christmas, and New Year's Day

ADMISSION: fee; student discounts

WHEELCHAIR ACCESSIBILITY: no

Grouseland

This twenty-one-room Federal-style mansion was home to William Henry Harrison from 1804 to 1812. The house is located on its original site, which was part of a 300-acre farm. Built between 1803 and 1804, the home was the first brick house in Vincennes. It is furnished with pre-1812 artifacts, including authentic Harrison pieces. Distinctive curved walls are found throughout the house, even in the dependency. The passageway between the great house and dependency is now a gallery of William Henry Harrison artifacts and exhibits.

Grouseland sits across from the southern edge of the Vincennes University campus. In addition to the mansion, the site includes a gift shop. Interpreters in period costume conduct guided tours of the home. December features "Christmas at Grouseland," with period decorations hung throughout the house.

Grouseland opened to the public in 1911 after being rescued from destruction by the Francis Vigo Chapter, D.A.R. It is still owned by this chapter but has been run by Grouseland Foundation since 1999.

NEAREST AIRPORT: Evansville, Indiana

GENERAL DIRECTIONS: Each exit into Vincennes will take you to Hart Street. Take Hart St. to 2nd St.; turn right. Cross the railroad tracks; go 1/4 block and turn left.

NEARBY ATTRACTIONS: George Rogers Clark National Historic Park, Vincennes State Historic Sites, Old French Home, Old Cathedral, Indiana Military Museum.

JOHN TYLER

1790–1862
10th President • 1841–1845

John Tyler was the first vice president to accede to the office of
president after the death of his predecessor; he assumed the role
upon the death of William Henry Harrison just one month after
Harrison's own inauguration. Tyler struggled for the remainder of
his term against those who believed his authority to be less than
complete, even being called "His Accidency" by some detractors.
Today Tyler's assertion that the vice president, in fact, becomes president in the event of death or assassination is considered constitu-
tionally mandated.

   Born at Greenway Plantation on Virginia's James River and
educated at the College of William and Mary, Tyler studied law
under his father and was admitted to the bar. After stints as both
governor of Virginia and a U.S. congressman and senator, Tyler was
chosen as the running mate to the Whig candidate, William Henry
Harrison, in 1840.

   The Constitution called for the vice president to assume the
duties and powers of the president in the case of a president's death,
but many believed it did not call for the vice president to assume the

office of the president. Tyler never received the complete support or respect of either his own cabinet or his own party, and he disagreed with the Whig party view on nearly every issue. In 1841, after Tyler refused to sign legislation creating the Third Bank of the United States, all but one member of his cabinet resigned, further weakening his already tenuous hold on presidential authority. Tyler was expelled from the Whig party and became a president without a party.

A year after his expulsion from the party and following yet another veto of a Whig-backed bill, the country's first impeachment resolution was introduced in the House of Representatives. The committee claimed Tyler had misused his veto power; the resolution failed. Tyler left office after one term, having managed to enact some positive legislation, including the Preemption Act and the annexation of Texas, despite his differences with the Whig party. An interesting byproduct of Tyler's presidency is that it prompted party members to take a closer look at their vice presidential candidates and their views.

John Tyler achieved another first in the White House; he was the first president to be married while in office. For Tyler it was a second marriage; his first wife, Letitia Christian, died during his administration. In 1844, nine months after the death of his first wife, the president married Julia Gardiner in a New York City ceremony kept secret from the public and all but one of Tyler's own children. With his two wives, Tyler had fifteen children—seven of whom were born after his term as president—more than any other American president. Tyler died in 1862 in Richmond, Virginia. He is remembered by historians not as a great president but as a man whose experience was one more test of the young nation's constitutional foundation.

I AM DETERMINED TO UPHOLD THE CONSTITUTION . . . to the utmost of my ability and in defiance of all personal consequences. What may happen to an individual is of little importance, but the Constitution of the country, or any of its great and clear principles and provisions, is too sacred to be surrendered under any circumstances whatever by those who are charged with its protection and defense.

—**John Tyler, 1842**

SHERWOOD FOREST PLANTATION

14501 John Tyler Memorial Highway, Charles City, Virginia 23030

PHONE: 804-829-5377

www.sherwoodforest.org

HOURS: daily; closed Thanksgiving and Christmas

ADMISSION: fee; student and senior discounts

WHEELCHAIR ACCESSIBILITY: limited

Known to be the longest frame house in America, the Sherwood Forest Plantation house is Virginia Tidewater in its architectural design and sits on twelve acres of terraced gardens and lawns. President John Tyler purchased the plantation in 1842 and lived there until his death in 1862. It has been continually owned by direct descendants of Tyler since that time. Tyler's grandson and his wife, the current owners, restored the residence in the mid-1970s. The house contains furnishings, paintings, and heirlooms belonging to President Tyler and his wife. Six original outbuildings surround the house.

Sherwood Forest Plantation

Sherwood Forest was damaged in the Civil War, as is evidenced by marks on the woodwork and doors plus the scars on the French Empire table used by Tyler in the White House. Legend has it that the house is home to a ghost known as the Gray Lady, who has been heard rocking in the Gray Room for more than 200 years.

Guided tours of the home are thirty to forty minutes in length, and visitors can take self-guided tours of the grounds. Large groups can request the Red Carpet and Tea Tour, with a tea in the Tippecanoe Room featuring traditional Virginia fare. Student groups can dance the Virginia Reel, churn butter, and play nineteenth-century lawn games as they learn about plantation life and politics of the 1840s. Box lunches are available to groups by reservation, and the grounds can be reserved for special events.

John Tyler's grandson and his family, who still reside on the estate, own and maintain the property with the assistance of admissions revenue and visitor support.

NEAREST AIRPORT: Richmond, Virginia
GENERAL DIRECTIONS: Located 18 miles west of Williamsburg and 35 miles east of Richmond on Virginia Route 5. From downtown Richmond, follow Main Street East (Route 5 East) approximately 30 miles. From the north, take I-95 south to I-295 South and take Exit 22A to Route 5. From the west, take I-64 East to exit 242A (Jamestown/Route 199) to Route 5.
NEARBY ATTRACTIONS: Berkeley, Westover, Shirley, and Evelynton plantations.

JAMES K. POLK

1795–1849
11th President • 1845–1849

James Knox Polk is often called by historians the greatest one-term president. He was a "dark horse"candidate but one behind whom both factions of the divided Democratic party could unite. An ardent believer in Manifest Destiny, Polk ran on a platform of expansionism. He was the last of the Jacksonian Democrats, and some say the last strong president prior to Abraham Lincoln. Polk stated four goals for his presidency and accomplished them all.

James K. Polk was born in Mecklenburg County, North Carolina, in 1795 but moved with his family to middle Tennessee early in his life. He served in the Tennessee state legislature, in the House of Representatives, and as governor of Tennessee before running for president. In fact, Polk had only aspirations of the vice presidency before Andrew Jackson, sensing the nation's desire for expansion, urged him to consider the presidency. Polk won the approval of his contemporaries and successors alike, among them thirty-third president Harry S Truman, who said of Polk: "A great president. Said what he intended to do and did it all."

Manifest Destiny was the guiding principle of the Polk administration. His Democratic party's slogan of "Fifty-four forty or fight!" referred to the northwestern land between 42° and 54°40' latitude, which most Americans believed should be their own. For years Great Britain had made similar claims, and the two nations were deadlocked. Polk fought hard to win the land and, in the end, agreed to the Oregon Treaty which, while it fell short of the famous parameters, guaranteed to the United States the land that is now the states of Washington and Oregon. Polk also led the United States into the Mexican War, which settled the conflict over the Texas-Mexico border and resulted in the acquisition of not only California but also the entire Southwest. In excess of 500,000 square miles, it was the largest addition to the Union since the Louisiana Purchase.

Despite his effective leadership, James Polk chose not to seek election to a second presidential term. After the inauguration of his successor, Zachary Taylor, Polk and his wife, Sarah, made their way to Nashville, where they intended to spend their retirement years in a newly purchased home they called Polk Place. The former president was weak from cholera by the time he arrived in Nashville, however, and within three weeks he was dead at the young age of fifty-four.

Who shall assign limits to the achievements of free minds and free hands under the protection of this glorious Union? No treason to mankind since the organization of society would be equal in atrocity to that of him who would lift his hand to destroy it. . . . If he say that error and wrong are committed in the administration of the Government, let him remember that nothing human can be perfect, and that under no other system of government revealed by Heaven or devised by man has reason been allowed so free and so broad a scope to combat error. Has the sword of despots proven to be a safer or surer instrument of reform in government than enlightened reason? Does he expect to find among the ruins of this Union a happier abode for our swarming millions than they now have under it? Every lover of this country must shudder at the thought of the possibility of its dissolution, and will be ready to adopt the patriotic sentiment, "Our Federal Union, it must be preserved."

–from James Polk's Inaugural Address, March 4, 1845

JAMES K. POLK MEMORIAL
STATE HISTORIC SITE

308 S. Polk Street, Pineville, North Carolina 28134

PHONE: 704-889-7145

www.ah.dcr.state.nc.us

HOURS: April through October, daily; November through March, Tuesday to Sunday; closed most holidays

ADMISSION: no fee, donations accepted

WHEELCHAIR ACCESSIBILITY: yes (visitor center only)

Located on the birthplace site of James K. Polk, the Memorial's exhibitions and programs commemorate the significant events of Polk's presidency as well as his life in Mecklenburg County. The site is twenty-four acres of the original 150 acres that belonged to Polk's father, Samuel. James Polk lived on the land on which the site is located from his birth in 1795 until his family moved to Columbia, Tennessee, in 1806.

The log buildings and their furnishings are not original to the Polk family, but they are reconstructions of a typical homestead of that time, including a log house, separate kitchen, and barn. The furnishings are period pieces that date back to the early 1800s.

The site includes a visitor center, museum, and gardens. Costumed guides lead tours on the half hour; an orientation film entitled *Who Is Polk?* is shown on the hour. Self-guided tours are also an option. Special activities include hands-on demonstrations for children's groups and living history programs. Picnic facilities are available on the property as well.

A reconstruction of a period homestead at the James K. Polk Memorial State Historic Site

The James K. Polk Memorial State Historic Site is owned and operated by the State of North Carolina, Department of Cultural Resources. The Polk Memorial Support Fund provides additional assistance to the site.

NEAREST AIRPORT: Charlotte, North Carolina

GENERAL DIRECTIONS: Five miles south of Charlotte in Pineville. South on old US 521 (Polk Street) in Pineville; the entrance is 1.5 miles on the left.

NEARBY ATTRACTIONS: Reed Gold Mine State Historic Site, Historic Latta Plantation, Historic Rosedale, Historic Brattonsville.

JAMES K. POLK ANCESTRAL HOME

301 West Seventh Street, Columbia, Tennessee 38401

PHONE: 931-388-2354

www.jameskpolk.com

HOURS: daily

ADMISSION: fee; student and
senior discounts; group discounts

WHEELCHAIR ACCESSIBILITY: yes, except
second floor of home

James K. Polk Ancestral Home

The James K. Polk Ancestral Home is the
only surviving original residence of the
eleventh president. Built by his father,
Samuel Polk, it was home to James following his graduation from college in 1818
until his marriage to Sarah Childress in 1824. Today, the Federal-style brick house
displays items from Polk's years in both Tennessee and Washington, D.C., including
furniture, paintings, and White House china.

In addition to the main home, the site includes the Sisters' House, where two of
Polk's married sisters lived at different times, and the detached kitchen building,
which was reconstructed in 1946 on its original foundation. The Sisters' House features a museum room, gift shop, and temporary exhibits; it also shows a short orientation video. Here visitors can view artifacts from the site's collection, including
White House gifts, campaign memorabilia, and Sarah Polk's Inaugural fan. In the
kitchen building, visitors will see period cooking implements and household pieces as
well as the occasional demonstration of nineteenth-century crafts and chores.

Outside, the grounds feature a formal boxwood garden, white azalea garden,
and wildflower garden. A cast-iron fountain from Polk's final residence—torn
down in 1901—was rescued and now resides in the courtyard.

The James K. Polk Ancestral Home offers outreach and community programs
throughout the year. Visitors can find a schedule of programs on the website.
Programs include Polk's America Discussion Group, a monthly meeting of individuals and scholars interested in topics of importance in the 1800–1850 time period,
and the Polk Academy Children's Summer Camp for fourth through sixth graders.

The State of Tennessee owns the home and its property, while the James K. Polk
Memorial Association, begun by a great-niece in 1924, maintains the property and its
collection. Membership is open to the public; details can be found on the website.

NEAREST AIRPORT: Nashville, Tennessee

GENERAL DIRECTIONS: Forty-one miles south of Nashville on U.S. Hwy 31; one
block west of Hwy 31 on 7th Street in downtown Columbia.

NEARBY ATTRACTIONS: Tennessee Antebellum Trail, The Hermitage, Tennessee
State Capitol, Tennessee State Museum, historic downtown Nashville district.

ZACHARY TAYLOR

1784–1850
12th President • 1849–1850

Known as "Old Rough and Ready" for his toughness and heroism during the Mexican War, Zachary Taylor was a good-hearted, unpretentious man who, due to a lifelong battle with stuttering, spoke in a slow, studied manner. A direct descendant of Mayflower Pilgrim William Brewster, Taylor was born in Orange County, Virginia, but grew up on his father's plantation in Kentucky, on the western edge of the American frontier. He later made his home in Baton Rouge, Louisiana, and owned a plantation in Mississippi.

Never a politician, Taylor considered the military his career. He fought in the War of 1812, the Black Hawk War, the Second Seminole War, and the Mexican War, all the while moving his wife, Peggy, and their children with him from fort to fort across the southeastern United States. In 1846, Taylor was promoted to the rank of major general for his service at Palo Alto and Resaca de la Palma. In a fierce battle, Taylor narrowly escaped serious injury on two occasions while courageously leading his men to victory over a much larger Mexican army.

Returning from war a hero, Taylor easily won the Whig nomination for president in 1848. In the national election, "Old Rough and Ready," who himself had never voted in a presidential election and had never run for public office, won a close three-way race, defeating Democrat Lewis Cass and former president Martin Van Buren, who represented the Free-Soil Party.

Taylor's time in office was consumed mostly by the issue of slavery. Although a slaveholder himself, he opposed its expansion while at the same time believing that preservation of the Union must be the ultimate goal of all Americans. He urged settlers in New Mexico and California to bypass the territorial stage and apply for statehood immediately. Since the territories were unlikely to permit slavery in their new state constitutions, this all but ensured the fulfillment of Taylor's desire to keep slavery out of new states. Southerners, who wanted slavery, and moderates, who wanted to preserve the Union, viewed Taylor's actions with equal disapproval.

Zachary Taylor served sixteen months as president. He died in office in July of 1850 of what the doctors called *cholera morbus*, a gastro-intestinal illness contracted after a meal of cherries and iced milk. Sanitation was poor in the hot, humid Washington summers, and Taylor's illness was not uncommon. Taylor's wife, Peggy, in poor health before her husband's death, lived only two more years. Three of their children survived them.

FOR MORE THAN HALF A CENTURY, during which kingdoms and empires have fallen, this Union has stood unshaken. The patriots who formed it have long since descended to the grave; yet still it remains, the proudest monument to their memory. In my judgment, its dissolution would be the greatest of calamities. . . . Upon its preservation must depend our own happiness and that of countless generations to come. Whatever dangers may threaten it, I shall stand by it and maintain it in its integrity to the full extent of the obligations imposed and the power conferred upon me by the Constitution.

–Zachary Taylor, speaking in 1848, the year he was elected president

No Zachary Taylor homes or libraries are open to the general public.

MILLARD FILLMORE

1800–1874
13th President • 1850–1853

Millard Fillmore, elected vice president in 1848, acceded to the presidency in the summer of 1850 upon the sudden death of President Zachary Taylor. Fillmore inherited the reins of a nation badly divided and on the verge of civil war. The highlight of his administration was the Compromise of 1850, a measure which Taylor had stubbornly opposed but which Fillmore believed was the best chance for securing peace between North and South.

Fillmore came to Washington, D.C., from New York's Finger Lakes region, where he was born in the year 1800 in a log cabin on his parents' farm. As a child, Fillmore received no formal education. Not until age seventeen, when a library opened in the small town of New Hope where he was serving as apprentice to a clothmaker, did Fillmore discover his love of books and learning. Two years later, he enrolled at a local school and later went on to study law. Fillmore's first teacher, Abigail Powers, would eventually become his wife. Together they had two children and amassed a personal library of over four thousand volumes. Mrs. Fillmore, as first lady, worked to create the first permanent library in the White House.

Fillmore brought to the presidency the skills of his years in law and as a member of the House of Representatives. Like many leaders of his day, Fillmore believed that the United States could survive half slave and half free; and he believed that the rights of slaveholders were protected by the Constitution. The Compromise of 1850, which Fillmore supported and Taylor had not, admitted California to the Union as a free state and abolished the slave trade in Washington, D.C. But it was no abolitionist's bill. The Compromise included the Fugitive Slave Law, which held northern states responsible for the return of escaped slaves found within their borders. At best, the Compromise was a temporary solution, forestalling but not preventing civil war.

Support of the Compromise of 1850 cost Fillmore the chance at a second term; northern members of the Whig party could not forgive him for his support of the Fugitive Slave Law. After one term, Fillmore retired from public life. Within sixteen months, personal tragedy struck twice: Abigail Fillmore died of pneumonia after catching cold at the Pierce inauguration; and one year later, the Fillmores' daughter, Mary, died suddenly of cholera. In his grief, the former president embarked on an extended trip across the United States and Europe. He later settled near his childhood home in Buffalo, New York, with his second wife, Caroline Carmichael McIntosh.

In 1856 Fillmore accepted the nomination of the American, or Know-Nothing Party—a group seeking to create stricter immigration laws—and ran again for the presidency. He garnered only 22 percent of the vote against James Buchanan. Throughout the Civil War, Fillmore opposed President Lincoln's administration, and he supported Andrew Johnson's stand against radical Reconstruction. Fillmore died in 1874 in Buffalo, New York.

OUR CONSTITUTION, THOUGH NOT PERFECT, IS DOUBTLESS THE BEST that ever was formed. Therefore, let every proposition to change it be well weighed and, if found beneficial, cautiously adopted. Every patriot will rejoice to see its authority so exerted as to advance the prosperity and honor of the nation, whilst he will watch with jealousy any attempt to mutilate this charter of our liberties or pervert its powers to acts of aggression or injustice. Thus shall conservatism and progress blend their harmonious action in preserving the form and spirit of the Constitution and at the same time carry forward the great improvements of the country with a rapidity and energy which freemen only can display.

—from Millard Fillmore's third Annual Message, December 6, 1852

THE MILLARD FILLMORE HOUSE ━━━━━━

24 Shearer Avenue, East Aurora, New York 14052

PHONE: 716-652-8875

www.millardfillmorehouse.org

HOURS: June through mid-October, Wednesday, Saturday, and Sunday (limited);
by appointment for groups

ADMISSION: fee; child discount

WHEELCHAIR ACCESSIBILITY: no

This Federal-style dwelling served as the first home of Millard Fillmore and his
first wife, Abigail, from 1826 to 1830. It stood in disrepair for many years until it
was purchased by artist Margaret Evans Price in 1930. Price had the house moved
to its current location and renovated it for use as her studio. After acquiring the
Fillmore House in 1975, the Aurora Historical Society set about restoring it to its
1826 appearance.

Much of the original woodwork is still in the house, which is furnished with
period pieces, including Fillmore's bed, scrub table, and tall law desk. Other pieces
are from Fillmore's time in the White House and his other homes in Buffalo. Colors
were selected based on research into the era and items that were uncovered during
the restoration process. A collection of period children's toys holds special appeal
for younger visitors.

The East Aurora Garden Club undertook the project of re-creating and car-
ing for a formal Presidential Rose Garden and a dooryard herb garden reminis-
cent of Abigail's. A carriage barn, constructed with beams from the Fillmore
family barn built by Millard's father, houses Fillmore's sleigh as well as a period
tool collection.

The Millard Fillmore House is owned, maintained, and staffed by the Aurora
Historical Society. It has been designated a National Historic Landmark.

NEAREST AIRPORT: Buffalo, New York

GENERAL DIRECTIONS: 25 minutes southeast of Buffalo via Route 400 off New
York State Thruway 90.

NEARBY ATTRACTIONS: Forest Lawn Cemetery (Fillmore's place of burial), Buffalo
and Erie County Historical Society, Roycroft Inn and Historic Campus.

MILLARD FILLMORE LOG CABIN ━━━━━━

FILLMORE GLEN STATE PARK

1686 State Route 38, Moravia, New York 13118

PHONE: 315-497-0130

HOURS: mid-May to mid-October

ADMISSION: fee; senior discount for New York residents

WHEELCHAIR ACCESSIBILITY: limited

Millard Fillmore Birthplace Log Cabin

Located in Fillmore Glen State Park, the Millard Fillmore Log Cabin is a replica of the cabin in which Fillmore was born about four miles away in Locke, New York. It is a quick stop on a trip through a park that offers hiking, water sports, and winter activities plus camping in the summer months.

The park and cabin are administered by the state of New York.

NEAREST AIRPORT: Syracuse, New York; Ithaca, New York; Rochester, New York
GENERAL DIRECTIONS: Route 38, one mile south of Moravia.
NEARBY ATTRACTIONS: St. Mathew's Church, Cayuga-Owasco Lake Historical Society, and New Hope Mills.

FRANKLIN PIERCE

1804–1869
14th President • 1853–1857

Franklin Pierce took office at a seemingly peaceful time in history. The 1850 Compromise had quieted the country for a brief time and the economy was prosperous. But this peace was not to last long and Pierce endured a troubled administration.

The son of a Revolutionary War veteran, Pierce was born in a log cabin on the banks of the Contoocook River in Hillsborough County, New Hampshire. He proved himself a superior student in childhood and later at Bowdoin College in Maine, where among his closest friends was the aspiring young author Nathaniel Hawthorne. After college Pierce returned to New Hampshire to set up a law practice.

Pierce did not actively seek the presidency; rather it fell into his lap at a time when the nation's political parties were as divided as the people they served. After a career in the New Hampshire legislature and later the Congress and Senate, Pierce had returned to his New Hampshire law practice. But in 1852, when his Democratic party could not agree upon a candidate, Pierce's name was put forth and accepted as a compromise candidate. Franklin Pierce won the national election and became the fourteenth president of the United States.

Only months before Pierce's inauguration, his eleven-year-old son was killed in a train accident. He and his wife, Jane, went to the White House in the depths of depression, and their experience of the presidency did little to lift their spirits. Pierce's push toward expansion was seen by northerners as an attempt on the part of the south to extend slavery into new areas, and conflict broke out anew. Like his immediate predecessors, Pierce proved powerless in his attempts to stem the tide of civil war. He gave his support to the Kansas-Nebraska Act in order to prevent the blocking of his own foreign policy measures, but he didn't believe in the act. Aimed at easing the conflict in the midwestern territories by allowing residents to choose for themselves whether their states would be slave or free, the results were disastrous. Kansas erupted into a bitter, bloody conflict, with northerners and southerners rushing into the state to fight for control of the territory. The nation needed strong, decisive leadership, but Franklin Pierce proved unequal to the task.

Pierce, disappointed in the Democrats' refusal to renominate him, left the White House after one term. He and Jane returned to New Hampshire, where they sought relief from their grief. In later years, Pierce openly opposed the Civil War, calling the bloodshed a tragedy and the goal of preserving the Union by force an impossibility. After the assassination of President Lincoln, an angry mob attacked Pierce's home, confusing his opposition to war with opposition to the Union. Pierce died in 1869 in Concord, New Hampshire, not far from the riverside log cabin where he was born.

WITH THE UNION MY BEST AND DEAREST EARTHLY HOPES ARE ENTWINED. Without it, what are we individually or collectively? What becomes of the noblest field ever opened for the advancement of our race in religion, in government, in the arts, and in all that dignifies and adorns mankind? From that radiant constellation that both illumines our own way and points out to struggling nations their course, let but a single star be lost, and, if these not be utter darkness, the luster of the whole is dimmed. . . . It is with me an earnest and vital belief that as the Union had been the source, under Providence, of our prosperity to this time, so it is the surest pledge of a continuance of the blessings we have enjoyed and which we are sacredly bound to transmit undiminished to our children.

–from Franklin Pierce's Inaugural Address, March 4, 1853

THE PIERCE HOMESTEAD

Route 31, Hillsborough, New Hampshire 03244

PHONE: 603-478-3165

www.franklinpierce.ws

HOURS: Memorial Day through Columbus Day,
Saturday and Sunday; July through August, daily

ADMISSION: fee; child discounts

WHEELCHAIR ACCESSIBILITY: first floor of house,
barn, and restroom; video of second floor available on request

The Pierce Homestead, the home of Franklin Pierce for thirty years, was built in 1804 by his father, Governor Benjamin Pierce. The house symbolized the elegance of the age with hand-stenciled walls, imported French wallpaper, and new furniture. It even boasts a ballroom on the second floor. The house was a gathering place of a number of great individuals, including Daniel Webster and Nathaniel Hawthorne.

The Franklin Pierce Homestead is maintained and operated by the Hillsborough Historical Society, a non-profit organization dedicated to the preservation of the history and historic properties of Hillsborough, New Hampshire. Monthly programs are featured by the Society from June to October.

NEAREST AIRPORT: Manchester, New Hampshire

GENERAL DIRECTIONS: Route 9 west from Concord, east from Keene. At junction of Routes 9 and 31, turn onto Route 31N.

NEARBY ATTRACTIONS: Pierce Manse, Daniel Webster Birthplace, Pierce grave site.

The Pierce Homestead

THE PIERCE MANSE

14 Horse Shoe Pond Lane, Concord, New Hampshire 03301

PHONE: 603-224-5957

HOURS: mid-June through Labor Day,
Monday to Friday; other times by appointment

ADMISSION: fee; child and student discounts

WHEELCHAIR ACCESSIBILITY: no

This Greek Revival house was the family home of Franklin Pierce from 1842 to 1848. It has been restored, and many of its furnishings belonged to Pierce or other members of his family. Some furnishings are known as "White House pieces." A portrait of young Franky Pierce, who died at age four, is one of the treasures of the Manse. In 1971, the structure was moved to its current location in historic Concord. A replica of the original barn and shed was added to the property in 1993.

Threatened with demolition by an Urban Renewal project in 1966, the only Concord house ever owned and occupied by Franklin Pierce was saved by The Pierce Brigade. The Brigade owns the house and maintains it as a memorial to New Hampshire's only president.

NEAREST AIRPORT: Manchester, New Hampshire

GENERAL DIRECTIONS: From I-93 north, take exit 15W. Turn left on Bridge Street. Go several blocks to Main Street; turn right. The Manse is located at the end of Main Street where it runs into Horse Shoe Pond Lane.

NEARBY ATTRACTIONS: Daniel Webster Birthplace, Pierce grave site, The Pierce Homestead.

The Pierce Manse

JAMES BUCHANAN
1791–1868
15th President • 1857–1861

James Buchanan entered the office of the presidency morally convinced that slavery was wrong but believing that the Constitution protected the rights of slave owners in those states in which it was established. He also believed that settlers in new territories should be able to decide for themselves whether they would be free or slave.

Born into a well-to-do family in 1791 in Cove Gap, Pennsylvania, Buchanan received an early education from his mother; he then went on to college and, later, law school. Buchanan, the only American president never to marry, had no biological children but did raise an orphaned niece, Harriet Lane, whom he took with him to the White House to serve as official hostess.

A gifted orator, Buchanan began his journey toward the presidency with a string of elected and appointed offices, including seats in the U.S. House of Representatives and Senate as well as appointments as minister to Russia and Great Britain and secretary of state. He ran as a Democrat and won the presidency in 1856 on a platform of conciliation. He took office convinced that he could avert civil war by working a compromise between North and South.

Buchanan supported the Supreme Court's controversial Dred Scott decision, which declared that blacks were not entitled to the rights guaranteed by the Constitution. Buchanan believed that this decision supported his view that slavery was protected by the Constitution, and he continued to work toward compromise with this as his basis. After Lincoln's victory and as Buchanan's term drew to a close, Buchanan stood by as South Carolina seceded from the Union, soon followed by six more states. He believed that the federal government had no constitutional authority to force any state to remain in the Union and believed himself powerless to act. Buchanan left office with the country fractured beyond compromise. Recent scholars have acknowledged that alternate policies would not likely have proven successful in averting the conflict.

An avowed optimist, Buchanan took on the presidency with high hopes, but he left after one term with words of foreboding for his successor, Abraham Lincoln: "My dear sir," Buchanan remarked to the sixteenth president, "if you are as happy on entering the White House as I am on leaving, you are a very happy man indeed."

James Buchanan lived a quiet life in retirement and remained, for the most part, on his Wheatland estate in Lancaster, Pennsylvania. He loyally supported the Union during the Civil War and spoke out in favor of President Johnson's post-war efforts at Reconstruction in the South. He died in 1868 at Wheatland.

IT MAY BE PROPER THAT ON THIS OCCASION I should make some brief remarks in regard to our rights and duties as a member of the great family of nations. In our intercourse with them there are some plain principles, approved by our own experience from which we should never depart. We ought to cultivate peace, commerce, and friendship with all nations, and this is not merely as the best means of promoting our own interests, but in a spirit of Christian benevolence toward our fellow men, wherever their lot may be cast. Our diplomacy should be direct and frank, neither seeking to obtain more nor accepting less than is our due. We ought to cherish a sacred regard for the independence of all nations, and never attempt to interfere in the domestic concerns of any unless this shall be imperatively required by the great law of self-preservation. To avoid entangling alliances has been a maxim of our policy ever since the days of Washington, and its wisdom no one will attempt to dispute. In short, we ought to do justice in a kindly spirit to all nations and require justice from them in return.

–from James Buchanan's Inaugural Address, March 4, 1857

WHEATLAND

1120 Marietta Avenue, Lancaster, Pennsylvania 17603
PHONE: 717-392-8721

www.wheatland.org

HOURS: April through October, daily; November, weekends only; December, limited hours daily; closed Easter, Thanksgiving, and Christmas

ADMISSION: fee; senior, student, child, and group discounts

WHEELCHAIR ACCESSIBILITY: no

Originally built in 1828 for Lancaster lawyer and banker William Jenkins, Wheatland was home to President James Buchanan from 1848 until his death in 1868. The mansion served as Buchanan's presidential campaign headquarters, and it was on the lawn of this Federal-style home that he gave

Wheatland's front hall

his first campaign address. Wheatland also provided the setting for the writing of both Buchanan's inaugural address and, later, his presidential memoirs.

Visitors to Wheatland receive guided tours of the house, which is furnished with Buchanan's original items and other period artifacts. In addition to the house tour, the site offers the Carriage House Visitors Center with a video and interpretive exhibits, self-guided tours of the grounds and gardens, and two gift shops. Educational programming at Wheatland includes a Children's Hands-On Tour and Summer Story Hour (reservations required), and Christmas candlelight tours, mansion mystery tours, and nineteenth-century fairs for families.

Wheatland opened to the public in 1936 as a result of a purchase and preservation effort led by the Junior League of Lancaster. It was named a National Historic Landmark in 1962 and currently operates under the stewardship of The James Buchanan Foundation for the Preservation of Wheatland. Membership in the foundation entitles members to free admission to Wheatland.

NEAREST AIRPORT: Harrisburg, Pennsylvania

GENERAL DIRECTIONS: From Route 30, take the exit for Route 741/Millersville/Rohrerstown, and take 741 east. Travel 0.6 miles to Marietta Avenue/23 East. Turn left onto Marietta Avenue and travel two miles. Wheatland is on the right.

NEARBY ATTRACTIONS: Railroad Museum of Pennsylvania, Strasburg Railroad, Landis Valley Museum, The People's Place.

Front façade of Wheatland

BUCHANAN'S BIRTHPLACE STATE PARK ———

6235 Aughwick Road, Ft. Loudon, Pennsylvania 17224

PHONE: 717-485-3948

www.dcnr.state.pa.us

HOURS: daily

ADMISSION: no fee

WHEELCHAIR ACCESSIBILITY: limited

(some paved areas, picnic areas, and path around lake)

This eighteen-and-a-half-acre state park is nestled near the village of Cove Gap in the Allegheny Mountains. In the late 1770s, anyone seeking a route west would have passed through this gap. In 1789, Buchanan's father bought the site, complete with cabins, barns, stables, store, and orchard—it was here that James Buchanan was born. Buchanan's father renamed the site Stony Batter after the family's home in northern Ireland and operated the business until moving it to Mercersburg when James was six.

Today, visitors can enjoy a picnic on the grounds, wander the trails, and fish. They can see the stone pyramid monument that was erected on the original site of the cabin in which Buchanan was born or visit the cabin itself on the grounds of the Mercersburg Academy where it was later moved. No staff is on site, but interpretive signs are being planned for the park.

It was the unwavering desire and persistence of Buchanan's niece, Harriet Lane Johnston, that led to the creation of the Buchanan memorials. In her will, Johnston set aside $100,000 earmarked for the James Buchanan Monument Fund. She chose a four-member board of trustees, and her will stipulated that the board had fifteen years from the time of her death to build a monument at Stony Batter and/or erect a statue in Washington, D.C. The stone pyramid monument in the park was completed in 1908. The nine-and-a-half-foot bronze James Buchanan Memorial was unveiled in Washington, D.C., in 1930.

The Buchanan Birthplace State Park is administered by the Cowans Gap State Park, which is fifteen minutes away and offers a variety of recreation activities.

NEAREST AIRPORT: Hagerstown, Maryland

GENERAL DIRECTIONS: Located just off PA Route 16 between Mercersburg and McConnellsburg in south central Pennsylvania.

NEARBY ATTRACTIONS: Mercersburg, Mercersburg Academy, Cowans Gap State Park.

ABRAHAM LINCOLN

1809–1865
16th President • 1861–1865

Abraham Lincoln has long been seen as a symbol of democracy and the American dream. Born in a tiny, one-room log cabin in Kentucky to an illiterate father, Lincoln taught himself to read and write and figure; and he grew up to become one of the country's most respected and memorialized leaders. His father, Thomas, moved the family a number of times during Lincoln's childhood, from Kentucky to Indiana and, later, to Illinois. Lincoln's mother, Nancy Hanks, died when he was ten and his father later married Sarah Bush Johnston. While Lincoln remembered his mother fondly, it was his stepmother who supported and encouraged him in his quest for education and self-improvement.

As a young man, Lincoln settled in New Salem, Illinois, not far from Springfield. Here he worked at a number of trades—sales clerk, surveyor, village postmaster—all while studying law. He was elected to the state legislature in 1834 and served four terms as a member of the Whig party. During this time, he married Mary Todd, with whom he had four sons. Lincoln entered national politics in 1847 when he won a term in Congress. After switching his allegiance to the newly emerging Republican Party in 1856, Lincoln lost his bid for Senate in the 1858 race against Stephen Douglas. He earned national recognition, however, through their debates and was soon considered a presidential candidate.

President Lincoln's election in 1860 and his known views on slavery prompted a number of southern states to secede from the Union. By the time of his Inaugural Address, seven states had already seceded, and others soon followed. Preserving and restoring the Union was Lincoln's overriding goal during the Civil War. The war began in April 1861 with the firing upon Fort Sumter and lasted four long years—tearing apart family and friends and very nearly the nation itself.

In his first presidential election, Lincoln's victory over his three competitors was modest; he won his second presidential election, which came as the war was winding down, with an overwhelming majority of the electoral vote. Lincoln lived to see the end of the Civil War and the preservation of the Union but not the implementation of his Reconstruction plans. Abraham Lincoln was assassinated by John Wilkes Booth on April 14, 1865, in Ford's Theatre, five days after Lee's surrender at Appomattox.

In addition to his strong leadership during the Civil War, Abraham Lincoln is remembered for his vision, his humanity, and his flair for public speaking. Among his most memorable speeches are the Emancipation Proclamation, declaring forever free those slaves within the Confederacy, and the Gettysburg Address, his dedication of the military cemetery at Gettysburg.

But in a larger sense, we cannot dedicate, we cannot consecrate, we cannot hallow this ground. The brave men, living and dead who struggled here have consecrated it far above our poor power to add or detract. The world will little note nor long remember what we say here, but it can never forget what they did here. It is for us the living rather to be dedicated here to the unfinished work which they who fought here have thus far so nobly advanced. It is rather for us to be here dedicated to the great task remaining before us—that from these honored dead we take increased devotion to that cause for which they gave the last full measure of devotion—that we here highly resolve that these dead shall not have died in vain, that this nation under God shall have a new birth of freedom, and that government of the people, by the people, for the people shall not perish from the earth.

–from Abraham Lincoln's Gettysburg Address, November 19, 1863

ABRAHAM LINCOLN BIRTHPLACE NATIONAL HISTORIC SITE

2995 Lincoln Farm Road, Hodgenville, Kentucky 42748

PHONE: 270-358-3137

www.nps.gov/abli

HOURS: daily; closed Thanksgiving, Christmas, and New Year's Day

ADMISSION: no fee

WHEELCHAIR ACCESSIBILITY: yes

Dedicated in 1911 by President William Howard Taft, the granite and marble Memorial Building is the centerpiece of this site. It is this structure that houses Lincoln's birthplace cabin. An obscure history, several moves, and a lack of proper documentation prevent the National Park Service from claiming this as the original cabin. In its index of parks, the National Park Service

The Birthplace Cabin

describes the cabin as "symbolic of the one in which Lincoln was born." Nevertheless, the site is acknowledged as the actual birthplace, and it is likely that the cabin is authentic as well.

In addition to the Memorial Building, visitors to this park will find a visitor center, which shows the movie *Lincoln: The Kentucky Years* on the hour and half-hour; exhibits that include the Lincoln family Bible, tools and utensils; and trails and picnic areas. Special programs take place throughout the year; information can be found on the website or by contacting the park. Staff within the visitor center provide orientation to the park's attractions and facilities.

The memorial and Sinking Spring Farm, as the 348 acres of land was called when Lincoln's father purchased it in 1808, were established as a national park in 1916 and designated as the Abraham Lincoln Birthplace National Historic Site in 1959. The site is owned and operated by the National Park Service.

NEAREST AIRPORT: Louisville, Kentucky

GENERAL DIRECTIONS: Three miles south of Hodgenville, Kentucky, on U.S. 31E and KY 61.

NEARBY ATTRACTIONS: Knob Creek Farm (Lincoln's Boyhood Home), Lincoln Boyhood National Memorial, historic Bardstown, Kentucky.

ABRAHAM LINCOLN'S BOYHOOD HOME ————

KNOB CREEK FARM

7120 Bardstown Road, Hodgenville, Kentucky 42748

PHONE: 502-549-3741

HOURS: April through October, daily

ADMISSION: no fee

WHEELCHAIR ACCESSIBILITY: limited

In an 1860 letter to Samuel Haycraft of Elizabethtown, Kentucky, Abraham Lincoln wrote, "My earliest recollection is of the Knob Creek Place." It is here that Lincoln lived as a boy from age two until he was almost eight years old. His family then had to move due to a title dispute.

The cabin on the site is not the original Lincoln cabin. Rather, it was rebuilt in 1931 with logs taken from the home of Lincoln's schoolmate Austin Gollaher and re-cut to the dimensions of the Lincoln cabin. Self-guided tours and limited interpretive opportunities are available.

The National Park Service assumed ownership of the site in 2001, and a gradual extension of services is anticipated. The site is registered with the National Register of Historical Places.

NEAREST AIRPORT: Louisville, Kentucky

GENERAL DIRECTIONS: Located on U.S. 31E just outside of Hodgenville, Kentucky.

NEARBY ATTRACTIONS: Historic Bardstown, Kentucky; Lincoln Museum.

Lincoln's Boyhood Home at Knob Creek

LINCOLN BOYHOOD NATIONAL MEMORIAL

Indiana Hwy 162, Lincoln City, Indiana 47552

PHONE: 812-937-4541

www.nps.gov/libo

HOURS: daily; closed Thanksgiving, Christmas Day, and New Year's Day

ADMISSION: fee; park passes

WHEELCHAIR ACCESSIBILITY: yes

This is the site of the home in which Abraham Lincoln spent fourteen years of his youth. It is also the site at which his mother, Nancy Hanks, died and was buried. The Memorial Visitor Center houses a museum and two memorial halls that commemorate Lincoln and his family. In addition, visitors can view the film, *Forging Greatness: Lincoln in Indiana*.

Lincoln Boyhood National Memorial

Trails in the park lead to the Lincoln Living Historical Farm, a re-created pioneer homestead. Here, rangers in period costume perform a variety of the activities associated with daily living in the 1820s. The homestead includes a cabin, outbuildings, split rail fences, farm animals, and vegetable and herb gardens. The Living Historical Farm is open daily mid-April through September and is closed October through mid-April. Although there is no staff and the buildings are closed, visitors can still wander the grounds during the winter months.

Call the park for details on special events, including the Lincoln birthday and holiday events. The park is operated by the National Park Service.

NEAREST AIRPORT: Evansville, Indiana

GENERAL DIRECTIONS: Located on Indiana Hwy. 162. From I-64, exit at U.S. 231 south through Dale and Gentryville, then east on Indiana Hwy. 162.

NEARBY ATTRACTIONS: Lincoln State Park, Colonel William Jones State Historic Site.

LINCOLN HOME NATIONAL HISTORIC SITE

413 South Eighth Street, Springfield, Illinois 62701

PHONE: 217-492-4241

www.nps.gov/liho

HOURS: daily; closed Thanksgiving, Christmas Day, and New Year's Day

ADMISSION: no fee; donations accepted; parking fee

WHEELCHAIR ACCESSIBILITY: yes, in visitor center, Dean House, and first floor of Lincoln Home

Among the sights at the park are a visitor center, which shows a short orientation film, a museum shop, the Dean House, the Arnold House, and, of course, the Lincoln Home. Constructed in 1839, the Lincoln Home is the only house Abraham Lincoln ever owned. He and Mary Todd Lincoln lived here from 1844 until Lincoln's election in 1861. The home has been restored to its 1860s appearance and stands in the midst of a four-block historic neighborhood that the National Park Service is in the process of restoring. The two-story dwelling includes a formal and back parlor, dining room, sitting room, kitchen, and a number of bedrooms.

After visiting the Lincoln Home, visitors can view the exhibit, "What a Pleasant Home Abe Lincoln Has," that was installed in the restored Harriet Dean House across the street from the Lincoln home in the summer of 1996. It features information on the Lincolns and their neighbors as well as models that show changes in the Lincoln Home from 1844 to 1861. Also located across the street is the restored Arnold House, which features the exhibit "If These Walls Could Talk." The exhibit explains the process of historic preservation in the United States.

Ranger-conducted tours of the home operate daily, with the last tour of the day beginning a half hour before closing. Tour tickets are free and are available at the visitor center. The visitor center lobby also contains exhibits and displays, and the staff can provide information on nearby Lincoln sites and attractions.

The Lincoln Home National Historic Site is operated by the National Park Service.

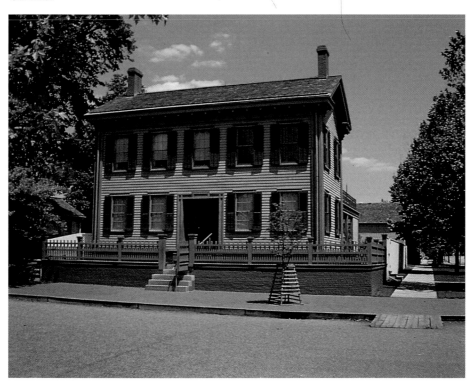

The Lincoln Home

The sitting room in the Lincoln Home

NEAREST AIRPORT: Springfield, Illinois

GENERAL DIRECTIONS: Accessible off I-55 for visitors traveling north/south; by I-72 for visitors traveling east/west. In addition, a trolley service provides transportation to eight historic sites and attractions in the area. Tickets can be purchased at the visitor center.

NEARBY ATTRACTIONS: Springfield is home to a number of historic sites. Among them are the Old State Capitol, the Lincoln-Herndon Law Offices, Lincoln's Tomb, and Lincoln's New Salem.

LINCOLN'S NEW SALEM STATE HISTORIC SITE ―

RR1, Box 244A, Petersburg, Illinois 62675

PHONE: 217-632-4000

www.lincolnsnewsalem.com

HOURS: daily; closed major winter holidays

ADMISSION: suggested donation

WHEELCHAIR ACCESSIBILITY: yes

The New Salem site is a 650-acre reconstruction of the village where Abraham Lincoln spent six years of his early adulthood. While here, Lincoln clerked in stores, split rails, served as postmaster and as a deputy surveyor, among other things. Visitors to the site can see re-creations of the shops, houses, stores, mills, school, and tavern that were part of New Salem in the 1830s. With the exception of the Onstot Cooper Shop, which is an original building, all structures are reproductions. The furnishings, equipment, and utensils are authentic period pieces, although not all are from the New Salem village.

The visitor center includes an auditorium, museum, gift shops, and exhibits, including some original Lincoln pieces. The center also shows an orientation film for visitors. All tours of the site are self-guided, and visitors can wander the park's trails and

Lincoln statue in front of the visitor center

use various picnic areas. Additionally, there are 200 campsites, about 100 of which have electricity.

Special events are many and varied at New Salem. In addition to holiday events, craft demonstrations, and educational programs for kids, the village hosts the Discovery series. These are hands-on workshops that highlight the natural and historical aspects of the site as well as provide information on pioneer life. The "Chautaqua" series and "Theater in the Park" series host plays, concerts, and lectures in the outdoor amphitheater and indoor auditorium. Visitors can check the website for upcoming events.

The New Salem State Historic Site is sponsored by the Illinois Historic Preservation Agency and the New Salem Lincoln League. The New Salem Lincoln

Onstot Cooper Shop at New Salem State Historic Site

League is a nonprofit group that sponsors special events, craft demonstrations, and fundraisers to benefit the site. Visitors can become members of the league.

The visitor center at New Salem

NEAREST AIRPORT: Springfield, Illinois
GENERAL DIRECTIONS: Located on Route 97, two miles south of Petersburg
NEARBY ATTRACTIONS: Springfield is home to a number of historic sites. Among them are the Old State Capitol, the Lincoln-Herndon Law Offices, Lincoln's Tomb, and Lincoln Home National Historic Site.

THE LINCOLN COLLEGE MUSEUM

300 Keokuk Street, Lincoln, Illinois 62656
PHONE: 217-732-3155, ext. 295
www.lincolncollegemuseum.org
HOURS: daily; closed holidays (except February 12)
ADMISSION: no fee, donations welcome
WHEELCHAIR ACCESSIBILITY: yes

Located on the campus of Lincoln College, the Lincoln College Museum is a vast repository of documents, artifacts, and memorabilia related to the sixteenth president. It was the collection of Judge Lawrence B. Stringer, an 1887 Lincoln University graduate, that formed the basis of the museum. The judge, who died in 1942, willed his collection to the school with the provision that a museum be built to house it. Since then, further acquisitions have made this a treasure trove of information for history buffs.

The collection includes a number of Lincoln's personal items: his Lincoln-Herndon law books, tools from his desk, and a lock of his hair. Visitors will also find articles relating to Mary Todd Lincoln, such as china, books, a lock of her hair, and mourning clothes. Documents on view range from an invitation to the 1865 Inaugural Ball to correspondence between Lincoln and his cabinet members and military leaders. In addition, there are several furniture pieces, a dinner bell from his Springfield house, and tassels from the covering of his coffin.

An exhibit at the Lincoln College Museum

The museum specializes in personalized tours. Staffers greet and lead each visitor on a tour, including a tour of the campus, if desired. They sponsor special programs and exhibits periodically and reach out to young people as an educational service. Picnic sites are also available on the campus.

Lincoln College sponsors the museum, and its collection is made possible by the donations of many. Plans are underway for a new 7,000-square-foot facility expected to be completed in 2004; it will rival the planned Lincoln Library in Springfield in terms of its collection.

NEAREST AIRPORT: Logan County Airport, Illinois
GENERAL DIRECTIONS: Lincoln, corner of Ottawa and Keokuk (Route 121 and Route 10)
NEARBY ATTRACTIONS: Numerous Lincoln sites are located in Springfield, a half-hour drive away.

ABRAHAM LINCOLN LIBRARY AND MUSEUM

Cumberland Gap Parkway, Harrogate, Tennessee 37752
PHONE: 423-869-6235
www.lmunet.edu/museum
HOURS: daily; closed some university holidays
ADMISSION: fee; student, senior, and group discounts
WHEELCHAIR ACCESSIBILITY: yes, except mezzanine (virtual tour available)

The Abraham Lincoln Library and Museum is situated on the campus of Lincoln Memorial University. The museum opened in 1977 to house a collection of authen-

The Abraham Lincoln Library and Museum

tic Lincoln and Civil War documents and artifacts. The collection now consists of more than 20,000 items plus a research library that houses over 6,000 rare books and countless documents. The university itself was founded by General Oliver Otis Howard, a Civil War general, as a memorial to Abraham Lincoln. Lincoln had requested that General Howard "do something for the loyal people of East Tennessee" if either survived the war.

Guided tours can be arranged, although the museum is mainly a look-and-wander experience that includes interactive areas. The museum's program director and education coordinator strive to offer family-oriented programming, including child-friendly performances. In addition, Camp Cumberland is a mock Civil War soldier's camp for children.

Special events are held throughout the year, including the Ostendorf Lecture (held in October) and Christmas with the Lincolns. Call or visit the website for an upcoming events calendar.

Lincoln Memorial University provides the major upkeep of the site. In fact, part of the criteria for establishing the university involved maintaining a collection of Lincoln and Civil War artifacts and documents.

NEAREST AIRPORT: Knoxville, Tennessee
GENERAL DIRECTIONS: From Knoxville, take Route 33 north to U.S. 25E north; from northbound I-75, pick up Hwy. 63 east through La Follette, Tennessee; from southbound I-75, pick up Hwy. 25E south at Corbin, Kentucky; westbound travelers follow Virginia Hwy. 58 west to Cumberland Gap, then U.S. 25E south.
NEARBY ATTRACTIONS: Cumberland Gap National Historic Park, Wilderness Road State Park, Great Smoky Mountains National Park.

THE LINCOLN MUSEUM

200 E. Berry Street, Fort Wayne, Indiana 46802
PHONE: 260-455-3864
www.thelincolnmuseum.org
HOURS: Tuesday to Sunday
ADMISSION: fee; student, senior, and group discounts; Lincoln Museum member discounts
WHEELCHAIR ACCESSIBILITY: yes

This 30,000-square-foot museum is dedicated to preserving and interpreting the history and legacy of our nation's sixteenth

Fiery Trial Theater at the Lincoln Museum

president. Its permanent exhibit, "Abraham Lincoln and the American Experiment," includes four theaters and eleven exhibit galleries. In addition, the museum hosts numerous interactive exhibits.

Among the museum's treasures is a rare edition of the Emancipation Proclamation signed by Lincoln in 1864—one of only eight in the world in public collections. The collection also includes thousands of books, prints, photographs, and media clippings. The research department fields e-mails, phone calls, and letters from students of Lincoln history, and research visits to the Reading Room can be arranged. The museum hosts a number of special events throughout the year as well.

The Lincoln Museum was founded in 1928 by the Lincoln National Insurance Company. The company had adopted the Lincoln name in 1905 with the permission of Robert Todd Lincoln and established the museum as a tribute to his father. Today, the museum is supported by museum members across the country as well as the Lincoln Financial Group Foundation and other corporate and individual supporters.

The Civil War Gallery at the Lincoln Museum

NEAREST AIRPORT: Fort Wayne, Indiana

GENERAL DIRECTIONS: The museum is on the southeast corner of Clinton and Berry streets. From I-69 south, take exit 112A to Coldwater Road (becomes Clinton Street). From I-95 north, take exit 102 east on Jefferson Blvd. to the downtown area. Turn left on Lafayette then left on Berry Street.

NEARBY ATTRACTIONS: Fort Wayne Museum of Art, Foellinger-Freimann Botanical Conservatory, and Allen County Public Library Genealogy Department.

ABRAHAM LINCOLN PRESIDENTIAL LIBRARY AND MUSEUM ——————

212 S. Sixth Street, Springfield, Illinois 62701

PHONE: 217-785-7930 (temporary pending museum opening)

www.state.il.us/hpa/preslib

HOURS: The library is currently scheduled to open in late 2002; the museum is scheduled for completion in mid 2004.

WHEELCHAIR ACCESSIBILITY: yes

The groundbreaking ceremony for the newest addition to the many sites honoring our 16th president took place on February 12, 2001.When completed, the facility will showcase Illinois' 46,000-item Lincoln collection. The library and museum are being built in downtown Springfield and will be constructed in two phases. The library will open in late 2002 and the museum will open approximately eighteen months later. The library building will also serve as the new home for the Illinois State Historical Library.

The 100,000-square-foot library will serve as the research arm of the complex with public areas, research carrels, and reading rooms. The building will also feature expanded archival and storage space for the Historical Library's current and future collections, including more than six miles of shelving for books.

The 98,000-square-foot museum will feature exhibits, audiovisual programs, a restaurant, and a gift shop. The museum will provide visitors from schoolchildren to scholars a new opportunity to explore the history of one of America's most widely recognized presidents.

The library and museum are being built with state, federal, and city funds plus private donations; it will be staffed and operated by the state of Illinois.

NEAREST AIRPORT: Springfield, Illinois

GENERAL DIRECTIONS: Located at the intersection of Sixth and Jefferson streets in downtown Springfield.

NEARBY ATTRACTIONS: Lincoln Home (home of Abraham Lincoln's father and stepmother), Old State Capitol, Lincoln-Herndon Law Offices, and Lincoln Tomb.

FORD'S THEATRE NATIONAL HISTORIC SITE ——

511 10th Street NW, Washington, D.C. 20004

PHONE: 202-426-6924

www.nps.gov/foth

HOURS: daily; closed Christmas Day

ADMISSION: no fee

WHEELCHAIR ACCESSIBILITY: Orchestra level

While not actually a home or library, Ford's Theatre preserves the site of the

Ford's Theatre National Historic Site

nation's first presidential assassination. On the night of April 14, 1865, a well-known actor, John Wilkes Booth, stepped into the president's box and shot Abraham Lincoln in the back of the head, altering the course of the nation's power to rebuild after the Civil War. This event took place a mere five days after the surrender at Appomattox. Lincoln was carried to the Petersen Boarding House across the street and died early the next morning.

A museum is located in the basement of the theatre, which still maintains a schedule of performances. (Call to be sure the theatre will be open on the day of your visit.) Park rangers give talks in the theatre fifteen minutes after the hour, except during matinees, rehearsals, and workshops. The museum and Petersen Boarding House remain open during these times. In addition to the talks, the events of the assassination are relayed through interpretive displays.

Ford's Theatre is part of the National Park Service.

NEAREST AIRPORT: Washington, D.C.
GENERAL DIRECTIONS: Located near the intersection of 10th and E streets in the northwest section of the city. Parking is extremely limited; using public transportation is recommended. The closest Metro Rail station is Metro Center at 11th and G streets.
NEARBY ATTRACTIONS: Washington, D.C., is home to many historic attractions; among them are the White House, presidential memorials, Stephen Decatur House Museum, Woodrow Wilson House Museum, and Smithsonian Institution.

ABRAHAM LINCOLN

ANDREW JOHNSON

1808–1875
17th President • 1865–1869

Andrew Johnson, who was named for former president Andrew Jackson, was born in 1808 in Raleigh, North Carolina. He came from common, southern roots. Johnson's father, Jacob, alternately a janitor, church sexton, and hotel porter, died when his son was three years old. His widow was left to support the family by taking in spinning and weaving. Johnson received no education in childhood and was the only president to be illiterate into adulthood. He began his career as a tailor in Greeneville, Tennessee. Through the tutelage of his wife, Eliza, whom he married when he was eighteen and she sixteen, Johnson eventually learned to read and won the position of alderman in Greeneville; thus he began a career in public service that would lead all the way to the White House.

Stirred by ambition and helped along by a flair for public speaking, Johnson went from alderman to mayor of Greeneville, the Tennessee House of Representatives, the United States House, governor of Tennessee, and, when the Civil War began, United States senator. His support of the president and the Union won him strong disapproval at home but gained the notice of a grateful President

Lincoln. In 1862 Lincoln appointed Johnson military governor of Tennessee, with the responsibility of maintaining order and reestablishing federal control. He held that post until 1865. Lincoln, hoping that a pro-Union southerner would add balance to his bid for reelection, chose Johnson as his vice presidential running mate in 1864. The two would serve together only a month before Lincoln was assassinated and Johnson inherited the highest job in the land.

Johnson took the reins of a nation finally at peace but battered by war and shocked by the assassination of its leader. He intended to follow the course of Reconstruction set out by Lincoln but met with opposition from all sides. Southerners resented federal presence in their states, and northerners believed the government was too lenient on the Confederates. The continuing conflict between Johnson and the Radical Republicans eventually led to Johnson's impeachment when he allegedly violated the Tenure of Office Act by dismissing Secretary of War Edwin M. Stanton. Although he was acquitted at trial of all charges, the acquittal was by just one vote and his presidency never recovered. Despite weakness in office, Johnson made one significant decision. In 1867 he agreed to purchase Alaska from Russia for just over seven million dollars. Considered a wasteland at the time, Alaska is today treasured for its unmatched natural resources and beauty.

Johnson retired to his adopted home state of Tennessee after his term in office. He remained active in public life and, in 1875, won election to the Senate, the only former president to do so. He died in office in 1875 of complications following a bout with cholera. Johnson was survived by his wife, Eliza, and their five children.

SLAVERY IS DEAD, AND YOU MUST PARDON ME IF I DO NOT MOURN over its dead body; you can bury it out of sight. . . . I desire that all men shall have a fair start and an equal chance in the race of life, and let him succeed who has the most merit. I am for emancipation, for two reasons: first, because it is right in itself; and second, because in the emancipation of the slaves we break down an odious and dangerous aristocracy. I think that we are freeing more whites than blacks.

**–President Andrew Johnson speaking
in Nashville, Tennessee, at the close of the Civil War**

ANDREW JOHNSON NATIONAL HISTORIC SITE

101 N. College Street, Greeneville, Tennessee 37743
PHONE: 423-638-3551
www.nps.gov/anjo
HOURS: daily; closed Thanksgiving, Christmas Day, New Year's Day
ADMISSION: fee; senior and child discounts
WHEELCHAIR ACCESSIBILITY: yes, visitor center and early 1830s home

The Andrew Johnson National Historic Site preserves two of Johnson's homes and his tailor shop. The national cemetery where Andrew Johnson and his wife Eliza are buried is less than a half mile from the home site.

Exhibits include Johnson's original tailor shop and tools, his two homes, and presidential gifts and artifacts. A short film depicting Johnson's life from boyhood to his return to the Senate in 1875 is available upon request at the visitor center. Upon entrance to the visitor center, guests are given a replica of the 1868 ticket used to gain access to Johnson's trial; they can cast their vote to acquit or find the president guilty at the "One Vote Counts" exhibit in the museum. During the annual celebration of Constitution Week in September, visitors have an opportunity to sign an oversized copy of the Constitution; their names are sent to the archives of the National Constitution Center in Philadelphia.

A block and a half up Main Street from the visitor center is the Homestead, where the Johnsons began living in 1851. Ten rooms of the home are open to the public; they are furnished with original family furnishings. When Johnson died in 1875, the Homestead passed to his son Andrew Jr. The buildings were later acquired one by one by the federal government and the site is now administered by the National Park Service.

NEAREST AIRPORT: Bristol/Johnson City, Tennessee
GENERAL DIRECTIONS: From I-81S, take exit 36 to Route 172 to Greeneville.
From I-81N, take exit 23 to Route 11E north to Greeneville. The visitor center is located on the corner of College and Depot streets in historic downtown Greeneville.
NEARBY ATTRACTIONS: President Andrew Johnson Museum and Library, General Morgan Inn, Nathanael Greene Museum, Davy Crockett Birthplace State Park.

PRESIDENT ANDREW JOHNSON MUSEUM AND LIBRARY

OLD COLLEGE—TUSCULUM COLLEGE

Route 107, Greeneville, Tennessee 37743
PHONE: 423-636-7348
www.tusculum.edu
HOURS: Monday to Friday; closed college holidays
ADMISSION: no fee
WHEELCHAIR ACCESSIBILITY: yes

Andrew Johnson, who lived much of his adult life in Greeneville, Tennessee, donated $20 in 1841 toward the construction of Old College. He served on the board of Tusculum Academy (later Tusculum College) until his death in 1875. Although never a student at the school, Johnson did visit often and engage in debates with students and faculty.

Old College—President Andrew Johnson Library and Museum

The museum and library are housed in Old College, one of ten campus buildings that are listed on the National Register of Historic Places. The museum displays family and political memorabilia related to Johnson and his family, as well as Johnson's personal library and 1,400 volumes of the college's original library collection. The museum provides guided discussions, or visitors can explore on their own.

The President Andrew Johnson Museum and Library is part of Tusculum College and operates with support from the President Andrew Johnson Memorial Association.

NEAREST AIRPORT: Bristol/Johnson City, Tennessee
GENERAL DIRECTIONS: I-81 to U.S. 11E, Greeneville, Tennessee.
Route 107 to Tusculum.
NEARBY ATTRACTIONS: Andrew Johnson National Historic Site, General Morgan Inn, Nathanael Greene Museum, Davy Crockett Birthplace State Park.

ANDREW JOHNSON BIRTHPLACE
MORDECAI HISTORIC PARK
1 Mimosa Street, Raleigh, North Carolina 27604
PHONE: 919-834-4844
www.capitalareapreservation.org
HOURS: Wednesday to Monday
ADMISSION: fee
WHEELCHAIR ACCESSIBILITY: yes, limited

Andrew Johnson Birthplace

The Andrew Johnson Birthplace is a late eighteenth-century structure that now resides on Mordecai Historic Park's "Village Street." At the time of Johnson's birth in 1808, the building served as a kitchen and residence behind Casso's Inn in downtown Raleigh where Johnson's parents were employed.

In addition to the birthplace, the centerpiece of Mordecai Historic Park is the Mordecai Plantation House, home to five generations of the Lane-Mordecai family. Once one of the largest plantations in Wake County, North Carolina, the house is now a museum that features an extensive collection of original furnishings.

The plantation house is the oldest house in Raleigh on its original site; other outbuildings have been relocated to the Village Street and include the 1810 Badger-Iredell law office; an antebellum plantation kitchen; and St. Mark's Chapel, a chapel constructed by slave carpenters in 1847.

NEAREST AIRPORT: Raleigh-Durham, North Carolina
GENERAL DIRECTIONS: From downtown Raleigh, take Person Street north approximately three miles until it becomes Wake Forest Road. Turn left onto Mimosa Street to enter the park.
NEARBY ATTRACTIONS: State Capitol, Governor's Mansion, North Carolina Museum of History, Joel Lane Museum House, Exploris, and the City Market/Moore's Square Art District.

ULYSSES S. GRANT

1822–1885
18th President • 1869–1877

General Ulysses S. Grant made a name for himself first as a soldier. As his military successes during the Civil War built one upon the other, he moved up the ranks of the army. After being appointed interim Secretary of War by President Andrew Johnson, Grant aligned himself with the Radical Republicans, thus becoming their choice for the Republican presidential candidate in 1868—a race he won over Democratic candidate Horatio Seymour.

Born in 1822 in Point Pleasant, Ohio, Ulysses S. Grant was a slight, quiet child. He showed few signs of aspiring to a military career; but following his father's wishes, Grant entered West Point where he was an average student, excelling in horsemanship and math but struggling with military science. After graduating from West Point in the middle of his class, Grant received his commission and began his career as a soldier. He served with distinction in the Mexican War, after which he married Julia Boggs Dent, a match that went against the wishes of both families. The abolitionist Grants disapproved of the slaveholding Dents; and the Dents, with high hopes for their daughter, saw little promise in the young Grant.

The Dents were to be proven wrong during the Civil War, which Grant began as an infantry colonel and finished as the commander of the Union Army. Displaying great bravery and undying commitment to the Union, Grant became a national hero. It was he who, in 1865, accepted the surrender of General Lee at Appomattox, showing the same grace in victory that he had in battle. After the war, President Lincoln promoted Grant to General of the Armies—the first man to hold that rank since George Washington.

As presidential candidate, Grant neither campaigned nor made promises. With the simple slogan "Let us have peace," Grant won a convincing electoral victory to become the eighteenth president. Inexperienced and unprepared for the demands of the presidency, Grant was an ineffective chief executive. Rocked by scandal, he struggled with the continuing problems of Reconstruction, which were compounded by a lengthy economic depression. Nonetheless, Grant, still a national hero, won reelection and served two full terms in office.

In retirement, Grant triumphantly traveled the globe but then struggled through financial hardship after investing in a business that failed. He died in 1885 in New York, a few days after finishing his *Personal Memoirs*, an acclaimed literary masterpiece he wrote in order to provide for his family financially. His final resting place, Grant's Tomb, is now a monument overlooking New York's Hudson River.

THE RESPONSIBILITIES OF THE POSITION I FEEL, but accept them without fear. The office has come to me unsought; I commence its duties untrammeled. I bring to it a conscious desire and determination to fill it to the best of my ability to the satisfaction of the people. . . .

I shall on all subjects have a policy to recommend, but none to enforce against the will of the people. Laws are to govern all alike—those opposed as well as those who favor them. I know no method to secure the repeal of bad or obnoxious laws so effective as their stringent execution.

The country having just emerged from a great rebellion, many questions will come before it for settlement in the next four years which preceding Administrations have never had to deal with. In meeting these it is desirable that they should be approached calmly, without prejudice, hate, or sectional pride, remembering the greatest good to the greatest number is the object to be attained.

–from Ulysses S. Grant's first Inaugural Address, March 4, 1869

ULYSSES S. GRANT NATIONAL HISTORIC SITE

7400 Grant Road, St. Louis, Missouri 63123

PHONE: 314-842-3298

www.nps.gov/ulsg

HOURS: daily; closed Thanksgiving, Christmas Day, New Year's Day

ADMISSION: no fee

WHEELCHAIR ACCESSIBILITY: yes, in the visitor center, main house, and stone building

There are five historic structures on the almost ten acres of land (out of an original 850 acres) that make up the site. Four buildings—the main house, stone building, chicken house, and ice house—have been restored to their 1875 appearance. The visitor center is currently located in the historic 1868 barn that will be undergoing restoration for use as the site's museum.

The homestead, which is known as White Haven, was a focal point in the lives of Ulysses and Julia Grant. They lived here on and off throughout the 1850s. Despite their residence in Galena, Illinois, during the 1860s, the Grants continued to think of White Haven as home. By 1870, Grant was readying the property for a relaxing retirement. Circumstances caused Grant to abandon those plans, but he retained ownership of the property until a few months before his death in 1885.

Guided interpretive tours of the house are offered daily, and the outbuildings and grounds are available for self-guided tours. A short orientation film is shown in

White Haven

the visitor center throughout the day. The visitor center also hosts a small exhibit area. Special programs, ranging from lectures to living history performances to children's activities, are held throughout the year. Children may also participate in the Junior Ranger program.

A successful local community effort preserved the property from development and led to government interest. The site was authorized as a unit of the National Park Service in 1989 and was established in 1990.

NEAREST AIRPORT: St. Louis, Missouri

GENERAL DIRECTIONS: On Grant Road off Gravois Road (Route 30).

NEARBY ATTRACTIONS: Grant's Farm, Sappington House, Hawken House, Oakland House, and Mudd Grove. The greater St. Louis area includes the Old Courthouse and Old Cathedral.

HARDSCRABBLE CABIN AT GRANT'S FARM

10501 Gravois Road, St. Louis, Missouri 63123

PHONE: 314-843-1700

www.grantsfarm.com

HOURS: Mid-April through mid-May, Wednesday to Sunday;
mid-May through Labor Day, Tuesday to Sunday and holiday Mondays;
Labor Day through October, Wednesday to Sunday

ADMISSION: no fee

WHEELCHAIR ACCESSIBILITY: yes

Hardscrabble is the name U. S. Grant gave to the cabin he built on the eighty acres of Dent family land he and his bride, Julia Dent, received as a wedding gift. The cabin is part of Grant's Farm, a 280-acre wildlife preserve and historical site that is located just across from the Ulysses S. Grant National Historic Site (see previous listing).

Grant did much of the work on the cabin himself; he sawed and notched the logs, laid the floors, built the staircase, and shingled the roof. With help from friends, the cabin was built in just three days. The Grants lived in the cabin for just a short time. They moved back to the Dent family home at White Haven following the death of Julia's mother. At that time, Grant took on the running of both his own and his father-in-law's farm.

In addition to the historical Grant's cabin, visitors to Grant's Farm will enjoy seeing the Busch family carriage collection. The carriage collection includes vehicles that date as far back as the 1700s and carriages that have transported individuals such as President Harry S. Truman, Yul Brenner, Frank Sinatra, and Prince Philip of England.

The Farm is perhaps best known for its wildlife preserve. Among the animals roaming the land are bison, North American Wapiti (elk), Black Buck Antelope, and Barbary sheep. In the Tier Garten, visitors can meet smaller animals up close.

The Tier Garten Amphitheater hosts a wide array of educational and entertaining bird, mammal, reptile, and elephant shows.

Hardscrabble Cabin passed out of the hands of the Grant family in 1885. It was owned by a number of people throughout the following years and was displayed at the 1904 World's Fair. Adolphus A. Busch purchased the cabin in 1907 and had it reassembled about a mile from its original location. Hardscrabble Cabin was restored to its current condition in 1977.

The whole of Grant's Farm is operated by the Anheuser-Busch Company.

NEAREST AIRPORT: St. Louis, Missouri

GENERAL DIRECTIONS: On Grant Road off Gravois Road (Route 30).

NEARBY ATTRACTIONS: Ulysses S. Grant National Historic Site, Sappington House, Hawken House, Oakland House, and Mudd Grove. The greater St. Louis area includes the Old Courthouse and Old Cathedral.

U. S. GRANT HOME

500 Bouthillier Street, Galena, Illinois 61036

PHONE: 815-777-3310

www.granthome.com

HOURS: daily; closed major holidays

ADMISSION: suggested donation

WHEELCHAIR ACCESSIBILITY: first floor only

When General Ulysses S. Grant returned home to Galena in 1865, after his impressive service in the Civil War, a group of local Republicans presented this home to

U. S. Grant Home

Grant and his wife. The Italianate-style dwelling was not Grant's home for long. He made only occasional visits to Galena after his election in 1868, but the home remained in the Grant family until it was deeded to the city of Galena in 1904. Grant's final visit to the home was in 1880.

Dining room in the U. S. Grant Home

As is typical of the style, the house features rectilinear lines, a low-pitched roof, and balconies over covered porches. The house was furnished when it was presented to the Grants; and following a major restoration in the 1950s, it was returned to its 1868 appearance. Many of the furnishings in the home today are original Grant-family pieces.

When the home was presented to the city of Galena in 1904, it was with the understanding that the house be maintained as a memorial to Grant. The maintenance soon proved too expensive for the city, and it was deeded to the state of Illinois in 1931. It is currently operated by the Galena State Historic Sites, a division of the Illinois Historic Preservation Agency.

NEAREST AIRPORT: Dubuque, Iowa; Quad Cities Airport

GENERAL DIRECTIONS: North on Park Avenue off U.S. 20; parking and information center at the corner of Park Avenue and Bouthillier Street.

NEARBY ATTRACTIONS: The Belvedere, Dowling House, The Old Market House State Historic Site, and Washburne House State Historic Site.

ULYSSES S. GRANT COTTAGE
STATE HISTORIC SITE

Mount McGregor Road, Wilton, New York

PHONE: 518-587-8277

www.nysparks.state.ny.us/planmytrip

HOURS: Memorial Day through Labor Day, Wednesday to Sunday; after Labor Day, weekends through Columbus Day; open all Monday holidays

ADMISSION: fee; senior and student discounts

WHEELCHAIR ACCESSIBILITY: yes

U. S. Grant Cottage

General Ulysses S. Grant lived in this cottage a few miles outside of Saratoga Springs in the summer of 1885 as he struggled to complete his memoirs before his death from throat cancer. Grant was motivated to do so in order to provide for his family after his death. Today, the cottage and its furnishings and personal items remain as they were during Grant's stay.

Visitors can take a guided thirty-minute tour of the downstairs of the dwelling; upstairs rooms are not open to the public. Rooms on the main level include the parlor, dining room, and sickroom. Additionally, there is a small gift shop in the house.

The cottage is located on the grounds of the Mount McGregor Correctional Facility, and visitors check in at the access gate to the facility. After taking the house tour, visitors can walk to the overlook that offers a view of the Hudson River Valley. The site sponsors a number of activities throughout the summer.

The cottage is owned by the New York state park system, and it is operated by the Friends of Grant Cottage.

NEAREST AIRPORT: Albany, New York
GENERAL DIRECTIONS: Exit 16 off I-87; follow signs to Grant Cottage.
NEARBY ATTRACTIONS: Nearby Saratoga Springs offers a wide array of historical sites.

GRANT BIRTHPLACE

U.S. Route 52 and State Route 232, Point Pleasant, Ohio 45153
PHONE: 513-553-4911
www.ohiohistory.org/places/grantbir
HOURS: April through October, Wednesday to Sunday; closed holidays
ADMISSION: fee; senior and student discounts
WHEELCHAIR ACCESSIBILITY: limited

Ulysses S. Grant was born in this three-room cottage in 1822, and the family soon moved to nearby Georgetown, Ohio. Built in 1817, the restored cottage sits near Big Indian Creek in Point Pleasant. Today, it is furnished with period pieces, some of which belonged to the Grant family. The structure itself has an unusual history: it not only traveled atop a river barge on an extensive tour of U.S. riverways but also traveled atop a railroad flatcar to the state fairgrounds in Columbus, Ohio.

The Ohio Historical Society owns the home, which is managed by Historic New Richmond, Ohio.

NEAREST AIRPORT: Covington, Kentucky (Greater Cincinnati Airport)
GENERAL DIRECTIONS: Three miles east of New Richmond, off U.S. Route 52.
NEARBY ATTRACTIONS: Grant's Boyhood Home, Grant's Schoolhouse, Underground Railroad Museum, and Grave of Diana Whitney.

GRANT'S BOYHOOD HOME

219 E. Grant Avenue, Georgetown, Ohio 45121
PHONE: 937-378-4222
HOURS: June through August, Wednesday to Sunday; September through October, Saturday to Sunday
ADMISSION: fee; child discount
WHEELCHAIR ACCESSIBILITY: limited

Now a national historic landmark, this house was built in 1823, completed in 1828, and served as the boyhood home of Ulysses S. Grant. It is the home to which the Grant family moved from U. S. Grant's birthplace in Point Pleasant. A restoration of the building was completed in 1982, and the house is furnished in period pieces.

The house is located near the tannery Grant's father built and two schoolhouses that young Ulysses attended.

NEAREST AIRPORT: Georgetown, Ohio (Brown County Airport); Covington, Kentucky (Greater Cincinnati Airport)
GENERAL DIRECTIONS: Forty miles from downtown Cincinnati on State Route 125 East. Two blocks east of Historic Courthouse Square.
NEARBY ATTRACTIONS: Grant's Schoolhouse, and John Rankin Historic Site (Ripley, Ohio).

RUTHERFORD B. HAYES

1822–1893
19th President • 1877–1881

A sturdy man with a long, full beard, Rutherford Birchard Hayes was a cheerful extrovert whose love of people made him perfectly suited for political campaigns. He was born in Delaware, Ohio, in 1822, shortly after the death of his father. The greatest influence on his youth was his older sister, Fanny, with whom he remained close throughout his life.

After graduating from Harvard Law School, Hayes settled back home in Ohio to practice law, first in Lower Sandusky and later in Cincinnati. His career was interrupted, however, by four years' service in the Union army during the Civil War. While still in the army, Hayes found himself nominated for a seat in the Ohio House of Representatives. Although he did not actively campaign, saying that it was unbefitting an officer to do so, Hayes was elected on his war record.

Shortly into his second term in Congress, Hayes was nominated to the office of governor of Ohio. He resigned his Congressional office to serve the first of three terms as governor. And it was from the governor's office that Hayes, now convinced that politics and not law was his calling, launched his run for the White House in 1876. In an election so close that Hayes went to bed on election night believing himself the loser, the Ohio governor became the nineteenth president. It was an election that is remembered by some historians as the most corrupt of its time. Hayes lost the popular vote; and he was not declared president until March 2, 1877, after an Electoral Commission of eight Republicans and seven Democrats determined the twenty disputed electoral votes belonged to Hayes, resulting in a victory of 185 votes to 184.

As president, Hayes's administration was noteworthy for bipartisan appointments made on the basis of merit; his administration marked the beginning of civil service reform. Hayes formally put an end to Reconstruction with the Compromise of 1877, which he secured in exchange for his promise to provide federal subsidies for internal improvements in the South—a promise he failed to fulfill. Hayes also laid the foundation for the construction of a U.S.-controlled canal across the Isthmus of Panama. In response to European intentions to build a canal through Central America, President Hayes vowed to Congress that, in accordance with the Monroe Doctrine, any canal built in the region would be constructed and controlled by the United States. The Panama Canal would not be built for another quarter century, but Hayes's pledge of American control was to be fulfilled.

Before his election, Rutherford Hayes announced his desire to be a single-term president. He remained true to his word, retiring in 1881 with his wife, Lucy, to Spiegel Grove, his Ohio estate, where he devoted his time to promoting causes such as public education and prison reform. Mrs. Hayes died in 1889, four years before her husband. Both are buried at Spiegel Grove.

LET ME ASSURE MY COUNTRYMEN OF THE SOUTHERN STATES that it is my earnest desire to regard and promote their truest interest—the interests of the white and of the colored people both and equally—and to put forth my best efforts in behalf of a civil policy which will forever wipe out in our political affairs the color line and the distinction between North and South, to the end that we may have not merely a united North or a united South, but a united country.

–from Rutherford B. Hayes's Inaugural Address, March 5, 1877

RUTHERFORD B. HAYES PRESIDENTIAL CENTER

Spiegel Grove, Fremont, Ohio 43420

PHONE: 419-332-2081 or 800-998-7737

www.rbhayes.org

HOURS: daily; closed Thanksgiving, Christmas Day, and New Year's Day

ADMISSION: fee; child discount

WHEELCHAIR ACCESSIBILITY: yes

Our nation's first presidential center, the Rutherford B. Hayes Presidential Center is located on twenty-five acres of wooded land known as Spiegel Grove. The land was part of the Hayes estate and the retirement home of Rutherford B. Hayes and his wife, Lucy. On the grounds are his thirty-one-room Victorian home, the Hayes Museum & Library, and the burial site of Hayes and his wife.

Guided tours lead through the Hayes home, which is filled with original family furnishings. One of the most spectacular features of the home is a four-story walnut and butternut staircase leading to a lantern offering a 360-degree view of Spiegel Grove. The museum, just a few steps from the house, is filled

Hayes Museum and Library at the Rutherford B. Hayes Presidential Center

with artifacts relating to President Hayes's life, including Civil War and Native American pieces. The traveling exhibit area hosts several national exhibits each year. The library occupies the third floor of the structure and contains over 70,000 volumes, including 12,000 from the president's own collection. It also has extensive genealogical and local history resources. Tours of the museum and library are self-guided.

Year-round special events include free lectures and concerts, traveling exhibits, an annual Civil War Encampment, and Victorian Teas. A complete listing is available on the website.

The Center is one of sixty-two Ohio Historical Society sites. It is funded by state funds and a trust set up by President Hayes.

The Hayes Home at the Rutherford B. Hayes Presidential Center

NEAREST AIRPORT: Detroit, Michigan

GENERAL DIRECTIONS: Located at the corner of Hayes and Buckland Avenues in Fremont, Ohio. Ten minutes from 91/6 of the Ohio Turnpike (I-80/I-90).

NEARBY ATTRACTIONS: Fort Meigs and the Ohio Historical Society.

JAMES A. GARFIELD

1831–1881
20th President • 1881

James Garfield, whose time in office as president was cut short by an assassin's bullet, had already earned recognition for his nearly twenty years in the House of Representatives before accepting the Republican presidential nomination in 1880. He is also remembered for his military service during the Civil War.

As a child in Orange Township, Ohio, James Abram Garfield dreamed of being a sailor not president of the United States. After a brief time aboard an Ohio canal boat, however, Garfield discovered himself ill-suited to life on the water and turned his attention to his education. Determined to succeed in school despite limited family finances, Garfield worked as a janitor, a carpenter, and a teacher to put himself through local private schools and Williams College in Massachusetts.

It was at Williams that Garfield heard a speech by Ralph Waldo Emerson that inspired him to leave his mark upon the world. After graduation, he taught classical languages for a time; bored with the quiet life of a teacher, he later took up the study of law. Upon admittance to the bar in 1860, Garfield was already a state senator. After serving in the House of Representatives for nearly twenty years, Garfield was elected to a term in the United States Senate beginning in March 1881; but he resigned before he began serving the term when he was nominated on the Republican presidential ticket in June 1880.

James A. Garfield was shot at the Baltimore and Potomac Railroad station in Washington, D.C., on July 2, 1881, not quite four months after his inauguration. He hung onto life for almost three months, dying on September 19, 1881. The latest medical technology of the day was used in an attempt to save the president, including an electronic device thought to be capable of finding the location of the bullet in the president's body. The device, which was used to no avail, was operated by Alexander Graham Bell, inventor of the telephone. Garfield's assassin was Charles J. Guiteau, a former supporter bitter because the president had passed over him for a diplomatic post.

Garfield had little time to accomplish much as president, and what time he did have was consumed by a scandal at the post office. Perhaps his assassination, while tragic, did provide the impetus for devising a less partisan means of awarding government jobs. Garfield was on his way to visit his wife, Lucretia, recovering from malaria in New Jersey, when he was shot. After the president's death, Lucretia and their five surviving children settled in Ohio.

THE SUPREMACY OF THE NATION AND ITS LAWS *should no longer be a subject of debate. That discussion, which for half a century threatened the existence of the Union, was closed at last in the high court of war by a decree from which there is no appeal—that the Constitution and the laws made in pursuance thereof are and shall continue to be the supreme law of the land, binding alike upon the States and the people. This decree does not disturb the autonomy of the States nor interfere with any of their necessary rights of local self-government, but it does fix and establish the permanent supremacy of the Union.*

The will of the nation, speaking with the voice of battle and through the amended Constitution, has fulfilled the great promise of 1776 by proclaiming "liberty throughout the land to all the inhabitants thereof."

–from James A. Garfield's Inaugural Address, March 4, 1881

JAMES A. GARFIELD NATIONAL HISTORIC SITE

8095 Mentor Avenue, Mentor, Ohio 44060

PHONE: 440-255-8722

www.wrhs.org; www.nps.gov/jaga

HOURS: daily; closed Memorial Day, Labor Day,
Thanksgiving, Christmas Eve, Christmas Day, New Year's Day

ADMISSION: fee; senior and child discount

WHEELCHAIR ACCESSIBILITY: yes, except small section of the house
tour for which video is available

This site is the location of the home acquired by James Garfield in 1876 to accommodate his large family. By spring of 1880, he had enlarged the home from a nine-room farmhouse into a twenty-room, two-and-a-half story structure. Four years after Garfield's assassination in 1881, his wife added the Memorial Library wing, setting the precedent for presidential libraries. The home was the site of the first "front porch" campaign and was named "Lawnfield" by the reporters camped out on the lawn during the campaign.

In addition to exhibits, the visitor center in the carriage house offers a short video about the life of President Garfield. Interpreters lead a short guided tour of the restored home. The 7.8-acre Lawnfield estate also houses structures such as the recently restored seventy-five-foot tall pump house/windmill, the restored barn, the chicken coop, and a tenant house.

Garfield's home recently underwent a top-to-bottom restoration. It is now nearly as it might have appeared in the 1880–1904 time period, during which Garfield campaigned for president and two major additions were made to the home. Interior work includes reproduction of the original wallpaper, preservation of all wood and finishes, restoration of original brass light fixtures, and conservation work on paintings and furnishings. Nearly 80 percent of the artifacts are original Garfield family pieces.

The exterior color scheme of the home is accurate to that time period as well. Exterior renovation work included restoration of the famous front porch, red cedar shingle roof, and gingerbread detailing. Major foundation improvements were made also.

The James A. Garfield National Historic Site is owned by the National Park Service and operated by the Western Reserve Historical Society.

NEAREST AIRPORT: Cleveland, Ohio

GENERAL DIRECTIONS: Located approximately twenty-five miles from Cleveland. From I-90 take SR 306 Mentor-Kirtland exit. North on SR 306 for two miles to Mentor Avenue (U.S. 20), then right and east for two miles.

NEARBY ATTRACTIONS: James A. Garfield Birthplace Site (marker), James A. Garfield Monument.

CHESTER A. ARTHUR

1829–1886
21st President • 1881–1885

Chester A. Arthur was elected to only one office during his life, that of vice president under James A. Garfield in 1880. His only other public office was the appointed post of Collector of the Port of New York. Arthur became president in September of 1881 after the assassination of President Garfield. In addition to the accomplishments of his administration, Arthur was renowned for his full mustache and side-whiskers, his tall, heavy-set build, and his sense of style.

Chester Arthur was born in Fairfield, Vermont, the son of an Irish immigrant and a descendant of English settlers in New Hampshire. After graduating from Union College in 1848, Arthur earned his living as a teacher in New York and Vermont, while at the same time studying law at home. He completed his legal training in New York City and went on to practice there. His most famous case was that of Lizzie Jennings, a black woman who filed suit against a New York street car company after being refused a seat on a "whites only" train. Arthur won the case for Ms. Jennings and forced the eventual desegregation of all public street cars in New York City.

As president, Arthur worked with Congress on civil service reform, an issue which became a priority after the backlash of the longstanding spoils system—the policy of awarding government jobs based on political connections—led to the assassination of President Garfield. Although Arthur himself had benefited from the spoils system earlier in his career—his political connections won him the lucrative and much sought-after position of Collector of the Port of New York—he signed into law the Pendleton Act of 1883, which provided for civil service exams, put an end to enforced political contributions for government employees, and discouraged nepotism. The Arthur administration also enacted the first federal immigration law, excluding paupers, criminals, and lunatics from immigrating.

Chester Arthur, suffering from Bright's Disease, a fatal kidney ailment that had troubled him since his days as president, did not actively pursue renomination in 1884. The Republican party, believing that he had gone too far in his efforts to reform the federal government, refused to give him a second nomination in any case. Arthur's wife, Nell, died before her husband became president and left him with the care of their son and daughter. Arthur died in 1886 at the age of fifty-six, just two years after leaving office.

Since the close of your last session the American people, in the exercise of their highest right of suffrage, have chosen their Chief Magistrate for the four years ensuing.

When it is remembered that at no period in the country's history has the long political contest which customarily precedes the day of the national election been waged with greater fervor and intensity, it is a subject of general congratulation that after the controversy at the polls was over, and while the slight preponderance by which the issue had been determined was as yet unascertained, the public peace suffered no disturbance, but the people everywhere patiently and quietly awaited the result.

Nothing could more strikingly illustrate the temper of the American citizen, his love of order, and his loyalty to law. Nothing could more signally demonstrate the strength and wisdom of our political institutions.

–from Chester A. Arthur's final address to Congress, December 1, 1884

PRESIDENT CHESTER A. ARTHUR STATE HISTORIC SITE

Off Route 36 or 108, Fairfield, Vermont

PHONE: 802-828-3051

www.historicvermont.org

HOURS: late May through early October, Wednesday to Sunday

ADMISSION: no fee, donation

WHEELCHAIR ACCESSIBILITY: yes

Chester Arthur was born in a small, primitive cabin in Fairfield while his family awaited the completion of the parsonage being built by his father's Baptist congregation. The family moved to the parsonage the next year, and it is this home that served as the model for the 1953 re-creation on this site. Rather than furnishing the home as the cramped quarters it must have been, the house offers a pictorial exhibit on Arthur's life.

The home is owned and operated by the State of Vermont's Division for Historic Preservation.

NEAREST AIRPORT: Burlington, Vermont; Manchester, New Hampshire

GENERAL DIRECTIONS: From the west, take Route 36 to Fairfield; head north at Fairfield, bearing right approximately one mile north of the village. Continue five miles to the site. From the east, take Route 108 approximately four miles from either Bakersfield or Enosburg. Go west on gravel road about two miles to the site.

NEARBY ATTRACTIONS: St. Alban's Historical Society, Highgate Falls Lenticular Truss Bridge (Canada).

Re-creation of Arthur family home at the President Chester A. Arthur State Historic Site

GROVER CLEVELAND

1837–1908
22nd President 1885–1889
24th President 1893–1897

The only president to be elected to two non-consecutive terms, Grover Cleveland was an ambitious, hard-working man who took his presidential responsibilities as the most serious commitment in his life.

Cleveland, born in New Jersey and raised in Clinton, New York, credited his success in life to his strict Presbyterian upbringing. An ambitious student, Cleveland had hopes of attending college; but when his father died in 1853, Cleveland set out toward Ohio, where he hoped to find work. He stopped along the way in Buffalo, New York, and went to work for an uncle who was a successful stock breeder. In his spare time, Cleveland began to study law. Six years later, Cleveland won admittance to the New York bar and began working as a lawyer, with aspirations of entering politics. His rise to the presidency began in 1882 with his election as mayor of Buffalo. The Cleveland administration was so immediately successful and popular that community leaders urged their mayor to run for governor. He won that job in 1882 and within two years was the Democratic nominee for the office of president.

In his first term in the White House, Cleveland worked to reduce tariffs on imported goods in hopes of increasing foreign trade. The tariff issue was being debated throughout America, and Cleveland's stand was a generally unpopular one. Most Americans believed that free trade would damage domestic industry. When Cleveland stood for reelection four years later, he won the popular vote but lost the electoral majority to his opponent, Benjamin Harrison. Defeated but not discouraged, Cleveland returned to his law practice in Buffalo. Four years later he challenged Harrison and won a second chance at the presidency.

Back in the White House after his four-year hiatus, Cleveland continued to push for lower tariffs, this time sure to insist that he was not in favor of absolute free trade. He also faced two major crises: the Panic of 1893 and the Pullman Strike in Chicago. Cleveland believed that the Panic was caused by the Sherman Silver Purchase Act of 1890 and the McKinley Tariff and had to be solved with a return to the gold standard. In the famous Pullman Strike, railroad workers in Chicago formed a union and shut down rail service between their city and the Pacific. Cleveland responded decisively and swiftly, using federal authority to end the strike.

In retirement, Cleveland moved to Princeton, New Jersey, where he was active for the remainder of his life in the affairs of Princeton University. Cleveland died in 1908, leaving his young children and his wife, Frances, whom he had married in the White House when she was only twenty-one.

HE WHO TAKES THE OATH TODAY TO PRESERVE, PROTECT, AND DEFEND the Constitution of the United States, only assumes the solemn obligation which every patriotic citizen—on the farm, in the workshop, in the busy marts of trade, and everywhere—should share with him. The Constitution which prescribes this oath, my countrymen, is yours; the suffrage which executes the will of freemen is yours; the laws and the entire scheme of our civil rule, from the town meeting to the State capitals and the national capital, is yours. . . . Every citizen owes to the country a vigilant watch and close scrutiny of its public servants and a fair and reasonable estimate of their fidelity and usefulness. Thus is the people's will impressed upon the whole framework of our civil polity—municipal, state, and federal; and this is the price of our liberty and inspiration of our faith in the Republic.

–from Grover Cleveland's first Inaugural Address, March 4, 1885

GROVER CLEVELAND BIRTHPLACE HISTORIC SITE

207 Bloomfield Avenue, Caldwell, New Jersey 07006

PHONE: 973-226-0001

HOURS: call for hours of operation

ADMISSION: no fee

WHEELCHAIR ACCESSIBILITY: no

President Grover Cleveland was born in this house in 1837 while his father was serving as pastor of the neighboring First Presbyterian Church of Caldwell. The downstairs of the two-and-a-half story structure is open to the public, and a curator is available to guide visitors through the house. The house is furnished much as it was in 1837 and includes some artifacts that date to the time of the Cleveland occupancy.

NEAREST AIRPORT: New York, New York; Newark, New Jersey

GENERAL DIRECTIONS: From the north, take Garden State Parkway south to I-80. Take I-80 west to State Route 23 and SR 23 south to Bloomfield Avenue. From the south, take Garden State Parkway north to I-280. Take I-280 west to exit 5B. Follow South Livingston Avenue to Eagle Rock Avenue. Turn right, then turn left on Roseland Avenue; follow Roseland till it dead-ends at Bloomfield Avenue.

NEARBY ATTRACTIONS: Edison National Historic Site.

BENJAMIN HARRISON

1833–1901
23rd President 1889–1893

The twenty-third president, Benjamin Harrison, was born with American politics in his blood. His great-grandfather signed the Declaration of Independence and his grandfather, William Henry Harrison, was the ninth president. He was not, however, born a natural politician. Stiff and often cold with people, Harrison succeeded by virtue of hard work, integrity, and intelligence.

Born on his grandfather's farm in North Bend, Ohio, Harrison was a bright and motivated student. He graduated from Miami University in Ohio in 1852 and embarked upon a law career in Indianapolis. His legal career was interrupted by three years' service in the Civil War, during which he rose to the rank of brigadier general. After the war, Harrison continued his law practice until 1881, when he began the first of three terms in the United States Senate representing his adopted home state of Indiana. Harrison remained in the Senate until 1887, when he defeated Grover Cleveland by winning the electoral vote despite Cleveland having won the popular vote.

While in office, Harrison signed into law the Dependent and Disability Pensions Act, which improved compensation to disabled veterans. In direct opposition to Grover Cleveland, who had served before him and would serve after him, Harrison supported an act to require the U.S. government to purchase silver from western mines. He believed this would increase the amount of money in circulation and stimulate the economy. Harrison, a protectionist, also disagreed with Cleveland's stand on tariffs; and during the Harrison administration, the tariff on imported goods rose to forty-eight percent. Both the Silver Purchase Act and the new tariff were overridden by measures in the second Cleveland administration. Harrison ran for reelection but lost to the same man he had defeated four years earlier, Grover Cleveland.

Benjamin Harrison married Caroline Lavinia Scott in 1853. During her husband's presidency, Mrs. Harrison supervised renovations at the White House, including the installation of modern plumbing and electricity. Although she was in favor of bringing electricity to the White House, she was reportedly afraid to touch the switches and had employees turn them on in the morning and off again at night. Caroline died during her husband's campaign for reelection. In retirement, Harrison married Mary Dimmick, a niece of his first wife. They lived in Indianapolis until the former president's death in 1901.

LET US EXALT PATRIOTISM AND MODERATE OUR PARTY CONTENTIONS. Let those who would die for the flag on the field of battle give a better proof of their patriotism and a higher glory to their country by promoting fraternity and justice. A party success that is achieved by unfair methods or by practices that partake of revolution is hurtful and evanescent even from a party standpoint. We should hold our differing opinions in mutual respect, and, having submitted them to the arbitrament of the ballot, should accept an adverse judgment with the same respect that we would have demanded of our opponents if the decision had been in our favor.

No other people have a government more worthy of their respect and love or a land so magnificent in extent, so pleasant to look upon, and so full of generous suggestion to enterprise and labor. God has placed upon our head a diadem and has laid at our feet power and wealth beyond definition or calculation. But we must not forget that we take these gifts upon the condition that justice and mercy shall hold the reins of power and that the upward avenues of hope shall be free to all the people.

–from Benjamin Harrison's Inaugural Address, March 4, 1889

PRESIDENT BENJAMIN HARRISON HOME ——

1230 N. Delaware Street, Indianapolis, Indiana 46202

PHONE: 317-631-1888

www.presidentbenjaminharrison.org

HOURS: daily; closed major holidays,
500 Race Day, and first three weeks in January

ADMISSION: fee; senior and student discounts

WHEELCHAIR ACCESSIBILITY: yes

This Victorian house of sixteen rooms was constructed in 1875 in the brick Italianate style. When the Harrisons moved into the home, their son Russell was twenty and daughter Mary was sixteen. The family occupied the home except during the periods 1881 to 1887, when Harrison was in the U.S. Senate, and again from 1889 to 1893, the presidential years. Caroline Harrison died in the White House in October of 1892, and Harrison returned to Indianapolis a widower. He remarried in 1896, and a daughter, Elizabeth, was born in 1897.

President Benjamin Harrison Home

Harrison's house figured prominently in his campaign. It was here that Harrison learned of his Republican nomination for president. During the following weeks Harrison gave eighty speeches to the over 300,000 people who marched to the home on Delaware Street. And it was in the library that election returns were received and tallied as they came across a specially installed telegraph. Among the other rooms visitors can tour are the parlors, dining room, nursery, bedrooms, sitting room, kitchen, and law office. The house is furnished with many of Harrison's paintings, furniture, and political memorabilia. The carriage house behind the home features the women's suffrage exhibit, "From Bustles to Ballots."

Dining room in the President Benjamin Harrison Home

The house is available for viewing by guided tour only (except for roped, self-guided tours for large groups). Tours are approximately an hour long and include ten rooms in the house. The third floor ballroom displays changing exhibits. A calendar of special events can be found on the website. Educational programs are also available.

The site is owned by the Arthur Jordan Foundation and managed by the President Benjamin Harrison Foundation.

NEAREST AIRPORT: Indianapolis, Indiana
GENERAL DIRECTIONS: 12th and Delaware streets off I-65.
NEARBY ATTRACTIONS: Morris-Butler House, James Whitcomb Riley House.

WILLIAM MCKINLEY

1843–1901
25th President • 1897–1901

William McKinley campaigned for the presidency without leaving his home in Canton, Ohio. In his "front porch" campaign, McKinley spoke daily to large gatherings outside his home but left the hard work of the campaign trail to a devoted group of supporters who spread out across the country on behalf of their candidate. McKinley's strategy worked. In 1897 he became the twenty-fifth president of the United States.

McKinley did not remain at home during the campaign due to any reticence on his part, for he was an outgoing, friendly man with a gift for storytelling and public speaking. Humble, yet confident, McKinley was popular with supporters and opponents alike.

Born in Niles, Ohio, McKinley was a happy, active child who found early success at his Methodist high school as a founding member of the debating club. McKinley attended Allegheny College for a short time but left because of illness.

After the Civil War McKinley worked for a Youngstown, Ohio, judge and studied law. He became a lawyer in 1867 and soon gained the notice of local Republican party members, who urged him to run for the House of Representatives in 1877. McKinley served a total of fourteen years in the House, where he became known as a fervent supporter of protectionism. He left the House in 1891 to become governor of Ohio and, in 1896, ran successfully against William Jennings Bryan for the presidency.

In his first term as president McKinley led the nation into the Spanish-American War with the goal of establishing stability and independence in Cuba. The war resulted in the acquisition of the Philippines, Puerto Rico, and Guam as United States territories and freed Cuba from Spanish control. McKinley also negotiated the annexation of Hawaii and, in the continuing battle between free trade advocates and protectionists, restored a high tariff on imported goods in hopes of boosting domestic industry. McKinley won a second term in 1900 but served only six more months before Leon F. Czolgosz, an anarchist and unemployed Detroit millworker, assassinated him in Buffalo, New York, on September 14, 1901.

McKinley was survived by his wife Ida, who had already suffered with her husband the tragedy of losing two daughters. Mrs. McKinley, to whom the president had been extremely devoted, died six years after her husband's assassination.

IN CONCLUSION, I CONGRATULATE THE COUNTRY upon the fraternal spirit of the people and the manifestations of good will everywhere so apparent. The recent election not only most fortunately demonstrated the obliteration of sectional or geographical lines, but to some extent also the prejudices which for years have distracted our councils and marred our true greatness as a nation. The triumph of the people, whose verdict is carried into effect today, is not the triumph of one section, nor wholly of one party, but of all sections and all the people. The North and the South no longer divide on the old lines, but upon principles and policies; and in this fact surely every lover of the country can find cause for true felicitation. Let us rejoice in and cultivate this spirit; it is ennobling and will be both a gain and a blessing to our beloved country. It will be my constant aim to do nothing, and permit nothing to be done, that will arrest or disturb this growing sentiment of unity and cooperation, this revival of esteem and affiliation which now animate so many thousands in both the old antagonistic sections, but I shall cheerfully do everything possible to promote and increase it.

–from William McKinley's Inaugural Address, March 4, 1897

NATIONAL McKINLEY BIRTHPLACE MEMORIAL

40 North Main Street, Niles, Ohio 44446

PHONE: 330-652-1704

www.mckinley.lib.oh.us

HOURS: September through May, daily; June through August, Monday to Saturday

ADMISSION: no fee

WHEELCHAIR ACCESSIBILITY: library (no wheelchair accessibility in museum)

McKinley statue in courtyard

This birthplace memorial is an excellent example of Greek classic architecture. The Court of Honor features a statue of William McKinley and is supported by twenty-eight imposing columns. Constructed of Georgian marble, it was built between 1915 and 1917. The Memorial library, which serves as the public library of Niles, is in one of two lateral wings, while the museum and an auditorium are in the other. The museum features memorabilia from President McKinley's early life, Civil War and Spanish-American War artifacts, and presidential and campaign items.

The McKinley Memorial Library began construction in 2002 of a replica of McKinley's birthplace house. It will be built on the site of the original birthplace and will contain a library dedicated to McKinley.

Tours are self-guided, although groups can book a guided tour in advance. Visitors can check the website for details on occasional special programs.

The National McKinley Birthplace Memorial Association owns and maintains the property. The Association was created by an act of Congress to build a memorial for President McKinley in the town where he was born. The library staff is responsible for both the library and museum.

NEAREST AIRPORT: Cleveland, Ohio; Pittsburgh, Pennsylvania

GENERAL DIRECTIONS: I-80 to State Route 46, north for four miles on State Route 46

NEARBY ATTRACTIONS: Butler Museum of American Art.

THEODORE ROOSEVELT

1858–1919
26th President • 1901–1909

Theodore "Teddy" Roosevelt was the most popular president of his era, and according to most historians, a fine president as well. The youngest man to take the oath of office at the time, he brought to the presidency a sense of excitement and energy. He is often called the first modern president, as he led the country toward progressive reforms in both domestic and foreign policy.

Roosevelt was born in New York City in 1858 to a family of great wealth. He was a sickly child; but by adulthood, through a devoted course of physical activity, Roosevelt had grown into a robust, energetic man fond of hiking, boxing, swimming, and tennis and ready to take on any challenge life could offer. He graduated Phi Beta Kappa from Harvard and went on to Columbia Law School; in 1881, he left school to run for the New York State Assembly. He won three consecutive terms in the Assembly, where his youth and energy quickly earned him a reputation. Roosevelt had found his life's calling in politics, but in 1884, grieving the deaths of his wife Alice and his mother, he left New York for the Dakota Territory, where he worked as a cattle rancher and a deputy sheriff. In 1886 Roosevelt returned to New

York and began his rise to the White House. He served as U.S. Civil Service commissioner, as police commissioner of New York City, as secretary of the navy, and as governor of New York. Roosevelt also served in the Spanish-American War, winning fame as leader of the Rough Riders, the volunteer cavalry regiment that led the U.S. charge up San Juan Hill in Cuba. Roosevelt became vice president in 1901, and, six months later upon the death of President McKinley, he acceded to the presidency.

For eight years, Theodore Roosevelt sat at the helm of the nation as it began the twentieth century, acting boldly and aggressively but also fairly and intelligently. He took up the cause of maintaining stability in Latin America, using U.S. power to enforce what he called "big stick" diplomacy. Roosevelt also presided over the planning and early construction of the Panama Canal and became known as a "trust buster" for his work to end large corporate monopolies. One of the most lasting legacies of the Roosevelt administration is its spirit of conservationism. A lover of the outdoors, Teddy Roosevelt did much to preserve the nation's natural beauty and resources. In 1906 he won the Nobel Peace Prize for his work toward peace between Russia and Japan.

In addition to his daughter Alice from his first marriage, Roosevelt had five children with his second wife, Edith. He never lost his love of the active life or his enthusiasm for public service. Upon retirement in 1909, Roosevelt embarked upon an African safari and a tour of Europe. The remainder of his retirement was no less active, including more trips abroad and continued involvement in politics—including a run for president in 1912 as a nominee of the Progressive Party. Roosevelt died in 1919 at Sagamore Hill, his estate on Long Island.

I PREACH TO YOU, THEN, MY COUNTRYMEN, that our country calls not for the life of ease, but for the life of strenuous endeavor. The twentieth century looms before us big with the fate of many nations. . . . Let us therefore boldly face the life of strife, resolute to do our duty well and manfully; resolute to uphold righteousness by deed and by word; resolute to be both honest and brave, to serve high ideals, yet to use practical methods. Above all, let us shrink from no strife, moral or physical, within or without the nation, provided we are certain that the strife is justified; for it is only through strife, through hard and dangerous endeavor, that we shall ultimately win the goal of true national greatness.

–from a speech delivered April 10, 1899, in Chicago while governor of New York

THEODORE ROOSEVELT BIRTHPLACE NATIONAL HISTORIC SITE

28 East 20th Street, New York, New York 10003

PHONE: 212-260-1616

www.nps.gov/thrb

HOURS: Monday to Friday

ADMISSION: fee; student discount

WHEELCHAIR ACCESSIBILITY: limited

This typical New York brownstone was the birthplace of and home to Theodore Roosevelt for the first fourteen years of his life. The house is a re-creation, as the original was demolished in 1916 to make room for a commercial building. After Roosevelt's death in 1919, a group of prominent New York citizens bought the site, razed the commercial building, and reconstructed Roosevelt's boyhood home. The building opened to the public in 1923.

Of the home's five floors, three are open to the public for guided tours of the period rooms. The museum gallery is open for self-guided tours, and the library is open by appointment only. Approximately 40 percent of the home's furnishings are from the original house. Another 20 percent are family pieces, and the remainder are period pieces. It was Roosevelt's wife and sisters who provided the information for color and decor schemes. The house is the country's first Victorian reconstruction.

The site hosts a Junior Ranger program for children ages four to twelve, and visitors can call for information on other special events. The Birthplace is owned and administered by the National Park Service.

NEAREST AIRPORT: New York, New York; Newark, New Jersey

GENERAL DIRECTIONS: In Manhattan, on 20th Street between Broadway and Park Avenue.

NEARBY ATTRACTIONS: The Bill of Rights Museum at St. Paul's National Historic Site, General Grant National Memorial, Federal Hall National Memorial, Ellis Island, Statue of Liberty, and Forbes Gallery.

SAGAMORE HILL NATIONAL HISTORIC SITE

20 Sagamore Hill Road, Oyster Bay, New York 11771

PHONE: 516-922-4447 or 516-922-4788

www.nps.gov/sahi

HOURS: summer, daily; Labor Day to Memorial Day, Wednesday to Sunday; closed Thanksgiving, Christmas Day, New Year's Day

ADMISSION: fee; child discount

WHEELCHAIR ACCESSIBILITY: limited

Sagamore Hill was the home of Theodore Roosevelt from 1886 until his death in 1919. It also served as Roosevelt's summer White House from 1902 to 1908. The site includes the home, the Old Orchard Museum, and a visitor center.

The Roosevelt home is a twenty-three-room, Queen Anne-style brick and wood shingle structure. It is now furnished much as it was during Roosevelt's lifetime, with an emphasis on Roosevelt's post-presidential period, and reflects the man's many interests and hobbies. The North Room is probably the most widely described of the house's rooms. Its dramatic entrance and design made it a natural setting for receiving visitors. It was also used for many important family occasions. The room was a favorite for gathering to read, to play the piano, or to sit by the fire and talk. The home is available for viewing by guided tour only. Tours are approximately forty-five minutes long and begin on the hour. Availability is limited to fourteen people per tour.

The Old Orchard Museum is a 1930s-style Georgian home built by Roosevelt's oldest son. It now serves as the park's museum and features films and exhibits on President Roosevelt's career, his family life at Sagamore, and the lives of his six children.

The National Park Service owns and operates Sagamore Hill National Historic Site.

NEAREST AIRPORT: New York, New York
GENERAL DIRECTIONS: Located 45 minutes to an hour from any of the three nearby airports. From Northern State Parkway exit 35N or Long Island Expressway/I-495 exit 41N. From either of these exits take Route 106 north for four miles. Turn east onto Route 25A for two-and-a-half miles. Turn left onto Cove Road, then right onto Cove Neck Road to Sagamore Hill.
NEARBY ATTRACTIONS: Raynham Hall Historic House Museum and Walt Whitman Birthplace.

Sagamore Hill

WILLIAM HOWARD TAFT

1857–1930
27th President • 1909–1913

Distinguished by a handlebar mustache and a weight that often exceeded three hundred pounds, Secretary of War William Howard Taft won the endorsement of outgoing president Theodore Roosevelt in his bid for the presidency in 1908. Pledging to continue the policies of his predecessor and close friend, Taft went on to win the election over William Jennings Bryan and became the twenty-seventh president.

Taft was born in 1857 in Cincinnati, Ohio. His father was a leader in the Republican party and a career diplomat. His mother, Louise Torrey Taft, came from a prominent Boston family. After attending Yale University, where he was graduated second in his class, Taft studied law at the Cincinnati Law School with hopes of following his father into government service. Taft worked in the Cincinnati legal community for twenty years before making his entry into national politics.

In 1900 President McKinley chose Taft to be governor-general of the Philippines. On the islands, newly acquired in the Spanish-American War, Taft was to oversee the establishment of a stable government. Taft left the Philippines in 1904 when President

Roosevelt called upon him to fill the post of Secretary of War. From there, four years later, he made his bid for the White House.

As president, Taft became known for his "dollar diplomacy," a policy which relied upon American industry investments to promote stability in Latin America. Taft also followed through on the anti-trust policies of Theodore Roosevelt, continuing the move to break up and prevent large corporate monopolies. However, Taft failed to follow through on Roosevelt's progressive agenda and eventually lost the support of his one-time mentor. Roosevelt even went so far as to campaign for the Republican nomination in 1912. Losing that bid to Taft, Roosevelt broke free from the party to run as the Progressive candidate. That split in the party led to the election of Democrat Woodrow Wilson in 1912.

Taft's wife, Nellie, made her own lasting impression on the city of Washington when she arranged for three thousand Japanese cherry trees to be planted along the Tidal Basin. The annual celebration of the cherry blossoms remains one of Washington's most cherished traditions. Taft himself began another longstanding tradition, that of the president throwing out the first ball to open the professional baseball season.

Following his exit from the White House, Taft went on to teach at Yale University. In 1921, President Warren Harding appointed Taft Chief Justice of the Supreme Court, a position Taft had desired since his early days in the legal profession. He served on the court until his death in 1930. William Howard Taft is buried at Arlington National Cemetery, alongside his wife, Nellie, with whom he had three children. He was the first former president to be honored with burial at Arlington and has since been joined only by John F. Kennedy.

THE PROGRESS WHICH THE NEGRO HAS MADE IN THE LAST FIFTY YEARS, from slavery, when its statistics are reviewed, is marvelous, and it furnishes every reason to hope that in the next twenty-five years a still greater improvement in his condition as a productive member of society . . . may come.

The Negroes are now Americans. Their ancestors came here years ago against their will, and this is their only country and their only flag. They have shown themselves anxious to live for it and to die for it. Encountering the race feelings against them, subjected at times to cruel injustice growing out of it, they may well have our profound sympathy and aid in the struggle they are making. We are charged with the sacred duty of making their path as smooth and as easy as we can.

–from William Howard Taft's Inaugural Address, March 4, 1909

WILLIAM HOWARD TAFT
NATIONAL HISTORIC SITE

2038 Auburn Avenue, Cincinnati, Ohio 45230

PHONE: 513-684-3262

www.nps.gov/wiho

HOURS: daily; closed Thanksgiving, Christmas Day, New Year's Day

ADMISSION: no fee

WHEELCHAIR ACCESSIBILITY: yes

The William Howard Taft National Historic Site is the birthplace and boyhood home of the only man to serve as both president and chief justice of the United States. The house that Taft was born in has been restored to its original appearance. A visit includes a tour of the restored birthplace and four rooms furnished with period pieces. The second floor of the home houses an exhibit commemorating Taft's life and career.

Taft House

The Taft Education Center, located adjacent to the home, features an orientation video and exhibits on later generations of the Taft family. Its signature exhibit is an animatronic figure of the president's son, Charlie, telling stories about various family members.

Guided tours are available by request; other exhibits are self-guided. Rangers and guides are available to answer questions at the house and the education center.

Special events include a celebration of the Constitution on Constitution Day (September 17th), a visit by Father Christmas, and a New Year's Day open house. Children ages five to twelve can participate in the Junior Ranger program.

The site is operated by the National Park Service.

NEAREST AIRPORT: Cincinnati, Ohio

GENERAL DIRECTIONS: Located in the Mt. Auburn section of Cincinnati. From I-71 north, take exit 2 (Reading Road/Eden Park Drive). From I-71 south, take exit 3 (William Howard Taft Road).

NEARBY ATTRACTIONS: U.S. Grant Birthplace, U.S. Grant Boyhood Home, William Henry Harrison Tomb and Harrison Family Shrine, and Harriet Beecher Stowe House.

WOODROW WILSON

1856–1924
28th President • 1913–1921

Woodrow Wilson dreamed all his life of a career in politics; in realizing that dream, he became one of the great leaders of his century.

Born in Staunton, Virginia, but raised mostly in Augusta, Georgia, Wilson was troubled by illness and poor eyesight in childhood. Nonetheless, he managed to earn a spot at the College of New Jersey (now Princeton University). From there he continued on to law school at the University of Virginia. Wilson never enjoyed his legal studies but kept at them as a means of entering politics. After graduation, he found the practice of law unfulfilling and for a time chose to pursue higher education and a career as a professor. Wilson earned a Ph.D. at Johns Hopkins and worked several years as a professor and scholar before becoming president of Princeton in 1902. Wilson set his alma mater on a course to become one of the leading universities in America before leaving to run for governor of New Jersey. After two successful years as governor, Wilson received the Democratic presidential nomination.

Woodrow Wilson quickly proved himself a skilled leader. Among the early achievements of his administration were the Clayton

Antitrust Act; Federal Reserve Act, which created a system of regional, federal banks to provide a measure of stability to the economy; the Federal Trade Commission, created to keep watch over interstate trade; and the Adamson Act, the first step toward the establishment of the eight-hour workday.

President Wilson will always be best remembered for his leadership during the First World War. With his pledge to help make the world "safe for democracy," Wilson reluctantly but confidently led American forces into the war in 1917, never losing sight of peace as his ultimate objective. In 1919 he sailed to Europe as head of the U.S. delegation to the Paris Peace Conference. The resulting Treaty of Versailles, which ended the war, did not fulfill Wilson's vision as outlined in his "Fourteen Points" presentation to Congress, but it did secure the adoption of a covenant establishing the League of Nations, which he hoped would avert future world conflicts. Ironically, the treaty was never ratified by the Senate, and the United States never became a member of the organization for which Wilson had campaigned so tirelessly.

During his second term, in 1919, Wilson suffered a stroke that left him incapacitated for months. He was cared for by his second wife, Edith, but never fully recovered. He died in 1924 in Washington, D.C.

THE WORLD MUST BE MADE SAFE FOR DEMOCRACY. Its peace must be planted upon the tested foundation of political liberty. We have no selfish ends to serve. We desire no conquest, no dominion. . . . There are, it may be, many months of fiery trial and sacrifice ahead of us. It is a fearful thing to lead this great peaceful people into war, into the most terrible and disastrous of all wars, civilization itself seeming to be in the balance. But the right is more precious than peace, and we shall fight for the things which we have always carried nearest our hearts—for democracy, for the right of those who submit to authority to have a voice in their own governments, for the rights and liberties of small nations, for a universal dominion of right by such a concert of free peoples as shall bring peace and safety to all nations and make the world itself at last free. To such a task we can dedicate our lives and our fortunes, everything that we are and everything that we have, with the pride of those who know that the day has come when America is privileged to spend her blood and her might for the principles that gave her birth and happiness and the peace which she has treasured. God helping her, she can do no other.

–from Woodrow Wilson's war message to Congress, April 2, 1917

WOODROW WILSON BIRTHPLACE

18–24 North Coalter Street, Staunton, Virginia 24402

PHONE: 540-885-0897

www.woodrowwilson.org

HOURS: daily; closed Thanksgiving, Christmas Day, New Year's Day

ADMISSION: fee; student and AAA discounts

WHEELCHAIR ACCESSIBILITY: yes (museum and two floors of the manse)

Set atop a hill in downtown Staunton, this Greek Revival house, formerly a Presbyterian Manse, is the birthplace of Woodrow Wilson. The home has been fully restored and is decorated with period furniture, some of which is the Wilson family's own. Gardens surround the house, offering a restoration of Victorian landscape style.

The Woodrow Wilson Museum, located in a mansion adjacent to the house, contains seven exhibit galleries that document Wilson's life and career through photos, documents, and objects. The building also contains a research library and archives, educational program space, and storage for collections. Also on display is Wilson's Pierce-Arrow limousine, which has been restored to full working order.

The site offers guided tours of the house and self-guided tours of the museum. In addition, special events and programming are offered year-round, ranging from a birthday celebration to Christmas festivities to summer music and living history.

The Woodrow Wilson Birthplace Foundation owns and maintains the site. It was designated a National Historic Landmark in 1965. A presidential library at the birthplace site is currently in the planning stages. It will serve as a central resource to which scholars, politicians, and others can look to understand Wilson's legacy.

Woodrow Wilson Birthplace Manse

Woodrow Wilson Birthplace Museum

NEAREST AIRPORT: Washington, D.C.; Shenandoah Valley Regional Airport

GENERAL DIRECTIONS: Five minutes from I-81; 20 minutes from Blue Ridge Parkway and Skyline Drive. Well-signed in all directions.

NEARBY ATTRACTIONS: American Museum of Frontier Culture, Blackfriars Playhouse (authentic replica of Shakespeare's indoor theater).

THE BOYHOOD HOME OF PRESIDENT WOODROW WILSON

419 Seventh Street, Augusta, Georgia 30901

PHONE: 706-722-9828

HOURS: Tuesday to Saturday

ADMISSION: fee; senior and student discounts

WHEELCHAIR ACCESSIBILITY: limited, first floor only

This site, home to Woodrow "Tommy" Wilson from age three to thirteen, opened in fall 2001 after a ten-year restoration. The house is situated on about an acre of land that is also the site of the Lamar House, the boyhood home of U.S. Supreme Court Justice Joseph R. Lamar. The Lamar House, undergoing restoration as of the publication date of this book, will be used as an interpretive center when complete. Lamar was Wilson's best friend in Augusta.

The Wilson House, originally the Presbyterian Manse, was purchased for the family by the First Presbyterian Church when Woodrow Wilson's father was pastor of the church. The home is a two-and-a-half story brick house with fourteen rooms. It has been restored with more than 90 percent original materials, original paint colors, and reproduction carpets and floor coverings. The house features thirteen pieces of original Wilson family furniture as well as a silver butter dish and book owned by the president. Other furnishings and accessories are 1860s period pieces.

Boyhood Home of Woodrow Wilson, Augusta, Georgia

Also on the grounds is a two-story brick service building containing the kitchen, laundry, wood storage room, and two servant's rooms. A brick carriage house is located in the backyard as well. All tours are guided and presentations are geared toward the age of the audience.

Library collections related to the boyhood home are maintained at Historic Augusta, 111 Tenth Street, Augusta, Georgia. Historic Augusta is in the process of developing both a schedule of special events and a website related to the site. Visitors can call for updates on the progress of these developments.

Historic Augusta, a community-based historic preservation organization, has operated the site since purchasing the property in 1991 to save it from an uncertain fate. Seventy-five percent of the restoration cost came from community donations.

NEAREST AIRPORT: Augusta, Georgia

GENERAL DIRECTIONS: Approximately 150 miles east of Atlanta and 70 miles west of Columbia, South Carolina. From I-20, take exit 199 and head east toward downtown Augusta. Follow Washington Road, John C. Calhoun Expressway, and Greene Street to the intersection of Seventh Street. The house is located on the corner of Seventh and Telfair streets.

NEARBY ATTRACTIONS: Meadow Garden (home of George Walton, a signer of the Declaration of Independence), Ezekiel Harris House, Augusta Canal National Heritage Area.

WOODROW WILSON BOYHOOD HOME

Tours begin at Robert Mills Welcome Center at
1616 Blanding Street, Columbia, South Carolina 29201
PHONE: 803-252-1770, ext. 24
www.historiccolumbia.org
HOURS: Tuesday to Sunday
ADMISSION: fee; senior and student discounts
WHEELCHAIR ACCESSIBILITY: ramp to main floor only

Woodrow Wilson Boyhood Home, Columbia, South Carolina

This is the home to which young Tommy, as Woodrow Wilson was called at the time, moved with his family when he was fourteen years old. Although the family only lived here for two years, the Wilson family maintained strong ties to the area.

The house is a Tuscan-villa style Victorian patterned after the designs of Andrew Jackson Downing. Wilson's mother, Jesse Woodrow Wilson, oversaw the construction of the home and the design of the gardens. The furnishings are period pieces from the 1870s, but few are original to the Wilson family. The most significant piece in the house is the birth bed, in which Wilson was born in 1856 in Virginia.

A grassroots effort in 1928 saved the home from destruction. Docent-led guided tours are available for visitors with "I-Spy" activities available for children.

The site is managed by the Historic Columbia Foundation, and the garden is maintained by the Columbia Garden Club.

NEAREST AIRPORT: Columbia, South Carolina
GENERAL DIRECTIONS: Parking is located off Henderson Street between Taylor and Blanding streets.
NEARBY ATTRACTIONS: Robert Mills House, Hampton-Preston Mansion, Mann-Simons Cottage, South Carolina State House, South Carolina State Museum, and Governor's Mansion.

WOODROW WILSON HOUSE

2340 S Street, Washington, D.C. 20008
PHONE: 202-387-4062
www.woodrowwilsonhouse.org
HOURS: Tuesday to Sunday;
closed major holidays
ADMISSION: fee; senior, student, and
National Trust member discounts
WHEELCHAIR ACCESSIBILITY: yes

The Woodrow Wilson House is Washington,
D.C.'s only presidential museum and a
National Trust Historic Site. Wilson retired
to this residence in 1921 and spent the final
three years of his life here.

Woodrow Wilson House

The Georgian revival-style house was
built in 1915, and after purchasing the prop-
erty in 1921, Wilson and his wife Edith remodeled it to suit their needs. The structure and its interior have been carefully preserved with authentic furnishings, White
House objects, and gifts of state from around the world. In the bedrooms, personal
and wardrobe items offer visitors an intimate picture of the lives of the former president and his wife. The house is also a living textbook of American life in the

Interior of Woodrow Wilson House

1920s — from sound recordings to silent
films, flapper dresses, and zinc sinks.

Programs consist of fully guided house
tours, school programs, public enrichment
programs, and special events. Wilson
House guides bring a variety of professional and educational backgrounds to
their presentations. Tours are preceded by
a video presentation, using historical
footage that enables visitors to understand
the house and artifacts in the context of
their time.

NEAREST AIRPORT: Washington, D.C.; Baltimore, Maryland
GENERAL DIRECTIONS: From Dupont Circle (served by METRO), travel north
on Massachusetts Avenue for five blocks, turn right onto 24th Street, then right
onto S Street.
NEARBY ATTRACTIONS: Washington, D.C., is home to many historic attractions;
among them are the White House, presidential memorials, Decatur House
Museum, Ford's Theatre, and the Smithsonian Institution.

WARREN G. HARDING

1865–1923
29th President • 1921–1923

Warren G. Harding, perhaps one of the country's least effective presidents, followed Woodrow Wilson into office, winning on a campaign of "A Return to Normalcy." Although Harding was affable and popular, historians often note that Harding failed to take a stand on any issue, preferring to follow party line or defer to his advisors.

The son of two self-taught, rural doctors, Harding was born in 1865 in Blooming Grove (then called Corsica), Ohio. He grew up on a farm and attended a one-room schoolhouse in a town called Caledonia. At fifteen, Harding left home to attend Ohio Central College in Iberia. It was there that he got his start in publishing as the editor of the campus paper. After graduation, Harding continued to work in the newspaper business, eventually buying the *Marion Star* and turning it into a popular and profitable paper.

Harding's ascension to the White House began in the Ohio State Senate in 1900. He went on to become lieutenant governor of Ohio but was defeated in his 1910 bid for governorship. In 1914 he was elected to the Senate. He delivered the nominating speech for President Taft at the Republican Convention in 1912 and won the 1920 Republican nomination for president late in the balloting at the party convention.

In the White House, Harding struggled to live up to the distinguished record of his predecessor, Woodrow Wilson. Scandal troubled his administration almost from the start as members of his cabinet were found guilty of accepting bribes and selling government oil reserves for personal gain. Harding also let the work Wilson had done to form the League of Nations go to waste by refusing to back U.S. membership.

On the positive side, Harding did speak out against discrimination in the South, demanding equal rights for African Americans at a speech at the University of Alabama. Nothing he could do, however, would lift the dark cloud of scandal from his administration.

Warren Harding died in August of 1923 while returning from a tour of the western states and Alaska. His vice president, Calvin Coolidge, assumed the oath of office from his father's home in Vermont. Harding's wife, Florence "Flossie" Harding, died sixteen months later.

TODAY, BETTER THAN EVER BEFORE, WE KNOW THE ASPIRATIONS of humankind, and share them. We have come to a new realization of our place in the world and a new appraisal of our Nation by the world. The unselfishness of these United States is a thing proven; our devotion to peace for ourselves and for the world is well established; our concern for preserved civilization has had its impassioned and heroic expression. There was no American failure to resist the attempted reversion of civilization; there will be no failure today or tomorrow.

The success of our popular government rests wholly upon the correct interpretation of the deliberate, intelligent, dependable popular will of America. In a deliberate questioning of a suggested change of national policy, where internationality was to supersede nationality, we turned to a referendum, to the American people. There was ample discussion, and there is a public mandate in manifest understanding. . . .

Mankind needs a world-wide benediction of understanding. It is needed among individuals, among peoples, among governments, and it will inaugurate an era of good feeling. . . . In such understanding men will strive confidently for the promotion of their better relationships and nations will promote the comities so essential to peace.

–from Warren G. Harding's Inaugural Address, March 4, 1921

WARREN G. HARDING HOME

380 Mount Vernon Avenue, Marion, Ohio 43302

PHONE: 740-387-9630 or 800-600-6894

HOURS: November to Memorial Day weekend, closed (groups by appointment); Memorial Day weekend through Labor Day weekend, Wednesday to Sunday; September through October, Saturday to Sunday

ADMISSION: fee; child and member discounts

WHEELCHAIR ACCESSIBILITY: no

This is the home from which Warren G. Harding launched himself into the White House with his "front porch" campaign. The restored house, originally built in 1891, features almost all original pieces owned by Harding and his wife. The adjacent press house, used during the campaign, now houses a museum dedicated to President and Mrs. Harding's lives.

Groups visiting the site can arrange for special programs such as teas served on the front porch. Special programs are also available for school groups.

The Harding Home is part of a group of historical sites owned and operated by the Ohio Historical Society. The house underwent construction and restoration in late 2001 and early 2002.

NEAREST AIRPORT: Columbus, Ohio

GENERAL DIRECTIONS: On State Route 95 (Mount Vernon Avenue), about two miles west of U.S. Route 23 in Marion County.

NEARBY ATTRACTIONS: Marion County Historical Society, Marion Union Station, Huber Machinery Museum, and Wyandot Popcorn Museum.

CALVIN COOLIDGE

1872–1933
30th President • 1923–1929

Known as "Silent Cal" for his quiet and stoic demeanor, Calvin Coolidge came to the office of president following the death of Warren Harding in 1923. He had emerged from the scandals that plagued the Harding administration with his reputation unsullied, and he restored some level of dignity to the office of president.

Born on July 4, 1872, in Plymouth, Vermont, John Calvin Coolidge—known throughout his life by his middle name to avoid confusion with his father—was fifty-one years old when he assumed the presidency. Like so many American presidents, Coolidge began his career as a lawyer. He earned a bachelor's degree at Amherst College and went on to study law in nearby Northampton. He was admitted to the Massachusetts bar in 1897 and soon thereafter began his own independent practice. Over the next two decades Coolidge worked his way up through the ranks of the Massachusetts Republican party, rising from the Massachusetts General Court to the governor's office. His use of the state guard to break a strike by the Boston police brought him to the attention of the general public, and in 1920 Coolidge won the office of vice president as the running mate of Warren Harding.

Coolidge became president three years later when Harding died in office and in 1924 won election to his own term. President Coolidge, who believed that thrift was the greatest of all virtues and that too much government was a danger to the people, earned public disapproval quickly with his veto of two very popular bills. Coolidge opposed the Veterans Bonus Bill, which promised World War I veterans a paid insurance policy, payable in two decades. This bill passed despite the president's veto. Coolidge also opposed, this time successfully, a farm relief bill aimed at helping farmers by requiring the government to buy surplus crops. Coolidge saw this as undue government interference and twice used his influence to kill both versions of the McNary-Haugen bill. One issue on which Coolidge and the American people were in agreement was the Kellogg-Briand Pact, in which fourteen countries joined the United States in a pledge to resolve all future international conflicts by peaceful means. While the pact had no means for enforcement, it did signify the nation's intent concerning future conflicts.

In the years of great national prosperity and optimism that followed America's leadership in World War I, Calvin Coolidge was a popular president despite many unpopular decisions. Nonetheless, he did not seek a second term; and as the Great Depression ensued, a certain amount of public sentiment turned against Coolidge, laying blame for the country's economic downturn on the policies of his administration. Upon leaving office, Coolidge retired with his wife, Grace, to Northampton. The former president devoted his time to the writing of his autobiography and to a regular newspaper column called "Talking Things Over with Calvin Coolidge." He died in 1933 at his home in Northampton.

THERE IS ANOTHER ELEMENT, MORE IMPORTANT THAN ALL, without which there cannot be the slightest hope of a permanent peace. That element lies in the heart of humanity. Unless the desire for peace be cherished there, unless this fundamental and only natural source of brotherly love be cultivated to its highest degree, all artificial efforts will be in vain. Peace will come when there is realization that only under a reign of law, based on righteousness and supported by the religious conviction of the brotherhood of man, can there be any hope of a complete and satisfying life. Parchment will fail, the sword will fail, it is only the spiritual nature of man that can be triumphant.

–from Calvin Coolidge's Inaugural Address, March 4, 1925

PRESIDENT CALVIN COOLIDGE STATE HISTORIC SITE

VT 100A, six miles south of U.S. 4, Plymouth Notch, Vermont

PHONE: 802-672-3773

www.historicvermont.org

HOURS: late-May to mid-October, daily

ADMISSION: fee; student discount, family pass

WHEELCHAIR ACCESSIBILITY: yes, most buildings

Plymouth Notch is essentially a small Vermont hill town of over 550 acres that includes about twenty-five buildings—eleven of which are open to the public. Foremost among these are the Calvin Coolidge Birthplace and the Coolidge Homestead.

Calvin Coolidge was born in the downstairs bedroom of the modest house attached to the general store. The Calvin Coolidge Birthplace was extensively renovated over the years, and in 1968, the Vermont Division for Historic Preservation purchased the building and restored it to its 1872 appearance. Original pieces donated by the Coolidge family furnish the home.

The Coolidges moved to the house known as the Coolidge Homestead when Calvin was four years old. It is here that Vice President Coolidge received word of President Harding's death in 1923. Coolidge's father, a notary public, administered the presidential oath of office to his son in this home. Coolidge built an addition to the home in 1931, which was later removed when the house was given to the State of Vermont. The house is currently furnished just as it was in 1923.

Calvin Coolidge Homestead

Among the other structures that are open to the public at the site are homes of Coolidge's family and neighbors, the village church, the general store, a cheese factory, and the community dance hall that served as the summer White House in 1924. The visitor center contains a museum, gift shop, and exhibits relating to Coolidge's life and presidency. The steep hillside cemetery is the resting place of Calvin Coolidge and seven generations of his family. Site tours are self-guided, but an extensive guidebook is provided and staff is available in principal buildings to assist visitors.

The President Calvin Coolidge State Historic Site is part of a system of sites owned and operated by the Vermont Division for Historic Preservation.

NEAREST AIRPORT: Burlington, Vermont; Manchester, New Hampshire
GENERAL DIRECTIONS: Six miles south of U.S. 4 on VT 100A, about midway across the state.
NEARBY ATTRACTIONS: Chester Arthur Historic Site, Billings Farm and Museum, and Marsh-Billings-Rockefeller National Historic Park.

THE CALVIN COOLIDGE PRESIDENTIAL LIBRARY & MUSEUM

FORBES LIBRARY
Route 9 at Route 66, Northampton, Massachusetts 01060
PHONE: 413-587-1014
www.forbeslibrary.org
HOURS: Monday to Wednesday; call before visit
ADMISSION: no fee
WHEELCHAIR ACCESSIBILITY: yes

The Calvin Coolidge Presidential Library & Museum is home to the largest collection of manuscript pages and photographs related to Calvin Coolidge. All of his vice presidential and presidential papers are housed here, along with over 4,000 photos, scrapbooks, speeches, and Coolidge's personal library. The collection covers the time from his days of reading law in the offices of Hammond and Young through his years in office and beyond.

The museum, which is housed within the library building, features an Indian headdress and memorabilia. Portraits by Howard Chandler Christy are among the other artifacts on display in the museum.

The Library & Museum underwent a renovation from 2001 to early 2002. It is owned and operated by the Forbes Library.

NEAREST AIRPORT: Hartford, Connecticut; Westfield, Massachusetts
GENERAL DIRECTIONS: At the intersection of Route 5 and Route 9, follow Route 9 west for about two blocks. Turn left at the intersection of Route 9 and Route 66. The library sits on the left, a large stone building on a semi-circular driveway.
NEARBY ATTRACTIONS: Old Sturbridge Village and Historic Deerfield.

HERBERT HOOVER

1874–1964
31st President • 1929–1933

Herbert Hoover was a hard-working man who trained as a mining engineer and first came to the notice of the American people for his relief efforts in Europe during World War I. He was in the White House only eight months before the October 1929 stock market crash sent the country into the Great Depression.

Born in 1874 in West Branch, Iowa, Hoover attended Quaker schools as a child and later worked to put himself through Stanford University. At Stanford, Hoover met his future wife, fellow mining major Lou Henry. After their marriage, the Hoovers lived for a time in China, where Hoover worked during the Boxer Rebellion. They had two sons, both of whom followed their parents into engineering.

Hoover was in London when World War I broke out in Europe. He was made chairman of the American Relief Commission, and the committee helped more than 120,000 Americans return from Europe to the United States. He next became chairman of the Commission for Relief in Belgium, where he helped to distribute food throughout war-ravaged Belgium and France. It was in these posts that Hoover earned his reputation as an efficient and skilled leader. After the war, his efforts were rewarded with an appointment as Secretary of Commerce. From there he won the presidency, his first-ever elective office, in 1928.

Herbert Hoover ran for president on the wave of prosperity sweeping the nation in the decade after World War I. His party's famous pledge of "a chicken in every pot and a car in every garage" reflected a mood of optimism and confidence across America. Hoover won the 1928 election in a landslide victory.

The Great Depression soon crushed the nation's optimism and quickly consumed Hoover's presidency. Hoover, unfortunately, held fast to his belief that government should not interfere with business and resisted cries for federal relief. As unemployment soared and farms failed, Hoover, insisting that the worst was over, became the focus of anger and frustration. Groups of homeless people set up cities of cardboard houses they called "Hoovervilles" and covered themselves with newspapers they mockingly called "Hoover blankets." More trouble came in the form of more than twenty thousand veterans who marched to Washington to demand early payment of the Veterans Bonus promised to them by the Coolidge administration. Hoover called in federal forces to disperse the angry men, a move that strengthened negative public opinion of him.

Hoover lost his bid for reelection to Franklin Roosevelt. He retired with Lou to California, where he openly opposed the reforms of the Roosevelt administration and remained active in public life. In 1947 President Truman appointed Hoover to a commission to reorganize the executive departments. He was appointed to a similar post by President Eisenhower in 1953. Among the recommendations of these committees was the establishment of the Department of Health, Education, and Welfare. Herbert Hoover died in 1964.

THE GREATNESS OF AMERICA HAS GROWN out of a political and social system and a method of control of economic forces distinctly its own—our American system—which has carried this great experiment in human welfare further than ever before in all history. We are nearer today to the ideal of abolition of poverty and fear from the lives of men and women than ever before in any land. And I again repeat that the departure from our American system by injecting principles destructive to it which our opponents propose will jeopardize the very liberty and freedom of our people, will destroy equality of opportunity, not alone to ourselves, but to our children.

–from a 1928 campaign speech by Herbert Hoover

HERBERT HOOVER NATIONAL HISTORIC SITE

110 Parkside Drive, West Branch, Iowa 52358

PHONE: 319-643-2541

www.nps.gov/heho

HOURS: daily; closed Thanksgiving, Christmas Day, New Year's Day

ADMISSION: fee; senior and student discounts

WHEELCHAIR ACCESSIBILITY: yes, with a few exceptions

This 186-acre site includes a number of structures relating to the early and public life of Herbert Hoover; most notable is the cottage where he was born in 1874. The Herbert Hoover Presidential Library & Museum is also located here, as is the hillside burial site of the president and his wife. The historic site is administered by the National Park Service.

Friends Meetinghouse

Herbert Hoover spent the first eleven years of his life in the area. After the death of his parents, he moved to Oregon, where he was raised by an aunt and uncle. He never returned to live in West Branch, but he visited often. The cottage changed hands many times until Hoover purchased and restored it in 1935. The blacksmith shop is not original but is similar to the one Herbert Hoover's father operated from

Herbert Hoover National Historic Site visitor center

1871 to 1879. The one-story frame schoolhouse was first used as a meeting house by the Quakers and it served as the primary school during Hoover's boyhood. The building has been moved a number of times and has been in its current location since 1971. The Friends Meetinghouse was built in 1857 and served as a place of worship for the Quakers and the Hoover family. It is located two blocks from its original site. The Presidential Library & Museum is administered by the National Archives and

President and Mrs. Hoover's gravesites

Records Administration (see listing below). It houses papers and collections relating to both the public and personal lives of President Hoover.

Guided tours can be arranged in advance, but the site is primarily self-guided. Guests can begin at the visitor center, where they view a short video and find exhibits and publications. Rangers are also on hand to aid visitors. Picnicking is available, as are hiking trails in the seventy-six-acre tallgrass prairie that surrounds the site. Special events include Hooverfest and Christmas Past celebrations.

NEAREST AIRPORT: Cedar Rapids, Iowa; Quad Cities Airport; Moline, Illinois
GENERAL DIRECTIONS: one-half mile north of I-80 off exit 254
NEARBY ATTRACTIONS: Kalona Historical Village (Kalona), Old Capitol Museum (Iowa City), University of Iowa Museum of Natural History (Iowa City), and Amana Colonies.

HERBERT HOOVER PRESIDENTIAL LIBRARY & MUSEUM

210 Parkside Drive, West Branch, Iowa 52358
PHONE: 319-643-5301
www.hoover.nara.gov
HOURS: daily; closed Thanksgiving, Christmas Day, New Year's Day
ADMISSION: fee; senior and student discounts
WHEELCHAIR ACCESSIBILITY: yes

Located on the Herbert Hoover National Historic Site, this library is not a traditional library. Rather it is a repository for making available papers and historical materials related to the presidency of Herbert Hoover. While the library collections are available to scholars of all levels through an application process, it is the museum that draws most visitors to the Herbert Hoover Presidential Library & Museum.

The museum opened to the public in 1962. Ten thousand square feet are devoted to seven galleries that detail Hoover's many years of public service. Examples of past changing exhibits are "Let's Play: Pastimes from the Past," "Revolutionary America," and "Christmas through the Decades." In addition to the exhibits, the museum includes a 180-seat auditorium, meeting and conference rooms, and a museum store.

Re-created Waldorf suite exhibit

The Library-Museum is one of ten libraries administered by the National Archives and Records Administration. A major expansion leading to the rededication of the library in 1992 was a joint partnership between private and public sources. The government supplied $5 million of the $8 million cost, with the remainder coming from the Hoover Presidential Association.

NEAREST AIRPORT: Cedar Rapids, Iowa; Quad Cities Airport; Moline, Illinois
GENERAL DIRECTIONS: one-half mile north of I-80 off exit 254
NEARBY ATTRACTIONS: Kalona Historical Village, Old Capitol Museum, University of Iowa Museum of Natural History, and Amana Colonies.

Herbert Hoover Library

FRANKLIN DELANO ROOSEVELT

1882–1945
32nd President • 1933–1945

Four times Americans went to the polls and elected Franklin Delano Roosevelt as their president. An inspirational and controversial leader, Roosevelt steered Americans through the dark, troubled days of the Great Depression and World War II.

Franklin Roosevelt grew up in the luxurious family home in Hyde Park, New York, and spent summers on beautiful Campobello Island. He was graduated from Harvard in 1903 and attended Columbia Law School, dropping out when he passed the New York bar exam. Despite his rather narrow experience of wealth and privilege, as president, Roosevelt became known as the champion of the poor and downtrodden. With the country in the throes of the Great Depression, Roosevelt, a former assistant secretary of the navy and governor of New York, ran for president on the promise of a "New Deal," a package of programs aimed at providing economic relief to a country in crisis.

In his twelve years as president, Roosevelt oversaw an unprecedented expansion of the federal government. The New Deal included programs to create jobs for the unemployed, to regulate banking and housing, to extend electric power to rural areas, and to stimulate business; he also began social security, the government program to provide income to the elderly and the disabled. Under Roosevelt, as never before, the federal government took on the responsibility of providing for those Americans who could not provide for themselves. His administration was not without controversy, and his programs were not universally embraced; but Franklin Roosevelt rose to the occasion at a time of great crisis in America and left an indelible mark on U.S. history. Despite his poor health, Roosevelt projected an image of strength and vitality and brought comfort and hope to countless American families—inspiring them with words such as, "We have nothing to fear but fear itself."

Roosevelt's wife, Eleanor, a niece of former president Theodore Roosevelt and a distant cousin to Franklin, was, like her husband, a popular and controversial figure. She was an outspoken advocate of civil and human rights and as first lady took an active role in American public life.

Stricken with polio at age thirty-nine, and thereafter confined to crutches or a wheelchair, Franklin Roosevelt defied his physical limitations for three terms in the White House. At the start of his fourth term, however, his health began to deteriorate. He died in office on April 12, 1945, only months before the end of World War II.

BUT HERE IS THE CHALLENGE TO OUR DEMOCRACY: *In this nation I see tens of millions of its citizens—a substantial part of its whole population—who at this very moment are denied the greater part of what the very lowest standards of today call the necessities of life. . . .*

It is not in despair that I paint you that picture. I paint it for you in hope—because the nation, seeing and understanding the injustice in it, proposes to paint it out. We are determined to make every American citizen the subject of his country's interest and concern; and we will never regard any faithful, law-abiding group within our borders as superfluous. The test of our progress is not whether we add more to the abundance of those who have much; it is whether we provide enough for those who have too little.

–from Franklin Delano Roosevelt's second Inaugural Address, January 20, 1937

Home of Franklin D. Roosevelt National Historic Site

4007 Albany Post Road, Hyde Park, New York 12538

PHONE: 845-229-9115

www.nps.gov/hofr

HOURS: daily; closed Thanksgiving, Christmas Day, New Year's Day

ADMISSION: fee; child discount

WHEELCHAIR ACCESSIBILITY: yes

James Roosevelt bought Springwood, the lifelong home of Franklin Delano Roosevelt, in 1867, fifteen years before Franklin's birth. Franklin and his mother, Sara Roosevelt, continued to live in the house after James's death in 1900; and in 1905, Franklin brought his bride, Eleanor, to the home. The couple continued to live at Springwood with Sara Roosevelt until her death in 1941. Despite frequent long absences due to Franklin's career, the couple sought to return to Springwood whenever possible. In 1943, Roosevelt donated the home and thirty-three surrounding acres to the American people on the condition that his family be allowed to use the home after his death. The home was transferred to the Department of the Interior in 1945, after the Roosevelt family relinquished their lifelong claim. The site currently comprises 290 acres on which both Springwood and the Franklin D. Roosevelt Presidential Library and Museum are situated. The site also includes hiking trails and the Rose Garden gravesite of Franklin and Eleanor Roosevelt. On the same grounds is the Eleanor Roosevelt National Historic Site, home to Val-Kill, Eleanor's private retreat and home.

Home of Franklin D. Roosevelt

Guided tours of the home are available. Visitors will be led through the main hallway, which houses Roosevelt's boyhood stuffed bird collection; the Birth Room, in which Roosevelt was born; and the Boyhood bedroom, which Roosevelt and each of his sons used. Bedrooms used by notable visitors are off the same hallway. Roosevelt's bedroom remains just as it was during his last stay in March 1945. Visitors will also see the Dresden Room and Dining Room in which formal entertaining took place and the Living Room/Library where the family liked to gather.

Tours of the library and museum are self-guided (see Library and Museum listing), as are strolls around the grounds. The site offers programs throughout the year; visitors can call for details on specific program themes. The visitor center is housed in what was once the carriage house. Along with a bookstore and gift shop, the center also houses the Duchess County Tourist Information Center.

The site is administered by the National Park Service. The Library and Museum is administered separately by the National Archives and Records Administration.

NEAREST AIRPORT: New York, New York; Newburgh, New York
GENERAL DIRECTIONS: Four miles north of Poughkeepsie on the left side of route 9
NEARBY ATTRACTIONS: Vanderbilt Mansion, West Point, Val-Kill (Eleanor Roosevelt National Historic Site), and Samuel Morse Estate.

THE ROOSEVELT COTTAGE

ROOSEVELT CAMPOBELLO INTERNATIONAL PARK

459 Route 774, Welshpool, New Brunswick, Canada E5E 1A4
PHONE: 506-752-2922
www.fdr.net
HOURS: Victoria Day (Saturday prior to Memorial Day) to
Canadian Thanksgiving (Columbus Day), daily; Visitor Center
open through October; Natural Area open year-round
ADMISSION: no fee
WHEELCHAIR ACCESSIBILITY: many areas are accessible; second floor of house is not

Located within the 2,800-acre Roosevelt Campobello International Park are the cottage and grounds that Franklin Delano Roosevelt visited first as a child and later as a father, husband, and public figure. The home was originally built in 1897; FDR and Eleanor spent summers there from 1909 to 1921, adding on to the cottage in 1915. It was at Campobello in 1921 that Roosevelt contracted polio. Although Eleanor and the children continued to visit each year, FDR's convalescence and political life kept him from making the trip. After an absence of twelve years, FDR made three brief visits in the 1930s.

The Roosevelt cottage measures 175 feet long by thirty-five feet wide. Eighteen of its thirty-four rooms are bedrooms and six are bathrooms. The first two floors of the structure are open to the public, while the third is not. Most of the furniture in the living and dining rooms are original Roosevelt pieces.

Historic photos, artifacts, and text and audio presentations are available in the visitor center, as is a short film, *Beloved Island*. Visitors can learn about the Roosevelt association with Campobello from the time Franklin and his parents first visited the island through his battle with polio, his presidency, and the establishment of the park.

The park's natural resource area preserves the woods, bogs, and beaches where FDR tramped and the waters where he sailed. Visitors can explore trails, drives (not suitable for large recreational vehicles), overlooks, and picnic areas.

Mulholland Point Lighthouse

The Roosevelt Campobello International Park Commission sets policy guidelines, oversees park administration, and submits annual budget requests to the Canadian and U.S. governments. Per the agreement between Canada and the United States, the two countries share equally in the costs of development, operation, and maintenance. Day-to-day management of the park is the responsibility of a superintendent appointed by the Commission.

Roosevelt Cottage

NEAREST AIRPORT: Bangor, Maine; Portland, Maine; Saint John, New Brunswick

GENERAL DIRECTIONS: Located on the southern end of Campobello Island in New Brunswick, Canada. Campobello is connected by the FDR International Bridge to Lubec, on the easternmost tip of Maine. During the summer, access is available by car ferry from Deer Island, New Brunswick; a second ferry from Eastport, Maine, travels to Deer Island. U.S. visitors must pass through Canadian Customs upon arrival on Campobello. The park is located 1.5 miles from the bridge.

NEARBY ATTRACTIONS: West Quoddy Head State Park, Ganong Chocolate Factory, and Saint Andrews.

THE FRANKLIN D. ROOSEVELT PRESIDENTIAL LIBRARY AND MUSEUM

4079 Albany Post Road, Hyde Park, New York 12538

PHONE: 845-229-8114

www.roosevelt.nara.gov; www.fdrlibrary.marist.edu

HOURS: daily; closed Thanksgiving, Christmas Day, New Year's Day

ADMISSION: fee

WHEELCHAIR ACCESSIBILITY: yes

The Franklin D. Roosevelt Presidential Library is the first of the presidential libraries administered by the government. It was conceived and built under President Roosevelt's direction on land donated by him and his mother. The Library/Museum is built close to the Roosevelt home on part of the original family estate. It is the result of Roosevelt's belief that a separate facility was needed to house the historical papers, books, and memorabilia he had accumulated during his many

Franklin D. Roosevelt Library

years of public service. Prior to this time, presidents took their papers with them upon leaving office. Some were sold or destroyed, others remained with families, while others found their way to the Library of Congress or private repositories.

The library houses over 200 collections containing more than 17 million pages from both Roosevelt, his wife, Eleanor, and his associates. The papers document his time as governor of New York as well as his presidency. Two wings were added in 1971 in memory of Eleanor Roosevelt. In addition to papers and books, the library's audiovisual collection includes photographs, motion pictures, and sound recordings.

The museum contains extensive displays on the lives and careers of both President and Mrs. Roosevelt. The desk Roosevelt used in the White House greets visitors to the museum, complete with mementoes and knickknacks arranged in much the same way as they were the day he died. A WWII exhibit features an introductory video, a replica of the Map Room, and interactive exhibits that allow visitors to take on the role of general or admiral directing Allied forces. Adjacent to this is the study Roosevelt used during his visits to Hyde Park.

A separate gallery in the museum devoted to Eleanor Roosevelt features a video presentation, a replica of her New York City apartment, and other displays highlighting her impact on the nation and the world. The President's 1936 Ford Phaeton, with special hand controls, is also on display.

Upon leaving the museum, visitors can make their way through the Rose Garden, where President and Mrs. Roosevelt are buried, to the family home that overlooks the Hudson River.

The Library/Museum is part of the Presidential Library system and is administered by the National Archives and Records Administration.

NEAREST AIRPORT: New York, New York; Newburgh, New York
GENERAL DIRECTIONS: Four miles north of Poughkeepsie on the left side of Route 9.
NEARBY ATTRACTIONS: Vanderbilt Mansion, West Point, Val Kill (Eleanor Roosevelt National Historic Site), and Samuel Morse Estate.

FDR's LITTLE WHITE HOUSE HISTORIC SITE

401 Little White House Road, Warm Springs, Georgia 31830
PHONE: 706-655-5870
HOURS: daily; closed Thanksgiving, Christmas Day, New Year's Day
ADMISSION: fee; senior and student discounts
WHEELCHAIR ACCESSIBILITY: yes, except guest house and servant quarters

Franklin Delano Roosevelt first visited Warm Springs in 1924 hoping to find a cure for his polio. He continued to visit the site yearly until his death in 1945. Roosevelt didn't find a cure; but swimming in the warm, buoyant spring waters did bring relief, and other sufferers soon followed him to the springs.

The Little White House is the only home Roosevelt ever owned outright. In 1945 he suffered a fatal stroke in the Little White House while sitting for a portrait. Today, the "Unfinished Portrait" is a focal point of the tour. The house and furnishings have been carefully preserved; all structures are original and all furnishings are authentic. The adjacent 2,500-square-foot museum displays memorabilia and presents a brief newsreel-style film compiled from home movies from the 1920s and 1930s. Visitors can also view the guest house, servant quarters, and garage where Roosevelt's 1938 Ford roadster is displayed.

FDR's Little White House

Tours are self-guided, and rangers are stationed in different areas of the site to answer questions. Visitors can drive to the pools that are a little over a mile away. Annual events include FDR's Birthday celebration, Franklin and Eleanor's Wedding Anniversary, and "A Warm Springs Thanksgiving." Details can be found on the website.

The Little White House is operated by the Georgia Department of Natural Resources. Fundraising is currently underway for the building of an 18,000-square-foot-museum to be dedicated in 2004.

NEAREST AIRPORT: Atlanta, Georgia

GENERAL DIRECTIONS: One-quarter mile south of Warm Springs, Georgia, on GA 85 alt and U.S. 27 alt.

NEARBY ATTRACTIONS: Warm Springs Village, Callaway Gardens and Day Butterfly Center, F. D. Roosevelt State Park, and Providence Canyon.

ELEANOR ROOSEVELT NATIONAL HISTORIC SITE

4097 Albany Post Road, Hyde Park, New York 12538

PHONE: 845-229-9115

www.nps.gov/elro

HOURS: May through October, daily; November through April, Thursday to Monday; grounds opened daily year-round; closed Thanksgiving, Christmas Day, New Year's Day

ADMISSION: fee; child discount

WHEELCHAIR ACCESSIBILITY: yes, first floor of home

Val-Kill is the only home that was ever truly Eleanor Roosevelt's. It is also the only National Historic Site dedicated to a first lady. Eleanor Roosevelt spent most of her childhood in her grandmother's mansion and moved into Springwood with Franklin Roosevelt after their marriage. Franklin's mother, Sara, expected to have the last word in household matters, and so it was not until the building of Val-Kill in 1925 that Eleanor could create and decorate a home as her own.

The idea for Val-Kill originated in 1924 when Eleanor invited two friends to picnic with the family on the Roosevelt estate. Hearing his wife lament the closing of the big house, Franklin suggested the trio build a small cottage that could be kept open year-round. The women accepted his offer of several acres of land, and by 1925, a small fieldstone house stood by the stream where the discussion had first taken place.

Eleanor's two friends, Nan and Marion, moved into the home and made it their permanent residence until 1947. Eleanor joined them for weekends and holidays and summers. In 1926, the women constructed a larger building nearby to house an experimental business of creating replicas of Early American furniture, pewter, and weavings. The business did not survive the Depression and closed in 1936. Eleanor converted the factory building into two apartments, and she retreated here when visiting Hyde Park unaccompanied by her husband.

As specified in Franklin's will, Eleanor turned the family home over to the U.S. government after his death, but she kept the converted factory, which she named Val-Kill Cottage, for her own use. She hosted numerous world leaders here, including Nikita Khrushchev, Marshal Tito, Adlai Stevenson, and John F. Kennedy. She also hosted a yearly picnic for students from the local Wiltwyck School for delinquent boys.

Visitors can tour Val-Kill Cottage and the grounds' outbuildings, gardens, pool, and pond. The house tour is guided, while tours of the grounds are self-guided. Stone Cottage, the original fieldstone cottage, now operates as a conference center; it is available to visitors when not in use. In addition, a biographical film of Eleanor Roosevelt is shown in the Playhouse and special events are scheduled year-round.

In May 1977, with the property in danger of being developed and the historic home lost, Jimmy Carter signed the bill creating the Eleanor Roosevelt National Historic Site. It is now operated by the National Park Service.

NEAREST AIRPORT: New York, New York; Newburgh, New York
GENERAL DIRECTIONS: Four miles north of Poughkeepsie on the left side of Route 9.
NEARBY ATTRACTIONS: Vanderbilt Mansion, West Point, Home of Franklin D. Roosevelt National Historic Site, and Samuel Morse Estate.

HARRY S TRUMAN

1884–1972
33rd President • 1945–1953

Harry S Truman acceded to the presidency upon the death of Franklin Roosevelt in 1945—just three months after becoming vice president. He took office at a critical point in history, with the world embroiled in the conflict of World War II. He was initially unprepared for what lay ahead, not even having been briefed on the development of the atomic bomb prior to Roosevelt's death. Truman told reporters, "I felt like the moon, the stars, and all the planets had fallen on me."

Born at the family home in Lamar, Missouri, in 1884, Truman grew up the son of a Missouri farm family in and around Independence, Missouri. As a child in Independence, Truman met his future wife, Elizabeth "Bess" Wallace. A high school graduate without the money to attend college, Truman tried unsuccessfully to make a start in business and spent a decade running the family farm before service in World War I revealed his skills as a leader and led him into a life of public service.

Truman served two years in World War I, rising to the rank of captain and discovering a knack for leadership. He returned to Missouri in 1919 with new connections and ambitions. After one failed business venture, Truman won election as judge of Jackson County,

Missouri. In 1934 Truman ran for Senate and, with the backing of powerful Missouri Democrats, won. After a decade of Senate membership, Truman was called upon by President Roosevelt to be his running mate in the 1944 election. Truman, at first hesitant, accepted the vice presidential nomination, and the two went on to victory.

Harry Truman's most difficult decision came within his first six months as president. In August of 1945 President Truman ordered atomic bombs dropped on Hiroshima and Nagasaki, Japan, aware of the likely devastation but believing that the bombs would end the war and save American soldiers inestimable suffering and death. His decision led to the end of World War II, and the United States emerged as a world leader with great power and great responsibilities.

President Truman then faced the difficult challenge of leading America into the Cold War era. Responding to the threat of Soviet aggression in Europe, Truman declared it U.S. policy to support people around the world in their fight against communism. He led the United States into the United Nations and, with Secretary of State George Marshall, devised the Marshall Plan for rebuilding Europe after the devastation of the war. In 1948 Truman won the confidence of the people and defied political odds to win election as president in his own right. In 1950 he ordered American troops into the Korean conflict under the aegis of the United Nations. It was a conflict that would last until after Truman left office; his successor, Dwight D. Eisenhower effected a truce in Korea in 1953.

Harry Truman left office after two terms and returned to Independence with Bess, where he lived until his death in 1972.

THE PEOPLES OF THE EARTH FACE THE FUTURE WITH GRAVE UNCERTAINTY, composed almost equally of great hopes and great fears. In this time of doubt, they look to the United States as never before for good will, strength, and wise leadership. . . .

The American people stand firm in the faith which has inspired this nation from the beginning. We believe that all men have a right to equal justice under law and equal opportunity to share in the common good. We believe that all men have the right to freedom of thought and expression. We believe that all men are created equal because they are created in the image of God.

From this faith we will not be moved.

–from Harry S Truman's Inaugural Address, January 20, 1949

HARRY S TRUMAN NATIONAL HISTORIC SITE

223 North Main Street, Independence, Missouri 64050

PHONE: 816-254-2720

www.nps.gov/hstr

HOURS: Memorial Day through Labor Day, daily; Labor Day through Memorial Day, Tuesday to Sunday; closed Thanksgiving, Christmas Day, New Year's Day

ADMISSION: fee; child discount

WHEELCHAIR ACCESSIBILITY: yes

A number of homes make up the Truman National Historic Site. Of greatest significance are the Truman Farm Home in Grandview, Missouri, and the Truman Home in Independence, Missouri. The site also includes the two adjacent homes of Mrs. Truman's brothers and, across Delaware Street, the home of the president's favorite aunt and cousins.

The white, Victorian-style Truman Home at 219 North Delaware Street was the president's residence from the time of his marriage to Bess in 1919 until his death. It was built by the maternal grandfather of Bess Truman and was known as the "Summer White House" during the Truman administration. Guided tours of the home reveal that it is much as Harry and Bess left it. Visitors must purchase tour tickets at the Ticket Center a few blocks from the home. Here they can also view a short slide program about the Trumans and their home.

Truman House

Truman Farm Home

During the summer months, rangers lead walking tours of the neighborhood. From the sidewalk, visitors can view the homes of George and Frank Wallace and the Nolands (relatives of Truman's). While not open to the public, these homes are historically significant.

Built in 1894 by Harry Truman's maternal grandmother, the Truman Farm Home is the centerpiece of the 5.25-acre remnant of the family's former 600-acre farm. Truman worked the farm as a young man from 1906 to 1917. Rangers lead tours of the farm homes on weekends in the summer; at other times tours are self-guided. Visitors can also explore the grounds, although the outbuildings on the site are closed.

The Truman Home was willed to the United States government by Bess Truman, while the Farm Home was added to the site in 1994 by an act of Congress. The entire site is now under the management of the National Park Service.

NEAREST AIRPORT: Kansas City, Missouri
GENERAL DIRECTIONS: To the Truman Home—from I-435 take exit 60 (Truman Road); from I-70 take exit 12 (Noland Road). To the Truman Farm—from I-435 take U.S. 71 to Blue Ridge Blvd.; from I-70 take exit 8A onto I-435 and proceed as above.
NEARBY ATTRACTIONS: Harry S Truman Library and Museum and Jackson County Courthouse—Truman Courtroom.

TRUMAN PRESIDENTIAL MUSEUM & LIBRARY

500 West U.S. Hwy 24, Independence, Missouri 64050
PHONE: 800-833-1225
www.trumanlibrary.org
HOURS: daily; closed Thanksgiving, Christmas Day, New Year's Day
ADMISSION: fee; senior and child discount
WHEELCHAIR ACCESSIBILITY: yes

The Truman Presidential Museum & Library is one of ten presidential libraries operated by the federal government. Its purpose is to preserve and make available historical materials relating to President Truman and his presidency. The Library currently houses over 15 million pages of manuscript materials, in addition to papers and books. Its audiovisual collection includes photographs, motion pictures, and sound recordings. President and Mrs. Truman are buried in the museum's courtyard.

The museum has about 35,000 objects in its collection, not all of which are on display at any given time. Among the permanent exhibits are a Thomas Hart Benton mural, a replica of Truman's Oval Office, and "Harry S Truman: The Presidential Years," which is an interactive exhibit providing an in-depth look at some of the most significant decisions of Truman's presidency.

Truman Memorabilia

The library was rededicated in December 2001 following more than $20 million in renovations.

The Library & Museum is part of the Presidential Library system and is administered by the National Archives and Records Administration.

NEAREST AIRPORT: Kansas City, Missouri
GENERAL DIRECTIONS: All major interstates will lead to U.S. Hwy 24.
NEARBY ATTRACTIONS: Harry S Truman National Historic Site, Mormon Visitors Center, and historic Independence Square.

HARRY S TRUMAN BIRTHPLACE STATE HISTORIC SITE

1009 Truman, Lamar, Missouri 64759
PHONE: 417-682-2279
www.mostateparks.com
HOURS: daily
ADMISSION: no fee
WHEELCHAIR ACCESSIBILITY: yes

Harry S Truman was born in the downstairs bedroom of this small frame house in Lamar, Missouri. His family moved from the area when he was only eleven months old.

Back view of the Truman Birthplace

Purchased by the Trumans in 1882 for $685, the house is called a story-and-a-half; it has four rooms downstairs and two upstairs. A smokehouse, well, and outhouse are located behind the house, which has no electricity or indoor plumbing. The interior furnishings are representative of a typical home of its style during the time the Trumans lived in Lamar.

President Truman attended the dedication of the site on April 19, 1959. It is listed on the National Register of Historic Places and is a Missouri State Park.

NEAREST AIRPORT: Joplin, Missouri; Kansas City, Missouri
GENERAL DIRECTIONS: 2 miles east of 71 highway
NEARBY ATTRACTIONS: Civil War Museum, Powers Museum, and Kendricks House Museum.

HARRY S TRUMAN LITTLE WHITE HOUSE MUSEUM

111 Front Street, Key West, Florida 33040
PHONE: 305-294-9911
www.trumanlittlewhitehouse.com
HOURS: daily
ADMISSION: fee
WHEELCHAIR ACCESSIBILITY: first floor

Little White House Museum

President Harry Truman used this house for 175 days during his administrations and spent eleven working vacations here as well. The house was originally a two-family dwelling. It was converted into a single family home before World War I. Presidents Eisenhower, Kennedy, and Carter also spent time in or visited the house.

The Little White House sits in a two-acre park with gardens. Eighty to 90 percent of the furnishings are original. In addition to the paid guided tour of the public and private rooms of the house, the site offers two free exhibit rooms as well as free tours of the gardens.

Two permanent exhibits are the "Harry Truman Story" and "The Florida Keys: Where Presidents Vacation." Additional temporary exhibits are added regularly.

The Harry S Truman Little White House is owned by the State of Florida. It is managed for the state by Historic Tours of America.

NEAREST AIRPORT: Miami, Florida; Key West, Florida
GENERAL DIRECTIONS: Located two blocks from Mallory Square at the corner of Front and Caroline streets.
NEARBY ATTRACTIONS: The Key West Shipwreck Historeum Museum, the Audubon House Museum, and the Custom's House.

DWIGHT D. EISENHOWER

1890–1969
34th President • 1953–1961

Dwight D. Eisenhower drew on his military success in World War II to propel himself to victory in the 1952 and 1956 presidential elections. Today, his foreign policy and leadership in the Cold War conflicts are remembered more favorably than his domestic policy.

Born in Texas and raised in Abilene, Kansas, David Dwight Eisenhower grew up in a poor family, one of seven boys. Known as Dwight David to avoid confusion with his father and nicknamed "Ike" from childhood, Eisenhower loved sports and military history. He enrolled at West Point at age twenty-one and from then on made the United States military his career. He held only one elected office in his life, that of president of the United States.

Eisenhower was graduated from West Point in 1915 with the rank of second lieutenant. For all but two of the next thirty-seven years, Eisenhower served in the United States Army. It was during World War II that he rose to prominence, becoming Supreme Allied Commander and, after the successful Allied landing at Normandy, a five-star general. In 1950 President Truman appointed Eisenhower supreme commander of NATO, a position he held until his nomination for president in July of 1952.

With Senator Richard M. Nixon as his running mate, Dwight Eisenhower won the 1952 presidential election based in great part on his war record and his strong, no-nonsense personality. Popular in office as he had been as a candidate, Eisenhower won re-election in a second landslide four years later. In office, he immediately lived up to his campaign promise and traveled to Korea to speed up the negotiations that ended the war. His administration was characterized by what is known as the Eisenhower Doctrine, a bold statement of the American stand against communism. Eisenhower believed that strength was necessary not for its own sake but for its power as a deterrent to war, and he began to build up the American nuclear arsenal. Eisenhower felt strongly that the United States had the right and obligation to protect any country threatened by the spread of communism.

Eisenhower, a goodhearted man, never lost the goodwill of the American people; he retired from public life in 1961 after attending the inauguration of his successor, John F. Kennedy. He and his wife, Mamie, then moved to Gettysburg, Pennsylvania, their first permanent home in almost forty-five years of married life. Eisenhower died in 1969 after a series of heart attacks. He was buried in his army uniform in Abilene, Kansas.

DOWN THE LONG LANE OF THE HISTORY YET TO BE WRITTEN, America knows that this world of ours, ever growing smaller, must avoid becoming a community of dreadful fear and hate, and be, instead, a proud confederation of mutual trust and respect. . . .

Disarmament, with mutual honor and confidence, is a continuing imperative. . . . As one who has witnessed the horror and lingering sadness of war—as one who knows that another war could utterly destroy this civilization which has been so slowly and painfully built over thousands of years—I wish I could say tonight that a lasting peace is in sight.

Happily, I can say that war has been avoided. Steady progress toward our ultimate goal has been made. But, so much remains to be done. As a private citizen, I shall never cease to do what little I can to help the world advance along that road. . . .

–from Dwight D. Eisenhower's Farewell Address, January 17, 1961

EISENHOWER CENTER

200 S.E. 4th Street, Abilene, Kansas 67410

PHONE: 785-263-4751 or 877-746-4453

www.eisenhower.utexas.edu

HOURS: daily; closed Thanksgiving, Christmas Day, New Year's Day

ADMISSION: fee; child discount

WHEELCHAIR ACCESSIBILITY: yes

The Eisenhower Center consists of five buildings located on the twenty-two-acre site. They are the Family Home, Museum, Library, Place of Meditation, and Visitor Center.

A typical nineteenth-century dwelling, the Family Home was occupied by the Eisenhowers from 1898 until Mrs. Ida Eisenhower's (Eisenhower's mother) death in 1946. Constructed of white pine clapboard and a cedar shingle roof, the rooms are furnished with a mix of styles that reflects the many decades the Eisenhowers lived there.

The Museum is designed to be self-guided and includes a number of galleries and over 35,000 artifacts. The Temporary Gallery showcases exhibits that are rotated every six months. The First Lady's Gallery contains artifacts relating to Mamie Eisenhower, including clothing and jewelry. The Military Gallery commemorates Eisenhower's life as a military man, while the Presidential Gallery features objects from the 1952 and 1956 campaigns and items relating to his administration.

The Eisenhower Library houses over 22 million pages plus photographs, films, and audio materials. It is open to researchers and includes archival stacks, a research

Eisenhower Boyhood Home at the Eisenhower Center

Eisenhower statue in center of complex

room, a photo lab, and an auditorium. A temporary exhibit gallery comprises part of the second floor.

The Place of Meditation is the final resting place of Dwight and Mamie Eisenhower and their first son. It is a quiet place offering visitors a spot for reflection and meditation.

The visitor center shows a short orientation film throughout the day in its auditorium. It also houses a gift shop.

The Eisenhower Center is administered by the National Archives and Records Administration. The Friends of Eisenhower Foundation was established in 1990 to assist the Library financially. Membership information is available on the website.

NEAREST AIRPORT: Salina, Kansas
GENERAL DIRECTIONS: 2 miles south off I-70, Abilene exit.
NEARBY ATTRACTIONS: local museums and antique stores.

EISENHOWER NATIONAL HISTORIC SITE

250 Eisenhower Farm Lane, Gettysburg, Pennsylvania 17325
PHONE: 717-338-9114
www.nps.gov/eise
HOURS: April through October, daily; November through March, Wednesday to Sunday; closed Thanksgiving, Christmas Day, New Year's Day
ADMISSION: fee; child discount
WHEELCHAIR ACCESSIBILITY: first floor of home, reception center, most of grounds

Eisenhower National Historic Site is the presidential and retirement home of Dwight D. Eisenhower. Purchased by the Eisenhowers in 1950, the 189-acre farm is the only place the president and his wife ever called home. They used it as a weekend retreat and meeting place during his presidency and lived here full-time during Eisenhower's retirement. In 1967, the Eisenhowers deeded the property to the National Park Service.

A tour of the Eisenhower home includes an up-close look at the nearly all original furnishings. The reception center, once a Secret Service office, now houses a bookstore and exhibits chronicling Eisenhower's life from his boyhood in Kansas

Eisenhower Home

through his presidency to his retirement at this Gettysburg farm. A biographical film is also shown here.

Upon arrival at the site, visitors take a fifteen-minute tour with a member of the park staff. A self-guided tour of the grounds is also available, as is a farm walking tour. The farm walking tour explores Eisenhower's cattle operation and includes a tour of the barn. Regularly scheduled ranger talks and living history programs are conducted seasonally. A living history program might include a historian portraying a reporter or Secret Service agent and offering his perspective on the Eisenhower presidency. The self-guided grounds tour includes a putting green, rose gardens, guest house, and garage that still houses several Eisenhower vehicles.

Located adjacent to the Gettysburg Battlefield, the site today comprises 690 acres and is still maintained as a working farm. It is managed by the National Park Service.

NEAREST AIRPORT: Harrisburg, Pennsylvania; Baltimore, Maryland
GENERAL DIRECTIONS: Due to limited parking, visitors must board shuttle buses at the Gettysburg National Military Park Visitor Center. Located about one mile south of Gettysburg on SR 134 (Taneytown Road) and US 15 (Steinwehr Avenue).
NEARBY ATTRACTIONS: Gettysburg National Military Park.

EISENHOWER BIRTHPLACE STATE HISTORICAL SITE

609 South Lamar Avenue, Denison, Texas 75020

PHONE: 903-465-8908

www.eisenhowerbirthplace.org

HOURS: Tuesday to Sunday; closed Christmas Day

ADMISSION: fee; child discount

WHEELCHAIR ACCESSIBILITY: yes

Dwight David Eisenhower was born in this modest two-story frame house in Denison, Texas, in 1890. The home is furnished with period pieces and is the focal point of the ten-acre park.

In addition to the house, the park features historic buildings, a hiking trail, flowers, and picnic areas. The covered pavilion and Red Store are available for use by the public. The visitor center features interpretive exhibits on Dwight D. Eisenhower's life and the history of the birthplace. The visitor center also has a gift shop and bookstore. The park hosts special community events each year, including an Easter egg hunt, Eisenhower's birthday, and a Victorian Christmas.

Eisenhower Birthplace

The Eisenhower Birthplace State Historical Site is part of the Texas Parks and Wildlife Department, and the park receives additional support from the United Supporters for Ike's Birthplace.

NEAREST AIRPORT: Dallas/Ft. Worth, Texas; Grayson County Airport, Texas

GENERAL DIRECTIONS: In downtown Denison, just off the corner of Crockett Avenue and Nelson Street.

NEARBY ATTRACTIONS: Red River Railroad Museum, Frontier Village, Eisenhower State Park, and Lake Texoma.

JOHN F. KENNEDY

1917–1963
35th President • 1961–1963

The youngest man ever elected president, and the first Roman Catholic, forty-three-year-old John Fitzgerald Kennedy won the White House with his pledge to lead America to meet the challenge and the promise of the future. Young, handsome, and charismatic, John Kennedy won a close race against Richard M. Nixon but would be denied, by an assassin's bullet, the chance to complete his term.

The son of Joseph Kennedy, a prominent Massachusetts businessman and diplomat, and Rose Fitzgerald Kennedy, whose father had been mayor of Boston, John Kennedy was born in Brookline, Massachusetts, in 1917 and lived a childhood of privilege. A fun-loving, active youth despite frequent illnesses, Kennedy did not take his education seriously until his junior year at Harvard, when he began to think of a future in politics. After graduation, Kennedy served in the navy, where his heroism after the bombing of his boat, the PT-109, won him the Purple Heart and national recognition.

After the war, Kennedy worked briefly as a journalist before a successful run for the House of Representatives as a Democrat from Massachusetts. From the House, Kennedy went on to the Senate, where he served for eight years before making his successful run for the presidency. In his race against Richard Nixon, Kennedy was helped immeasurably by the advent of extensive television campaign coverage, which gave the advantage to the attractive, charismatic Kennedy.

In his three years in office, John Kennedy, along with his wife, Jacqueline Bouvier Kennedy, and their children, captured the imagination of the American people and brought new life to Washington, D.C. Admired as much for his style as for his skills, Kennedy enjoyed great popularity. He inherited a nation near crisis with the Soviet Union and continued to struggle with the threat of communism that had troubled his predecessor. During the Kennedy years, U.S. involvement in the Vietnam conflict grew quickly. The Berlin Wall went up, and tensions with the Soviets rose to near crisis during the standoff over Soviet missiles in Cuba. Kennedy is remembered for his strong stand against spreading communism and for the development of the Peace Corps and the space program.

John F. Kennedy was assassinated on November 22, 1963, in Dallas, Texas, in what has proven to be one of the most controversial crimes in American history. Lee Harvey Oswald was arrested for the shooting but was himself shot and killed before he could be tried.

IN THE LONG HISTORY OF THE WORLD, only a few generations have been granted the role of defending freedom in its hour of maximum danger. I do not shrink from this responsibility—I welcome it. I do not believe that any of us would exchange places with any other people or any other generation. The energy, the faith, the devotion which we bring to this endeavor will light our country and all who serve it—and the glow from that fire can truly light the world.

And so my fellow Americans, ask not what your country can do for you—ask what you can do for your country. My fellow citizens of the world: ask not what America will do for you, but what together we can do for the freedom of man.

Finally, whether you are citizens of America or citizens of the world, ask of us here the same high standards of strength and sacrifice which we ask of you. With a good conscience our only sure reward, with history the final judge of our deeds, let us go forth to lead the land we love, asking His blessing and His help, but knowing that here on earth God's work must truly be our own.

–from John F. Kennedy's Inaugural Address, January 20, 1961

JOHN F. KENNEDY NATIONAL HISTORIC SITE

83 Beals Street, Brookline, Massachusetts 02446

PHONE: 617-566-7937

www.nps.gov/jofi

HOURS: May through October, Wednesday to Sunday

ADMISSION: fee; child discount

WHEELCHAIR ACCESSIBILITY: no (pending as of 2002)

Repurchased, restored, and given to the National Park Service by Rose Kennedy in 1969, this home was the birthplace of John F. Kennedy. Park rangers lead visitors on tours through the modest home, in which the living room was the center of most family activity. Many of the objects in the room were used by the Kennedy family from 1914 to 1921. Included are the piano given to Mrs. Kennedy as a wedding gift, an original mahogany gateleg table, and the Oriental rug used by the family when they lived here.

John F. Kennedy Birthplace

The master bedroom, in which John F. Kennedy was born, has been arranged in much the same way it was on the day of his birth. The furniture and decorative pieces in the room belonged to the family, as did the childhood pictures. The bassinet in the nursery was used by Rose Kennedy for all her newborn children; in later years, it cradled grandchildren. Other rooms include the guest room, study, kitchen, and dining room, which features much of the china and silver service used by the Kennedy family.

Outside the house, the neighborhood is home to a number of significant sites: The Naples Road Residence, on the corner of Abbottsford and Naples Roads, is the home to which the Kennedys moved after outgrowing the house on Beals Street. (It is a private residence and can be viewed only from the sidewalk or across the street.) The Kennedy children were all baptized in and attended Sunday mass at nearby St. Aidan's Catholic Church. Joseph Jr. and John first attended the Edward Devotion School and, later, the Dexter School.

The site is owned and operated by the National Park Service.

NEAREST AIRPORT: Boston, Massachusetts

GENERAL DIRECTIONS: Near Coolidge Corner area of Brookline, off Harvard Avenue. Visitors can take the MBTA Green Line to Coolidge Corner.

NEARBY ATTRACTIONS: John Fitzgerald Kennedy Library and Museum; Freedom Trail sites; and USS *Constitution*.

JOHN FITZGERALD KENNEDY LIBRARY AND MUSEUM

Columbia Point, Boston, Massachusetts 02125

PHONE: 617-929-4500; 877-616-4599

www.jfklibrary.org

HOURS: daily; closed Thanksgiving, Christmas Day, New Year's Day

ADMISSION: fee

WHEELCHAIR ACCESSIBILITY: yes

Dedicated in 1979, the John Fitzgerald Kennedy Library and Museum is one of ten presidential libraries administered by the National Archives and Records Administration (NARA). Its stated purpose is to advance the understanding of President Kennedy's life and career and the times in which he lived. The museum houses twenty-one exhibits covering Kennedy's life, his administration, and his family. The library, with its multitude of manuscript, audiovisual, and documentary

John Fitzgerald Kennedy Library and Museum

holdings, offers research, educational and outreach programs, and activities to scholars, students, journalists, and visitors of all ages.

A visit to the John F. Kennedy Library and Museum might begin with a seventeen-minute introductory film that is narrated by President Kennedy. After entering the galleries, which begin with a mock 1960 Democratic National Convention floor, visitors pass through a 1960-style street scene that includes campaign headquarters. A re-creation of the studio in which the first Kennedy-Nixon debate took place features cameras, lighting, and backgrounds that duplicate the original studio. An election map and tally board mimic the television studio in which Walter Cronkite covered the 1960 election returns.

Exhibits are arranged as "rooms" off the main White House exhibit corridor and include a Peace Corps exhibit, Kennedy's press conferences, the Cuban Missile Crisis, and the space program. In addition to the White House exhibits, there are a re-creation of the Justice Department office of Robert Kennedy and an exhibit detailing the life of Jacqueline Bouvier Kennedy. All exhibits except for those in the Ceremonial Room are permanent. The Ceremonial Room exhibit changes approximately every six months.

In addition to the introductory film, a twenty-minute film on the Cuban Missile Crisis is shown as part of that particular exhibit each day. Special events are often held at the Library and Museum and include such events as music recitals and speaking engagements.

As part of the NARA presidential library system, the John F. Kennedy Library and Museum receives federal funding; however, the funding does not fully support all of the site's activities. The John F. Kennedy Library Foundation, which was founded in 1984, works to supply additional funding to the Library and Museum.

NEAREST AIRPORT: Boston, Massachusetts

GENERAL DIRECTIONS: Located on Columbia Point in Boston, close to I-93. Follow signs to the University of Massachusetts and JFK Library.

NEARBY ATTRACTIONS: John F. Kennedy National Historic Site, Freedom Trail sites, and USS *Constitution*.

THE SIXTH FLOOR MUSEUM
AT DEALEY PLAZA

411 Elm Street, Dallas, Texas 75202

PHONE: 214-747-6660

www.jfk.org

HOURS: daily; closed Christmas Day

ADMISSION: fee; senior and student/child discount

WHEELCHAIR ACCESSIBILITY: yes

The museum is located on the sixth floor of the Dallas County Administration Building, formerly the Texas Book Repository. Evidence related to the 1963 assassination of John F. Kennedy was found here and two evidentiary areas have been preserved, including the alleged sniper's nest.

The 9,000-square-foot exhibit area houses over 400 photographs, six documentary films, and a range of artifacts and interpretive displays. One section of the permanent exhibit is devoted to the early 1960s and briefly chronicles Kennedy's presidency. The majority of the space, however, is devoted to the assassination, including sections on The Crisis Hours, The Investigations, and The Legacy.

The museum can be experienced by self-guided tour or by an award-winning audio tour that enhances the exhibit with eyewitness accounts and historic news broadcasts. A children's audio tour is also available.

The Sixth Floor Museum is operated by the Dallas County Historical Foundation, a nonprofit organization established in 1983. In February 2002, the seventh floor of the building opened to the public with expanded exhibition space and space for after-hours facility rental.

NEAREST AIRPORT: Dallas/Ft. Worth, Texas

GENERAL DIRECTIONS: From I-35 north or south or I-30 east or west, exit at Commerce Street/Reunion Boulevard. Market Street north two blocks to Elm Street, then the Elm extension. The museum is on the corner of Elm and Houston streets.

NEARBY ATTRACTIONS: Dealey Plaza and Kennedy Memorial Plaza.

Dallas County Administration Building (formerly the Texas Book Repository)

LYNDON B. JOHNSON

1908–1973
36th President • 1963–1969

Vice President Lyndon Baines Johnson took the oath of office aboard Air Force One on a runway at Dallas's Love Field airport just hours after the assassination of President John F. Kennedy. A big, strong man with roots in Texas and more than a quarter century's worth of experience in public office, Johnson assumed the presidency amid great turmoil and served during one of the most tumultuous periods in American history.

Born in the family farmhouse on the Pedernales River near Johnson City, Texas, Lyndon Johnson grew up on Texas legends and Texas politics. His father, a farmer and a state legislator, was an early role model for his son. Johnson worked himself through college and taught high school briefly before beginning his own career in public service. His first job was as secretary to a Democratic representative from Texas. Soon thereafter he himself won election to the House. For the next twenty-two years Lyndon Johnson represented Texas in the House and then the Senate, rising to become Senate majority leader in 1955 and earning a reputation as a persuasive and powerful legislator. Johnson's great influence in Washington and his popularity in Texas convinced John Kennedy to choose him as his running mate in 1960.

After completing John Kennedy's unfinished term, Johnson won reelection in his own right. In all he served as president for five years. President Johnson's greatest achievements came in the areas of civil rights, social welfare, and the space program. With his strong support, the Civil Rights Act of 1964, the Voting Rights Act of 1965, and the Civil Rights Act of 1968 all passed in Congress. Johnson's social and welfare programs included the creation of Medicare, aid to education, and wide-scale anti-poverty programs. His support of the space program, which he had overseen since his time as vice president, led to vast exploration, including the 1968 manned moon orbit.

Johnson's greatest burden was the Vietnam conflict. Although there was no official declaration of war, American involvement in the conflict increased during his administration. Increasingly violent protests erupted at home, and despite scaling back the bombing of North Vietnam in spring 1968, Johnson was unable to put an end to the conflict or to complete the withdrawal of American forces.

Worn down by the strains of the presidency, Lyndon Johnson surprised Americans by announcing that he would neither seek nor accept a second complete term. He retired in January of 1969 to his LBJ Ranch in Texas, where he died in January of 1973. He is survived by his wife, Claudia "Lady Bird" Johnson, and their two daughters, Lynda Bird and Luci Baines Johnson.

THE TIME HAS COME FOR AMERICANS OF ALL RACES AND CREEDS and political beliefs to understand and respect one another.

Let us put an end to the teaching and preaching of hate and evil and violence. Let us turn away from the fanatics of the far left and the far right, from the apostles of bitterness and bigotry, from those defiant of law, and those who pour venom into our nation's bloodstream. . . .

These are the United States—a united people with unity of purpose.

Our American unity does not depend upon unanimity. We have differences; but now, as in the past, we can derive from those differences strength, not weakness, wisdom, not despair. Both as a people and as a government we can unite upon a program which is wise and just, enlightened and constructive.

–from Lyndon B. Johnson's address to Congress, November 27, 1963

LYNDON B. JOHNSON NATIONAL HISTORICAL PARK

100 Ladybird Lane, Johnson City, Texas 78636
PHONE: 830-868-7128
www.nps.gov/lyjo
HOURS: daily; closed Thanksgiving, Christmas Day, New Year's Day
ADMISSION: no fee for Johnson City District; fee for LBJ Ranch District
WHEELCHAIR ACCESSIBILITY: yes

Lyndon B. Johnson National Historical Park comprises two distinct areas: the seventy-eight-acre Johnson City District and the 594-acre LBJ Ranch. The two areas provide a comprehensive look at Johnson's life from birth and boyhood to his presidency, retirement, and even his final resting place.

The Johnson City District

The park's visitor center is located within the Johnson City District and it is recommended that visitors begin here. The center features photographic exhibits and presents films depicting the lives of President and Mrs. Johnson. The center also has a bookstore and gift shop.

The Boyhood Home is one of the focal points of the Johnson City District. It was the home of the president from age five to twenty-six. Johnson announced his candidacy for the House of Representatives from the front porch of the home in 1937. During the presidential years, the house was used as a community center and public tours were offered. The house was designated a part of the park in 1969 and was restored to its 1920s appearance and reopened to the public in 1973. Tours are conducted every half hour and last approximately twenty minutes.

The Johnson Settlement is a quick walk from the visitor center. The settle-

The Texas White House at the LBJ Ranch

ment includes Dog-trot Cabin, the homestead of President Johnson's grandfather Sam Ealy Johnson Sr. The building also served as headquarters for Sam Johnson Sr.'s open-range cattle business.

Also within the Johnson settlement is an exhibit center that tells the story of Texas frontier life. Additional structures in the settlement that were added by descendants of Sam Johnson Sr. include the James Polk Johnson Barn and a windmill, a water tank, and a cooler house.

Maps are available for self-guided walking tours of the settlement. Costumed rangers demonstrate period living skills in spring and fall months.

The LBJ Ranch District

Access to the LBJ Ranch and its structures is limited to National Park Service bus tours during the day and after-hours auto tours that include part of the ranch. Tours begin at the visitor center of the neighboring Lyndon B. Johnson State Park and Historic Site, where visitors can view exhibits and a film relating to Johnson's life. Tours last approximately an hour and a half.

The most significant structure in the LBJ Ranch District is the ranch house, or the Texas White House, as it came to be known during Johnson's presidency. Johnson purchased the home and its 250-acre ranch from his widowed aunt Frank Martin in 1951 and greatly enlarged it over the years. He and his wife, Lady Bird Johnson, retired to the ranch house in 1969 upon leaving Washington, D.C., Mrs. Johnson still calls the ranch home and resides here part of the time.

The Reconstructed Birthplace is a memorial to the home to which Johnson's father brought his bride in 1907. Lyndon B. Johnson, the first of the family's five children, was born on August 27, 1908. Two of his siblings were also born in the home before the family moved to Johnson City when Johnson was five years old. In 1964 Johnson hired architect J. Roy White to reconstruct his birthplace home. Johnson and White relied on old photos and family members to guide the project. The result follows the original architectural style of the house but is a much nicer rendition of the original. White added a modern kitchen and bathroom, running water, and electricity. The home is furnished with some family heirlooms and original childhood toys and mementoes. The birthplace was used as a guest house between 1964 and 1966 for overflow guests to the ranch.

Other stops on the LBJ Ranch tour are Junction School, the one-room schoolhouse in which Johnson began his formal education; the Grandparents' Farmhouse, the home to which Johnson's grandparents moved after leaving their homestead in the Johnson Settlement; the Johnson Family Cemetery, where President Johnson was laid to rest on January 25, 1973; and the Show Barn, the center for the present-day ranching operations.

Lyndon B. Johnson National Historical Park is operated by the National Park Service. It operates in close conjunction with the neighboring Lyndon B. Johnson State Park and Historic Site.

NEAREST AIRPORT: Austin, Texas

GENERAL DIRECTIONS: Johnson City District—on Ladybird Lane between F and G streets, just off Hwy 290 in Johnson City. LBJ Ranch District—tours begin at the Lyndon B. Johnson State Park and Historic Site off U.S. Highway 290 between Stonewall and Johnson City.

NEARBY ATTRACTIONS: Lyndon B. Johnson State Park and Historic Site, the National Museum of the Pacific War, and Pedernales Falls State Park.

LYNDON B. JOHNSON STATE PARK AND HISTORIC SITE

U.S. Highway 290 between Stonewall and Johnson City, Stonewall, Texas 78671

PHONE: 830-644-2252

www.tpwd.state.tx.us

HOURS: daily; closed Thanksgiving, Christmas Day, New Year's Day

ADMISSION: no fee

WHEELCHAIR ACCESSIBILITY: yes

This 732-acre park lies in the heart of Hill Country, where President Johnson spent much of his life. The focal point of the park is the visitor center, which showcases memorabilia from Johnson's boyhood and photos from the presidential years. The visitor center is also the departure point for the National Park Service tours of the nearby Lyndon B. Johnson National Historical Park.

Attached to the visitor center is the Behrens Cabin, a two-room, dogtrot cabin built in the 1870s. The cabin and its furnishings are authentic to that time period.

The Sauer-Beckmann Farm, located east of the visitor center, is a living history farm. Interpreters wear period costumes and perform chores as they would have in the early twentieth century. The interpreters also conduct visitor tours of the complex, which includes the smokehouse, the Victorian-style house, a log house, and a garden.

The Farm was acquired by the Texas Parks and Wildlife Department in 1966. Following nearly ten years of archaeological surveying and restoration work, the farm opened to the public in 1975.

In addition to the historical significance of the site, the park offers visitors nature activities ranging from fishing and wildlife viewing to picnics and wildflower displays.

The park is operated by the Texas Parks and Wildlife Department in conjunction with the National Park Service.

NEAREST AIRPORT: Austin, Texas

GENERAL DIRECTIONS: Off U.S. Highway 290 between Stonewall and Johnson City.

NEARBY ATTRACTIONS: Lyndon B. Johnson National Historical Park, the National Museum of the Pacific War, and Pedernales Falls State Park.

LYNDON BAINES JOHNSON LIBRARY AND MUSEUM

2313 Red River Street, Austin, Texas 78705
PHONE: 512-916-5137
www.lbjlib.utexas.edu/johnson
HOURS: daily; closed Christmas Day
ADMISSION: no fee
WHEELCHAIR ACCESSIBILITY: yes

One of ten libraries administered by the National Archives and Records Administration (NARA), the Lyndon Baines Johnson Library and Museum is dedicated to preserving the record of Lyndon Johnson's political career and presidency. The library, a research facility, includes 46 million pages of documents relating to Johnson's political career and those of his close associates. Additional photos, audiovisual materials, and oral history materials are available for research as well.

Lyndon Baines Johnson Library

The museum's collection is 50,000 items strong and ranges from head-of-state gifts to personally used items. The permanent exhibits include photos from the six decades of Johnson's life, Johnson's presidential limousine, a 1910 Model T Ford given by Henry Ford II, a White House exhibit, and a replica of Johnson's Oval Office. A special First Lady's Gallery honors Lady Bird Johnson. Changing American history exhibits are often borrowed from other institutions and private collections and presented at the museum. A recent example is "From Gutenberg to *Gone with the Wind:* Treasures from the Ransom Center."

The museum is part of the NARA system of presidential libraries; additional funding for special exhibits and events as well as for two past renovations is supplied by the Friends of the LBJ Library and its parent organization, the LBJ Foundation.

NEAREST AIRPORT: Austin, Texas
GENERAL DIRECTIONS: Located on the campus of the University of Texas at Austin; one block west of I-35, between Martin Luther King Jr. and 26th streets.
NEARBY ATTRACTIONS: Texas State Capitol, Bob Bullock Texas State History Museum, and Texas Memorial Museum.

RICHARD M. NIXON

1913–1994
37th President • 1969–1974

Despite his accomplishments in office—particularly in foreign affairs—Richard Milhous Nixon will always be remembered for his role in the Watergate scandal and his subsequent resignation from the office of president. He remains the only president who resigned his office.

Born in 1913 in Yorba Linda, California, Nixon grew up in poverty, rising each morning to work in his family's grocery store before school. He attended Whittier College before heading east for Duke Law School, where he graduated with honors and was elected president of his class. After law school, Nixon returned to California and joined a Whittier law firm. World War II interrupted his law career, and after four years in the navy, he once again returned to California, this time with political ambitions.

In 1947 Nixon won a seat in the House of Representatives, where he gained recognition for his work on the House Un-American Activities Committee. His success helped him win a seat in the Senate in 1950; two years later, he was the Republican party's choice as running mate for Dwight Eisenhower. Nixon served eight years as vice president before making a failed bid for the White House in 1960.

Narrowly defeated by John Kennedy, Nixon returned once more to California. After failing in his 1962 bid for governor, he retired from public life for six years. In 1968, with the country torn apart by the conflict in Vietnam, Nixon finally won the presidency with a promise to bring back law and order to a country in turmoil.

The Nixon administration had two great international successes. In 1972 Nixon became the first president ever to visit China when he journeyed there to meet with Chairman Mao Tse-tung. The two leaders agreed to increase trade and cultural contacts between their countries. Nixon began the Strategic Arms Limitations Talks with the Soviet Union, signing the first SALT Treaty along with Soviet leader Leonid Brezhnev. Nixon also oversaw final American withdrawal from Vietnam in 1973.

Nixon won reelection in 1972 but within months was embroiled in one of the worst political scandals in American history. In June of 1972, members of the Committee to Reelect the President were arrested for a break-in at Democratic National Headquarters in the Washington office building known as Watergate. Over the next two years, news reporters discovered that Nixon himself played a role in the plot and in the cover-up that followed. Maintaining his innocence, Nixon resigned on August 9, 1974, to avoid impeachment. In September 1974, Nixon was pardoned of all criminal wrongdoing by Gerald Ford, whom Nixon had nominated as vice president following Spiro Agnew's resignation in 1973. Nixon and his wife, Pat, retired to San Clemente, California.

In the years after leaving office, Richard Nixon regained some measure of respect from many Americans in government and used his knowledge of international relations to serve as an unofficial American ambassador, traveling to nearly twenty foreign countries and meeting with many heads of state. He died on April 22, 1994.

EACH MOMENT IN HISTORY IS A FLEETING TIME, PRECIOUS AND UNIQUE. But some stand out as moments of beginning, in which courses are set that shape decades or centuries. This can be such a moment. . . .

What kind of nation will we be, what kind of world will we live in, whether we shape the future in the image of our hopes, is ours to determine by our actions and our choices.

–from Richard M. Nixon's first Inaugural Address, January 20, 1969

THE RICHARD NIXON LIBRARY & BIRTHPLACE

18001 Yorba Linda Boulevard, Yorba Linda, California 92886

PHONE: 714-993-3393

www.nixonlibrary.org

HOURS: daily; closed Thanksgiving and Christmas Day

ADMISSION: fee; senior and student discount

WHEELCHAIR ACCESSIBILITY: no (pending as of 2002)

Situated on nine acres in Southern California, the Richard Nixon Library & Birthplace offers visitors a glimpse into the events, the people, and the world that shaped and were shaped by the thirty-seventh president. The site includes the faithfully restored 1912 farmhouse in which Nixon was born, the First Lady's Gardens, the museum's twenty-two galleries, and the presidential limousine used by Presidents Johnson, Nixon, Ford, and Carter.

The museum's galleries trace Nixon's path from his Yorba Linda childhood to his early Congressional and Senate races, his vice presidency and presidency, and his later role as a diplomat. Interactive video and touchscreen technology are present throughout the many exhibits. Highlights of the galleries include life-sized statues of ten world leaders accompanied by mini-biographies on each, dresses and gowns worn by Nixon's wife and daughters, and a re-creation of the Lincoln sitting

Richard Nixon Library entrance

room, Nixon's favorite room in the White House. A timeline narration of key Watergate events is available, including the opportunity to listen to the "smoking gun" audiotape. Outside is the Memorial, the final resting place of President and Mrs. Nixon that is surrounded by an English country-style garden.

The Library's year-round programming features national policy conferences, town meetings, and speakers from politics, the media, and national affairs. Additionally, the site hosts community events such as family concerts, Christmas celebrations, and special exhibits.

The Nixon Center is an independent arm of the Richard Nixon Library & Birthplace Foundation, which is based in Washington, D.C. The Center is a bipartisan foreign policy insti-tute committed to the study of

Structure of Peace Gallery in the Richard Nixon Library

policy changes in the United States. The Center and Library sponsor three awards given to honor distinguished public service. Previous honorees include Gerald Ford, George H. W. Bush, and Alan Greenspan.

The Richard Nixon Library is the only presidential museum to be built and operated without taxpayer funds. It is operated by the Richard Nixon Library & Birthplace Foundation.

NEAREST AIRPORT: Orange County, California

GENERAL DIRECTIONS: From downtown Los Angeles, take I-5 south to Highway 91. Take Highway 91 east to Highway 57 north; exit at Yorba Linda Boulevard. Turn right on Yorba Linda Boulevard and proceed to museum.

NEARBY ATTRACTIONS: Old Town Yorba Linda, George Key Ranch, Historic Bradford House, Old Towne Orange, and Bryant Ranch Museum.

GERALD R. FORD

1913–
38th President • 1974–1977

Gerald Rudolph Ford had been a member of the House of Representatives for nearly twenty-five years and was planning to retire after one more term when an unprecedented series of events elevated him to the office of vice president and then that of president within a ten-month period. Ford, the House minority leader, was appointed vice president following the resignation of Spiro Agnew in October 1973. The following August, he acceded to the presidency to replace Richard Nixon, who had resigned during the Watergate scandal. He is the only person to have become president without having been elected to a position in the executive branch.

Gerald Ford was born Leslie Lynch King Jr. in Omaha, Nebraska, in 1913. His name was legally changed in 1916 when his mother remarried. Ford always considered his stepfather, Gerald R. Ford Sr., to be his true father. Ford spent his childhood in Grand Rapids, Michigan, where he was a hard-working, popular, and athletic youth. From 1949 to 1973, Ford, an honest and unpretentious man, represented the state of Michigan in Washington. A navy veteran and University of Michigan college football star who chose Yale

Law School over a career in professional football, Ford was a committed public servant who had never had presidential ambitions. Married since 1948 to his wife Betty, Ford was father to four children. He was chosen by Nixon to replace Agnew because of his moderate Republican reputation in the House and his clean-cut, honest image with the American people.

In the White House, Ford immediately pardoned Richard Nixon for all connections to the Watergate break-in and the subsequent cover-up. This action was received by many with suspicion as to Ford's political motives. During his three-year term he struggled against inflation, a recession, and a chronic energy shortage as well as the lingering distrust of the American people. Ford won the Republican nomination in 1976 over Ronald Reagan, but he lost the election to Jimmy Carter. He retired to California and a life of writing, speaking, and recreation with his wife, Betty.

To THE PEOPLES AND GOVERNMENTS OF ALL FRIENDLY NATIONS, and I hope that encompasses the whole world, I pledge an uninterrupted and sincere search for peace. America will remain strong and united, but its strength will remain dedicated to the safety and sanity of the entire family of man, as well as to our own precious freedom. I believe that truth is the glue that holds the government together, not only our government but civilization itself. That bond, though strained, is unbroken at home and abroad. In all my public and private acts as your President, I expect to follow my instincts of openness and candor with full confidence that honesty is always the best policy in the end.

My fellow Americans, our long national nightmare is over.

Our Constitution works; our great Republic is a government of laws and not of men. Here the people rule. But there is a higher power, by whatever name we honor Him, who ordains not only righteousness but love, not only justice, but mercy. . . .

With all the strength and all the good sense I have gained from life, with all the confidence my family, my friends, and my dedicated staff impart me, and with the good will of countless Americans I have encountered in recent visits to forty states, I now solemnly reaffirm my promise I made to you . . . to uphold the Constitution, to do what is right as God gives me to see the right, and to do the very best I can for America.

God helping me, I will not let you down.

–Gerald Ford, speaking in 1974

GERALD R. FORD LIBRARY

1000 Beal Avenue, Ann Arbor, Michigan 48109

PHONE: 734-741-2218

www.ford.utexas.edu

HOURS: Monday to Friday; closed federal holidays

ADMISSION: no fee

WHEELCHAIR ACCESSIBILITY: yes

The Gerald R. Ford Library collects and preserves documents, audiotapes, photographs, videotapes, and films relating to the administration of Gerald Ford. The approximately 21 million pages of documents include materials from the president and his staff as well as those of his wife, Betty, and senior government officials. Many of the materials relate to the policy issues of the Cold War era.

In addition to maintaining its collection, the library coordinates the award of research grants by the Gerald R. Ford Foundation and partners with the Foundation to present programs on public affairs and history.

The Ford Library opened in 1981. The building was financed with private money and was built by the University of Michigan. The library is managed by the National Archives and Records Administration (NARA) as part of its system of presidential libraries. The Ford Library is unique within the NARA system in that it is geographically separate from its associated museum.

NEAREST AIRPORT: Detroit, Michigan

GENERAL DIRECTIONS: Located on the University of Michigan North Campus, just off Fuller Road on Beal Avenue.

NEARBY ATTRACTIONS: Mattkei Botanical Gardens, Nichols Arboretum, and University of Michigan.

GERALD R. FORD MUSEUM

303 Pearl Street NW, Grand Rapids, Michigan 49504

PHONE: 616-451-9263

www.ford.utexas.edu

HOURS: daily; closed Thanksgiving, Christmas Day, New Year's Day

ADMISSION: fee; senior and child discounts

WHEELCHAIR ACCESSIBILITY: yes

The Gerald R. Ford Museum is an interactive delight. Its ten permanent exhibits utilize holographic technology, multimedia re-creations, and synchronized lighting and audio—all in addition to the traditional audio, video, and artifact displays.

In "The 1970s, an Overview" gallery, visitors will be immersed in the pop culture of that decade, from tie-dye and MIA bracelets to bell bottoms and eight-track tapes. The "Constitution in Crisis" gallery showcases the history of the Watergate scandal, including the actual burglary tools used in June 1972. The "New Mood at the White House" exhibit features a holographic device that allows visitors to feel like they are in one of ten White House rooms. Head-of-state visits, the family quarters, and state dinners are part of this display. The "1976 Campaign" gallery presents the 1976 Republican Convention and allows visitors the opportunity to stand behind a podium and read one of Ford's speeches from a teleprompter. Other galleries cover Ford's earlier career and life, his transition to the White House, and life in the Oval Office.

In addition to the permanent galleries, the museum hosts temporary exhibits that draw on the holdings of the Smithsonian Institution, other presidential libraries, and NARA. In 2002, the featured temporary exhibit was "Mount Vernon in Miniature," a replica of George Washington's home that is 1/12 scale. The museum periodically hosts special events and programs and opens for public events such as naturalization ceremonies for new citizens and fireworks on the Fourth of July.

The Gerald R. Ford Museum will be constructing an 8,000-square-foot addition to be completed in spring 2004; the museum will remain open throughout the construction period.

The Ford Museum is part of the National Archives and Records Administration. It is the only museum in the system that is geographically distant from its associated library. Despite the distance, the library and museum operate as one institution with one director.

NEAREST AIRPORT: Grand Rapids, Michigan
GENERAL DIRECTIONS: U.S. 131 to Pearl Street; east on Pearl to museum entrance.
NEARBY ATTRACTIONS: Van Andel Museum Center, Frederick Meijer Gardens, and Grand Rapids Art Museum.

Gerald R. Ford Museum

JIMMY CARTER

1924–
39th President • 1977–1981

James Earl Carter Jr., a Georgia peanut farmer who even as president signed his name "Jimmy," took office in 1977 under the dark clouds of rising inflation, unemployment, and an ongoing energy shortage. Despite successes in his administration, he left under the burden of the Iranian hostage crisis.

Jimmy Carter was born in 1924 in Plains, Georgia, where he grew up on a farm and attended public schools in the area. Carter learned his early lessons from his father, James Earl Sr., a farmer and state legislator, and his mother, Lillian, a nurse and outspoken civil rights advocate. Inspired by an uncle who was a navy radio operator, Carter accepted an appointment to the U.S. Naval Academy in 1943. After graduation and seven years in the service, he returned to Plains.

Carter's career in public service began in 1963 after he won a seat in the Georgia State Senate. His success there led to a run for governor in 1970. As governor, Carter gained prominence as a leader of the "New South" as he fought to improve education and put an end to segregation and discrimination. In 1976 Carter won the Democratic nomination and defeated incumbent Gerald Ford to win the presidency.

From the beginning of his term, Carter sought to reduce the "pomp and circumstance" of the presidency—he walked to the White House after his inauguration rather than ride in a limousine and he halted the playing of "Hail to the Chief" during public appearances. He was an outspoken proponent of international human rights, condemning Soviet aggression in Afghanistan and joining with sixty-three nations in a boycott of the 1980 Olympic Games in Moscow. Carter was also instrumental in the Camp David Accords of 1978 between Israel and Egypt, which led to the end of a thirty-one-year-old war between the two nations. The darkest hour of the Carter years, however—and the one for which he may always be remembered—was the taking of more than sixty American hostages at the United States embassy in Tehran, Iran, on November 4, 1979. Fifty-two American hostages remained in captivity four hundred and forty-four days. Carter's attempts at gaining their freedom were unsuccessful. The hostages were not released from Iran until January 20, 1981, the very day that Carter left office.

Jimmy Carter lost his bid for reelection in 1980 and retired to Georgia. Although he left office an unpopular president, Carter has since become one of the nation's most visible and beloved former leaders. His Carter Presidential Center in Atlanta works to promote human rights; and he and Rosalynn, with whom he has three sons and one daughter, are active members of the group Habitat for Humanity International, which builds houses for low-income families.

Our nation can be strong abroad only if it is strong at home, and we know that the best way to enhance freedom in other lands is to demonstrate here that our democratic system is worthy of emulation. . . .

The passion for freedom is on the rise . . . we will maintain strength so sufficient that it need not be proven in combat—a quiet strength based not merely on the size of the arsenal but on the nobility of the ideas . . . we will fight our wars against poverty, ignorance, and injustice, for those are the enemies against which our forces can be honorably marshaled.

We are a proudly idealistic nation, but let no one confuse our idealism with weakness. . . . When my time as your president has ended . . . I would hope that the nations of the world might say that we had built a lasting peace, based not on weapons of war but on international policies which reflect our own most precious values.

–from Jimmy Carter's Inaugural Address, January 20, 1977

JIMMY CARTER NATIONAL HISTORIC SITE ——

300 North Bond Street, Plains, Georgia 31780

PHONE: 229-824-4104

www.nps.gov/jica

HOURS: daily; closed Thanksgiving, Christmas Day, New Year's Day

ADMISSION: no fee

WHEELCHAIR ACCESSIBILITY: yes

The Jimmy Carter National Historic Site comprises four individual sites: Plains High School, the Carter Boyhood Home, Plains Train Depot, and the current Carter residence (not open to the public). Additional sites of interest are located throughout the small town of Plains.

Both Jimmy and Rosalynn Carter attended grammar school and high school in Plains High School, which graduated its last class in 1979. The school reopened in 1996 as the visitor center for the site. The center features exhibits on Carter's life and administration and is a good starting point for visitors.

The Plains Train Depot served as Carter's campaign headquarters during his run for the presidency in 1976; it has been restored and holds exhibits pertaining to the 1976 campaign.

The Carter Boyhood Home is located on a seventeen-acre parcel of the land that was part of the original Carter family farm southwest of Plains. Carter was just four years old when the family moved to the farm in 1928, and it wasn't until 1938 that electricity came to the farm. The Carters grew cotton, peanuts, and corn, and young Jimmy worked in the fields alongside African-American employees. It

Carter Boyhood Home

was this experience which led to Carter's opposition to racial segregation in later years. Carter resigned from the navy to take over the farming business after the death of his father in 1953. In 1962, Rosalynn Carter took on a greater role in the family business, thus enabling her husband to pursue a bid for the Georgia State Senate. The boyhood home is original, but some of the outbuildings are reconstructions. Furnishings are authentic to the 1930s time period.

The Carters live in the 1960s ranch home on Woodland Drive, which is closed to the public. It is the only home the Carters have ever owned.

All tours are self-guided; brochures, wayside exhibits, and audio stations are available to help visitors understand what they are seeing. Interpreters are on hand at the High School and Boyhood Home to aid visitors as well. Alternatively, visitors can rent an audio driving tour of the area. The biggest special event of the year is the Plains Peanut Festival in September.

The site is part of the National Park Service.

NEAREST AIRPORT: Albany and Columbus, Georgia
GENERAL DIRECTIONS: Located 9 miles from Americus on Highway 280. Turn north on Highway 45; visitor center is one block north in the Plains High School building.
NEARBY ATTRACTIONS: Andersonville National Historic Site; Habitat for Humanity International Headquarters.

JIMMY CARTER LIBRARY AND MUSEUM

441 Freedom Parkway, Atlanta, Georgia 30307
PHONE: 404-331-3942
www.jimmycarterlibrary.org
HOURS: museum, daily; research library, Monday to Friday
ADMISSION: fee, senior and child discount
WHEELCHAIR ACCESSIBILITY: yes

One of the ten libraries administered by the National Archives and Records Administration (NARA), the 70,000-square-foot Jimmy Carter Library and Museum, like all NARA libraries, is not a library in the usual sense, but rather it is a research facility that is home to millions of pages of documents relating to the Carter administration. The library also houses a museum. The library and museum are part of the Carter Presidential Center, which also includes the Carter Center, a non-governmental organization founded by President and Mrs. Carter in 1982. The Center houses the offices of President and Mrs. Carter and a staff of 150 who are working to improve peace and health in some sixty-five countries.

Contained in the archives of the library are about 27 million pages of Carter's White House materials and administration papers. These include documents and correspondence relating to the Carters, major figures in his administration, and political and personal friends. In addition to documents, the library houses thousands of photographs and hours of video and audiotape. Approximately one-third of the holdings are currently open to the public for research purposes; a large portion of the holdings are still undergoing the rigorous archiving process whereas others are unavailable due to security classification issues.

The museum houses artifacts relating to President Jimmy Carter and his administration. One such exhibit is an exact replica of Carter's Oval Office. Another is a display of White House gifts received by the Carters. The permanent museum exhibit features photographs and interpretative text relating to significant events in Carter's career.

Changing museum exhibits are theme-based and are drawn from the Smithsonian Institution, other presidential libraries, and museums around the world. Past exhibits have included "From Jimmy Who? to Mr. President," a celebration of Carter's campaign, and "Freedom's Journey," a collection of artifacts from events leading up to the signing of the Declaration of Independence. "American Originals: Treasures from the National Archives" is on display from September 2002 to January 2003. This exhibit includes some rarely seen holdings from the National Archives. Prominent in the exhibit are the signed Emancipation Proclamation, the Louisiana Purchase Treaty, and the official German Surrender document from World War II.

NEAREST AIRPORT: Atlanta, Georgia

GENERAL DIRECTIONS: About two miles east of downtown Atlanta. From north or south, take I-75/85 to exit 248C, Freedom Parkway. Follow signs to the Carter Center. From east or west, take I-20 to Moreland Avenue North exit. Follow Moreland Avenue north to Freedom Parkway and follow signs.

NEARBY ATTRACTIONS: Martin Luther King Jr. National Historic Site, World of Coca-Cola Museum, and CNN Studio Tour.

Carter Presidential Center

RONALD REAGAN

1911 –
40th President • 1981 – 1989

Known as the "Great Communicator" for the skill with which he used radio and television to speak to the American people, Ronald Reagan defeated Jimmy Carter with one of the largest electoral landslides in American history. In his two terms in the White House, Reagan maintained his hold on the affections of the American people. His leadership brought a renewed sense of patriotism to Americans at home and a renewed respect for America throughout the world.

Ronald Wilson Reagan was born in 1911 in Tampico, Illinois. After attending local public schools, Reagan went on to Eureka College, where he discovered his love of acting. Upon graduation, Reagan worked briefly as a radio announcer before beginning a thirty-year career as a Hollywood movie actor. He had two children, one of whom was adopted, with his first wife, Jane Wyman, and two more with his second wife, Nancy Davis.

Throughout his acting career Reagan maintained an interest in politics and was often urged by friends to run for office. Prior to political office, he served six terms as president of the Screen Actors Guild. It was during this time that Reagan's political views began to move from the liberal views of his youth to the conservative stand of his presidency. He joined the Republican Party in 1962. A successful speech delivered by Reagan for Barry Goldwater in 1964 convinced Reagan and his supporters that he could win the governor's office in California. In 1967 Ronald Reagan became governor of California and, in two terms, gained national prominence as a strong, conservative leader.

In 1976 Reagan mounted an unsuccessful challenge to incumbent Republican Gerald Ford for the party's presidential nomination. Four years later, Reagan won the nomination and ran against President Jimmy Carter, who was crippled by the deepening recession and his inability to gain the release of the hostages in Iran. Winning 489 electoral votes to Carter's 49, Reagan took office in January of 1981.

At nearly seventy years of age, Ronald Reagan was the oldest man ever to begin a presidency. Yet his charm and speaking skills inspired the confidence of the American people. On Reagan's inauguration day, the American hostages were freed in Iran after more than a year in captivity, and his administration was not much more than a year old when the economy began to expand. Reagan oversaw the build-up of American defenses to match Soviet strength. When Mikhail Gorbachev came to power, Reagan moved to improve relations, meeting Gorbachev in the famous Iceland summit. At home and abroad, Reagan was seen as a skilled leader, equal to America's position as a world superpower.

After eight years in office, Reagan left the White House in 1989. He and his wife, Nancy, retired to California.

I HAVE OFTEN WONDERED ABOUT THE SHYNESS OF SOME OF US in the West about standing for these ideals that have done so much to ease the plight of man and the hardships of our imperfect world. This reluctance to use those vast resources at our command reminds me of the elderly lady whose home was bombed in the blitz. As the rescuers moved about, they found a bottle of brandy she'd stored behind the staircase, which was all that was left standing. And since she was barely conscious, one of the workers pulled the cork to give her a taste of it. She came around immediately and said, "Here now—there now, put it back. That's for emergencies."

Well, the emergency is upon us. Let us be shy no longer. Let us go to our strength. Let us offer hope. Let us tell the world that a new age is not only possible but probable.

–from a speech by Ronald Reagan to British Parliament, June 8, 1982

RONALD REAGAN PRESIDENTIAL LIBRARY & MUSEUM

40 Presidential Drive, Simi Valley, California 93065

PHONE: 800-410-8354

www.reagan.utexas.edu; www.reaganfoundation.org

HOURS: daily; closed Thanksgiving, Christmas Day, New Year's Day

ADMISSION: fee; senior and child discount

WHEELCHAIR ACCESSIBILITY: yes

Situated in Simi Valley, about forty-five minutes from Los Angeles, the Ronald Reagan Presidential Library & Museum comprises the library archives (with its fifty-five million pages of government documents and personal papers), the museum (with its 100,000 artifacts related to Ronald Reagan), the Center for Public Affairs, and the Presidential Learning Center.

Along with the millions of pages of documents in the archives are more than 1.5 million photographs, 20,000 videotapes, 25,000 audiotapes, and 670,000 feet of film. Reagan's handwritten notes to heads of state, his cabinet meeting notes, and correspondence from world leaders are part of the collection as well.

Museum exhibits include temporary exhibits that change every few months and permanent exhibits such as an exact replica of the Oval Office, furnished just as it was during Reagan's terms in office. In addition to personal items, the museum's collection also features "head-of-state" gifts that were presented to President and Mrs. Reagan. Tours are led by docents each hour.

The Center for Public Affairs hosts conferences and programs welcoming

Ronald Reagan Presidential Library entrance

some of the world's great leaders—Margaret Thatcher, Mikhail Gorbachev, Colin Powell, and Billy Graham, among others. The Presidential Learning Center strives to teach children about leadership, character, and the dignity of the presidency through holiday celebrations, historical re-enactments, and roundtable discussions.

Special events are held monthly and range from Nancy Reagan book signings to the annual Kite Festival. A calendar of events can be found on www.reaganfoundation.org.

Two expansions are planned for the site in the next few years. The first expansion project involves the Presidential Learning Center and is a 25,000-square-foot expansion of the current building to accommodate a new multi-purpose room, classroom, lunchroom, and exhibit space. The second project is a new building to be called Air Force One Pavilion. The new space will house *Air Force One 27000* (the plane on which Reagan flew), Reagan's presidential limousine, and presidential travel-related artifacts.

Oval Office exhibit

The Ronald Reagan Presidential Library & Museum is operated by the National Archives and Records Administration with additional support from the Ronald Reagan Presidential Foundation.

NEAREST AIRPORT: Burbank, California; Los Angeles, California
GENERAL DIRECTIONS: From 118 west, exit Madera South; right on Madera, then three miles to Presidential Drive and turn right. From 23 north, exit Olson to right; left on Presidential Drive.
NEARBY ATTRACTIONS: Thousand Oaks Civic Art Plaza, Gardens of the World, and Santa Barbara Zoo.

RONALD REAGAN BIRTHPLACE

111 South Main, Tampico, Illinois 61283
PHONE: 815-438-2130
www.tampico-areahistoricalsociety.cityslide.com
HOURS: April through December 1, daily; February through March, Saturday to Sunday
ADMISSION: no fee; donation
WHEELCHAIR ACCESSIBILITY: limited, gift shop and museum only

This second-floor, six-bedroom apartment was the birthplace of President Ronald Reagan and his home for a short time thereafter. It is one of three homes in Tampico in which the family lived, and the only one which is open to the public.

The home is sometimes called the "honorary campaign headquarters," as Ronald Reagan stopped here during the 1976 campaign.

The rooms of the apartment — three bedrooms, living room, dining room, and kitchen—are furnished with pieces authentic to the 1911 time period, although they are not original to the Reagan family. The downstairs was a bakery at the time of Reagan's birth and, later, a bank; it now serves as museum and gift shop. The museum features artifacts from the first ten years of Reagan's life, including numerous photos and Reagan's fourth-grade school report. Tours of the upstairs are guided, although self-guided tours are permitted as needed. Each year the nearby historical museum hosts a birthday celebration with cake and showings of videos and documentaries while tours are given at the birthplace.

Ronald Reagan Birthplace

The Ronald Reagan Birthplace is privately owned by Mrs. Paul Nicely. It is operated by volunteers from the Tampico Historical Society.

NEAREST AIRPORT: Moline, Illinois

GENERAL DIRECTIONS: About twenty miles north of I-80 and 14 miles south of I-88. Take State Route 40 to State Route 172 or 92.

NEARBY ATTRACTIONS: Dutch windmill in Fulton, Illinois, Hennepin-Feeder Canal, Ronald Reagan Boyhood Home, and John Deere Historical Site.

RONALD REAGAN BOYHOOD HOME

816 South Hennepin Avenue, Dixon, Illinois 61021

PHONE: 815-288-3404

HOURS: April through November, daily; February through March, weekends only; closed Easter and Thanksgiving; closed December and January

ADMISSION: no fee

WHEELCHAIR ACCESSIBILITY: limited to visitor center

The Reagan family moved to this home, one of five in which they lived in Dixon, when Ronald Reagan was nine years old. It is the only home mentioned in Reagan's autobiography, *Where's the Rest of Me?* Reagan shared a second-floor bedroom with his brother, Neil; a second bedroom was used by his parents. The third and final bedroom was used by Reagan's mother as a sewing room. Mrs. Reagan took in sewing to supplement the family's income.

In addition to the bedrooms, the house features a kitchen, sitting room, parlor, and dining room. Although none of the furniture is original to the Reagan family, it is authentic to the time period in which the Reagans lived in the house.

Visitors to the site can begin at the visitor center and gift shop, where volunteers give a little background on the Reagan family and show a short video. Tours of the home are guided.

The Reagans never owned this house, and later it was turned from a one-family rental into a two-family rental. In the summer of 1980, after Reagan's nomination at the Republican National Convention, a mail carrier noticed the house was for sale. He put $250 down at the real estate office; and donations were collected to finance the house, which opened to the public in the fall of 1980. The house was restored and the barn was reconstructed to its 1920 appearance for Reagan's

Ronald Reagan Boyhood Home

birthday visit in 1984. The site has been open to the public since that time.

In 1982, Ronald Reagan's Boyhood Home was added to the National Register of Historic Places. It is owned and operated by the nonprofit Ronald Reagan Home Preservation Foundation, which has over seventy volunteer interpreters and tour guides.

The nearby South Central School, which Reagan attended, is currently undergoing development to become the Dixon Historic Center. The Center, which has no scheduled opening as of yet, will feature displays about President Reagan's life in Dixon.

NEAREST AIRPORT: Chicago, Illinois
GENERAL DIRECTIONS: On South Hennepin Avenue, between 8th and 9th streets.
NEARBY ATTRACTIONS: John Deere Historical Site and Ronald Reagan Birthplace.

RONALD REAGAN MUSEUM AT EUREKA COLLEGE

300 E. College Avenue, Eureka, Illinois 61530
PHONE: 309-467-6407
www.eureka.edu
HOURS: mid-August through May, daily; June through mid-August, Monday to Saturday
ADMISSION: no fee, donation
WHEELCHAIR ACCESSIBILITY: yes

Bronze bust in the Ronald Reagan Peace Garden

Ronald Reagan earned a Bachelor of Arts degree in sociology and economics during his four years at Eureka College. While a student at Eureka he participated in drama, sports, publications, and student government—all interests that played a role in his later career choices. Reagan returned to the campus for thirteen official visits, including two as president.

The Ronald Reagan Museum is located in the Donald Cerf Center on the campus. It houses approximately two thousand items from Reagan's student days, his Hollywood career, and his days as governor and president. The gallery is organized chronologically; all of the collection pieces are original and most were donated by President Reagan or his office. Items range from childhood photographs and school mementoes to movie items to inauguration items.

Tours of the museum are self-guided although a directory of the galleries is available. At present, no special events or children's activities are being offered at the museum.

Outside the museum is the Ronald Reagan Peace Garden. The garden was dedicated in May 2000 to celebrate the leadership of the president. A bronze bust of Reagan is featured; its pedestal bears quotes from Reagan's START (Strategic Arms Reduction Treaty) speech, which was delivered at the college's 1982 commencement. A four-foot by five-foot piece of the Berlin Wall, a gift from the Federal Republic of Germany, is a highlight of the garden.

The Ronald Reagan Museum and Peace Garden are maintained by Eureka College.

NEAREST AIRPORT: Peoria, Illinois (regional airport)
GENERAL DIRECTIONS: I-474 east to I-74 east to Goodfield exit. Take Route 117 north to Eureka; turn right on College Avenue.
NEARBY ATTRACTIONS: Lakeview Museum, Wildlife Prairie Park, Ewing Manor, and Illinois Shakespeare Festival.

GEORGE H. W. BUSH

1924–
41st President • 1989–1993

After serving loyally as vice president under Ronald Reagan for eight years, George Herbert Walker Bush won the presidency in his own right in 1988. In one of the roughest campaigns in American history, Bush shook off his reputation for weakness and came from behind to defeat Democrat Michael Dukakis. In the four years that followed, Bush proved himself a strong leader in a tumultuous international arena.

George Bush was born to wealth and privilege in 1924 in Milton, Massachusetts, and soon thereafter the family moved to Greenwich, Connecticut. Bush attended prestigious Phillips Academy in Andover, Massachusetts, and upon graduation enlisted in the navy. Bush flew fifty-eight navy combat missions in World War II, one of which ended in near disaster when his plane was shot down off the Bonin Islands. He was rescued after more than three hours in the Pacific Ocean and was awarded the Distinguished Flying Cross. After his return from the war, Bush enrolled in Yale University. He also married Barbara Pierce, by whom he had six children.

George Bush's rise to the presidency began in the oil fields of Texas where he went with hopes of making his own fortune in business. For nearly twenty years, Bush worked in the oil business, eventually building a million-dollar company and a reputation as a savvy businessman. In 1967 he made a successful run for a seat in the House of Representatives and served two terms in the House. A failed bid for the Senate in 1970 was followed by a series of political appointments. President Nixon appointed Bush ambassador to the United Nations; later he served as Chairman of the Republican National Committee and as chief liaison to China. In 1976 Bush was appointed director of the Central Intelligence Agency, a position he held for two years. In 1980, after his own unsuccessful run for the Republican presidential nomination, Bush accepted nomination as vice president and ran with Ronald Reagan against Jimmy Carter.

After eight years under the shadow of Ronald Reagan, in 1988, Bush emerged as a tough-minded, confident president. He shone in the world arena at a time when international issues dominated the news. In Panama, Bush launched a strong U.S. attack in retaliation to hostilities perpetrated by General Noriega. Bush led the United States in a war to liberate Kuwait from the invading forces of Saddam Hussein's Iraq. The Gulf War was President Bush's greatest hour. Patriotic pride swept the nation, and the president's popularity soared. Bush also reaped the benefits of the end of the Cold War.

As the Gulf War receded from popular memory, however, and Americans began to focus on the economic troubles at home, George Bush faced a difficult battle for reelection. In November of 1992, he lost that battle to Arkansas Democrat Bill Clinton.

WE STAND TODAY AT A UNIQUE AND EXTRAORDINARY MOMENT. The crisis in the Persian Gulf, as grave as it is, also offers a rare opportunity to move toward an historic period of cooperation. Out of these troubled times . . . a new world order can emerge: a new era, freer from the threat of terror, stronger in the pursuit of justice, and more secure in the quest for peace. An era in which the nations of the world, east and west, north and south, can prosper and live in harmony. . . . Today that new world is struggling to be born. A world quite different from the one we've known. A world where the rule of law supplants the rule of the jungle. A world in which nations recognize the shared responsibility for freedom and justice. A world where the strong respect the rights of the weak.

—George Bush, speaking on the crisis in the Persian Gulf in 1990

GEORGE BUSH PRESIDENTIAL LIBRARY AND MUSEUM

1000 George Bush Drive West, College Station, Texas 77845

PHONE: 979-260-9552

http://bushlibrary.tamu.edu

HOURS: daily; closed Thanksgiving, Christmas Day, New Year's Day

ADMISSION: fee; senior, student, child discounts

WHEELCHAIR ACCESSIBILITY: yes

Opened to the public in 1997, the George Bush Presidential Library and Museum is the newest of the presidential libraries administered by the National Archives and Records Administration (NARA). The library and museum are located on a ninety-acre site on the edge of the Texas A&M University campus.

The Bush Library serves as a research institution and is integrated into the academic environment of Texas A&M. The library's collection includes 38 million pages of personal and official papers, a million photographs, thousands of hours of videotape, and 80,000 museum objects. These extensive documents trace George Bush's career from congressman to chairman of the Republican National Committee to director of the CIA to vice president and president.

The Bush Museum provides 21,000 square feet of permanent and temporary exhibit space. Among the larger artifacts in the museum are a World War II Avenger Torpedo Bomber, a slab of the Berlin Wall, and replicas of President Bush's Camp David and Air Force One offices. Included in the permanent exhibit

Entrance to the George Bush Presidential Library

hall are displays detailing Bush's days at Yale; his marriage to Barbara; the family's move to Texas; and Bush's many roles in government, including his performance during the reunification of Germany, the collapse of the Soviet Union, and the Gulf War. The changing exhibits draw from various sources and celebrate American history, the presidency, and the Bush administration. Recent temporary exhibits have included "The White House in Miniature;" a stop on the cross-country tour of an original copy of the Declaration of Independence; and "Fathers and Sons: Two Families, Four Presidents," a look at the Bush and Adams families.

The museum offers tours for students that are customized to each grade level in keeping with the Texas Essential Knowledge and Skills program. These educational tours vary in length from an hour to an hour and a half. All tours, both guided and self-guided, are by reservation, and the museum recommends booking reservations two months in advance, especially for large groups.

Special events take place throughout the year; the Fourth of July celebration is one of the biggest events sponsored by the museum. Summer, family, and classroom programming are also available to students throughout the year.

The George Bush Presidential Library and Museum was built with funds from private donations. It is administered by the National

A slab of the Berlin Wall in the museum

Archives and Records Administration and supported, in part, by the nonprofit George Bush Presidential Library Foundation.

NEAREST AIRPORT: Houston, Texas; San Antonio, Texas; Dallas/Ft. Worth, Texas
GENERAL DIRECTIONS: From Highway 6 south, exit west on University Drive. Turn left onto Texas Avenue, then right onto George Bush Drive.
NEARBY ATTRACTIONS: Brazos Valley Museum of Natural History, Carnegie Center of Brazos Valley History, Texas A&M University Horticultural Gardens and Field Laboratory, and Bryan's Historical District.

WILLIAM JEFFERSON CLINTON

1946–
42nd President • 1993–2001

Forty-second president William Jefferson Blythe Clinton won the office in November 1991, running on a campaign that promised to bring renewed focus to the faltering U. S. economy. He served two terms, during which the economy grew at an unprecedented rate. Unfortunately, his accomplishments were marred by the personal scandals that followed him throughout this time.

Clinton was born in Hope, Arkansas, in 1946. He grew up in Hope and nearby Hot Springs with his mother, Virginia Blythe Clinton, and his stepfather, Roger Clinton. Inspired by the sixties leaders John F. Kennedy and Martin Luther King Jr., Clinton took an early interest in public service. At Georgetown University, Clinton was active in student government and served as an intern for Senator Fulbright of Arkansas. After graduation, Clinton went to Oxford University in England as a Rhodes Scholar and traveled through much of Europe and the Soviet Union. Upon his return, he enrolled in Yale Law School, where he earned his law degree in 1973.

Bill Clinton began his career as a law professor, but within four years he won his first elected office, that of the attorney general of Arkansas. Two years later, in 1978, at the age of thirty-two, Clinton won Arkansas's highest office and became the youngest governor in the United States. Governor Clinton was voted out of office after only one term, but he returned to the office of governor in 1983, where he would remain for nine years.

Bill Clinton's 1992 presidential campaign focused on the nation's domestic troubles. While his opponent, President George H. W. Bush, had achieved great popularity for his leadership in the Gulf War, the recession was worsening across the country and Americans blamed Bush. Bill Clinton won a comfortable victory in a three-way race that included, along with Bush, Independent Texas businessman Ross Perot. Clinton assumed the presidency with an ambitious pledge to revive the economy, reduce the national debt, and create a national health care system that guarantees insurance to all Americans.

During his two terms as president, Clinton presided over a period of economic growth during which the national budget went from enormous deficit to the largest surplus in history. Unemployment reached a forty-year low as well. He failed to institute the national health care system that he had promised but did have success with several related measures, including the Family and Medical Leave Act and the Children's Health Insurance Program.

The Clinton presidency will likely be remembered best, however, for the personal scandals that threatened his tenure. In 1999, Clinton became the second American president in history to face impeachment. Tried by the Senate on charges of perjury and obstruction of justice stemming from what Clinton himself called an "inappropriate relationship" with a White House intern, the president was acquitted in February 1999.

To renew America we must be bold. We must do what no generation has had to do before. We must invest more in our own people—in their jobs and in their future—and at the same time cut our massive debt. And we must do so in a world in which we must compete for every opportunity. It will not be easy. It will require sacrifice. But it can be done and done fairly. Not choosing sacrifice for its own sake but for our own sake, we must provide for our nation the way a family provides for its children.

–from Bill Clinton's Inaugural Address, January 20, 1993

WILLIAM J. CLINTON PRESIDENTIAL CENTER —

Little Rock, Arkansas

www.clintonpresidentialcenter.com

HOURS: The center is currently scheduled to open in late 2004; check website for construction progress.

WHEELCHAIR ACCESSIBILITY: yes

The William J. Clinton Presidential Center, when complete, will comprise a library, archives, and a museum commemorating the life and administration of the country's forty-second president. The groundbreaking for the site took place on December 5, 2001; completion is scheduled for late 2004. A virtual presidential library is being developed at the same time at www.clintonpresidentialcenter.com; it will host the world's most comprehensive digital archive of presidential materials to date.

The Presidential Center will be situated along the bank of the Arkansas River in downtown Little Rock. It will replace an area of old and vacant industrial warehouses and will provide access to a revitalized riverfront.

The Clinton collection includes approximately 80 million documents, nearly two million photographs, and over 75,000 artifacts. As of the date of this publication, the Central Arkansas Library System is sponsoring occasional preview exhibits of a number of the many items in the collection. The free preview exhibits take place in the Cox Building at 120 Commerce Street in the Historic River Market District. Visitors can call 501-918-3090 to find out when exhibits are taking place.

The Clinton Presidential Center is being funded through donations to the nonprofit Clinton Presidential Foundation.

NEAREST AIRPORT: Little Rock, Arkansas

GENERAL DIRECTIONS: In downtown Little Rock, along the south bank of the Arkansas River.

NEARBY ATTRACTIONS: Arkansas State Capitol, Old State House, Little Rock Central High School, Historic Arkansas Museum, and Daisy Bates Home.

THE CLINTON CENTER AND BIRTHPLACE

117 South Hervey Street, Hope, Arkansas 71801

PHONE: 870-777-4455

www.clintonbirthplace.com

HOURS: spring and summer, Tuesday to Sunday; fall and winter, Tuesday to Saturday

ADMISSION: fee; student and senior discounts

WHEELCHAIR ACCESSIBILITY: yes

The Clinton Center and Birthplace includes the first home in which Bill Clinton lived, a visitor center, a gift shop, and the Virginia Clinton Kelley Memorial

Garden. The 1917 wood-frame house was the home of Clinton's maternal grand-parents, with whom he lived while his mother studied nursing in New Orleans. Clinton lived here from the time of his birth in 1946 until his mother's return from New Orleans and marriage to Roger Clinton in 1950.

On display in the living room is a telephone identical to the one on which Clinton's mother received the call informing her of her husband's tragic death three months prior to Clinton's birth. Visitors can then move upstairs to tour the nursery and Clinton's mother's bedroom.

Visitors can trace the history of Clinton through photos and other artifacts in the visitor center. An "FOB" (Friends of Bill) Room is being planned as of the date of publication of this book, and it will feature campaign memorabilia, photographs, and temporary exhibits on loan from other sources. A chronology of Clinton's jour-ney from Hope, Arkansas, to the White House is featured on the wall of the Time Line Room. This room also displays an exact replica of the Oval Room rug designed by Kaki Hockersmith of Little Rock and used by Clinton while in the White House.

The Clinton Center and Birthplace is owned and operated by the Clinton Birthplace Foundation.

NEAREST AIRPORT: Texarkana or Little Rock, Arkansas
GENERAL DIRECTIONS: Exit 30 off I-30, located at the intersection of Hervey and 2nd streets.
NEARBY ATTRACTIONS: Old Washington State Park.

The First Home of President Bill Clinton

GEORGE W. BUSH

1946–
43rd President • 2001–

Georve W. Bush, the forty-third American president, entered the
White House in January 2001, part of only the second father and son
pair in American history to serve as presidents. His father, George
Herbert Walker Bush, held the same office from 1989 to 1993.

Born in Connecticut but raised mostly in Texas, George W. Bush
did not immediately enter politics. After earning an undergraduate
degree at Yale and an MBA at Harvard, Bush began a career in the
Texas oil business. He founded an oil and gas exploration company
and throughout the 1980s focused on building that company. In 1989,
after a failed bid for a seat in Congress, Bush became managing general partner of the Texas Rangers baseball team. In 1994, he won his
first elected office as governor of Texas. In 1998 he won a second term
but interrupted this term to seek the American presidency in 2000.

As governor of Texas, Bush characterized himself as a "compas-
sionate conservative" and cited beliefs in limited government, personal responsibility, strong families, and local governmental control
as his guiding principles. These same issues were the cornerstones of
Bush's presidential campaign against Vice President Al Gore Jr.

When voting polls closed on November 7, 2000, and the votes were tallied, Gore was the winner of the national popular vote by just over 400,000 ballots; but because of disputes in Florida, neither candidate had earned sufficient electoral votes to be declared victorious. The candidates and the nation awaited final word from Florida, where twenty-five electoral votes remained uncommitted.

It would be thirty-six days and a number of legal maneuvers before a winner emerged. On December 13, 2000, the United States Supreme Court reversed a Florida Supreme Court decision requiring a statewide manual recount of more than 170,000 undervotes—ballots for which the machine registered either no vote for president or a double vote. After this ruling, Vice President Gore conceded the Florida contest, thus giving George W. Bush the necessary electoral votes to become the first American president of the twenty-first century.

Initially, Bush's greatest challenge appeared to be repairing the party divisions created by the closely contested election. It was not long, however, before the tragic events of September 11, 2001, overshadowed any remaining animosity. Following terrorist attacks at the World Trade Center and the Pentagon on that fateful day—actions that claimed nearly 3,000 lives—the country and the Congress united behind the president against its common enemy.

George Bush and his wife, Laura Welch Bush, have twin daughters.

TODAY, OUR FELLOW CITIZENS, OUR WAY OF LIFE, OUR VERY FREEDOM came under attack in a series of deliberate and deadly terrorist acts. . . . Thousands of lives were suddenly ended by evil, despicable acts of terror. . . .

These acts of mass murder were intended to frighten our nation into chaos and retreat. But they have failed. Our country is strong. A great people has been moved to defend a great nation.

Terrorist attacks can shake the foundations of our biggest buildings, but they cannot touch the foundation of America. These acts shatter steel, but they cannot dent the steel of American resolve.

America was targeted for attack because we're the brightest beacon for freedom and opportunity in the world. And no one will keep that light from shining.

–George W. Bush, September 11, 2001

No sites are yet planned for George W. Bush.

WASHINGTON, D.C.

The city of Washington, D.C., is known throughout the world as the seat of the United States government, but it was not always so. George Washington and John Adams, the first two U.S. presidents, took their oaths of office in New York City and Philadelphia. Adams moved into the partially completed White House in Washington, D.C., in 1800. The U.S. Congress, which had met first in New York City and then in Philadelphia, met for the first time in the not-yet-completed U.S. Capitol in Washington, D.C., in November 1800. Thomas Jefferson, the third U.S. president, was the first to take the oath of office in Washington, D.C., in 1801.

The selection of Washington, D.C., as the new U.S. capital city was fraught with controversy. Both northern and southern states vied for the honor, and political compromises ensued. In return for locating the capital in the southern region, the northern states were relieved of significant debts they had incurred during the Revolution. In 1790, following the passage of the Residence Act which gave him the authority to do so, President George Washington chose as the site of the new U.S. capital the junction of the Potomac and Anacostia rivers. Congress named the city Washington in the Territory of Columbia. The term "District" replaced "Territory" when the capital city was incorporated in 1871.

President Washington enlisted the services of Pierre Charles L'Enfant in designing the new federal city. L'Enfant was a strong-willed personality who brooked no interference with his plans. He was later dismissed by Washington, but to this day the city follows L'Enfant's grand design.

Washington, D.C., faced a number of challenges over the course of its development: the burning of the Capitol and the White House during the British invasion of 1812; the doubling of the population during the Civil War years; a call for the beautification and revitalization of the city during the late 1800s; and the deterioration of the foundation, plumbing, and flooring in the White House in the 1940s. In each instance, millions of dollars and a commitment to maintaining the historical integrity of the city's design resulted in a city that is still largely true to L'Enfant's original vision.

Today, Washington, D.C., is home to a variety of impressive buildings that house the workings of the U.S. government: the White House, the Supreme Court, the Capitol, and countless office buildings that house thousands of federal workers. The U.S. Capitol remains the geographic and metaphoric center of the city with the National Mall, a gathering place for millions of tourists each year, extending out from the base of the Capitol as L'Enfant had envisioned. The mall is home to monuments and memorials, cultural institutions, and foreign ministry residences and offices; and its open grassy area serves as a gathering place for those who come to Washington, D.C., to be heard, whether in celebration or in protest.

I CONGRATULATE THE PEOPLE OF THE UNITED STATES on the assembling of Congress at the permanent seat of their Government, and I congratulate you, gentlemen, on the prospect of a residence not to be changed. Although there is cause to apprehend that accommodations are not now so complete as might be wished, yet there is great reason to believe that this inconvenience will cease with the present session. . . .

May this territory be the residence of virtue and happiness! In this city may that piety and virtue, that wisdom and magnanimity, that constancy and self-government, which adorned the great character whose name it bears be forever held in veneration! Here and throughout our country may simple manners, pure morals, and true religion flourish forever!

–from John Adams's annual message, November 22, 1800

THE WHITE HOUSE

1600 Pennsylvania Avenue NW, Washington, D.C. 20500

PHONE: 202-456-7041

WHITE HOUSE VISITOR CENTER

1450 Pennsylvania Avenue NW, Washington, D.C. 20230

PHONE: 202-208-1631

www.whitehouse.gov or www.nps.gov/whho

HOURS: As of the publication date of this book, the White House is open for school tours only; these can be arranged through the school's congressional representative. The White House Visitor Center is open daily; closed Thanksgiving, Christmas Day, and New Year's Day. Call for updated information on tour availability.

ADMISSION: no fee

WHEELCHAIR ACCESSIBILITY: yes

The White House has been home to all but one U.S. president—George Washington. Although Washington was involved in the planning and construction of the White House, John and Abigail Adams were its first occupants in 1800. Since that time, each president has had the opportunity to personalize the residence through choice of furnishings, decorations, and the occasional structural addition. The White House was rebuilt following its burning by the British in 1814. The interior of the building was again rebuilt during Harry Truman's presidency because of structural deterioration over the years.

The White House

Among the rooms open to the public during tours are the Library, the Vermeil (or Gold) Room, the East Room, the Green Room, the Blue Room, the Red Room, the State Dining Room, and the Cross Hall. The rooms contain portraits of various presidents and their wives, authentic period furniture, and an extensive array of decorative items.

The West Wing, which houses the Oval Office and the executive staff offices, along with the private residence portions are not open to the public.

The White House Visitor Center offers the opportunity to learn more about the White House and the presidency through exhibits, artifacts, videos, ranger-led talks, lectures, and living history programs. The six permanent exhibits relating to the White House include "First Families," "Symbols & Images," "White House Architecture," "White House Interiors," "Working White House," and "Ceremonies and Celebrations."

NEAREST AIRPORT: Washington, D.C.; Baltimore, Maryland

GENERAL DIRECTIONS: On-street parking is not permitted near the White House. The closest Metro stations are Federal Triangle and Metro Center (White House Visitor Center); Farragut West, Farragut North, and McPherson Square (White House).

NEARBY ATTRACTIONS: Washington Monument, Jefferson Memorial, Lincoln Memorial, Vietnam Veterans Memorial, Smithsonian Institution, National Archives and Records Administration, Library of Congress, and many more sites in the Washington, D.C., area.

NATIONAL ARCHIVES AND RECORDS ADMINISTRATION

IN WASHINGTON, D.C. (ARCHIVES I)

700 Pennsylvania Avenue NW, Washington, D.C. 20408

PHONE: 866-325-7208

IN COLLEGE PARK, MARYLAND (ARCHIVES II)

8601 Adelphi Road, College Park, Maryland 20740

PHONE: 866-272-6272

www.archives.gov

HOURS: Monday to Saturday; closed federal holidays. The Rotunda in Washington, D.C., is closed for renovation until mid-2003; the research room remains open.

ADMISSION: no fee

WHEELCHAIR ACCESSIBILITY: yes

The National Archives and Records Administration (NARA) was established in 1934 to facilitate the preservation of federal government records. Prior to the establishment of NARA, the records were maintained by the various agencies that had

National Archives

accumulated them, resulting in the loss and destruction of innumerable records. In addition to the preservation of records, NARA is also charged with ensuring the public has easy access to the documents that chronicle the history of the United States.

The National Archives and Records Administration consists of the National Archives in Washington, D.C., and College Park, Maryland, ten presidential libraries, two presidential materials projects, nineteen regional records facilities, the office of the Federal Register, the Information Security Oversight Office, and the National Historical Publications and Records Commission. (Individual presidential libraries are profiled within the listings for each president.)

Visitors to the National Archives in Washington, D.C., can arrange to work in the research rooms, where they will have access to billions of pieces of paper, or in the Microfilm Reading Room, where they will have access to census records, ships' passenger lists, and other family history materials on microfilm. The Rotunda exhibit halls in Washington, D.C., are closed for renovation until mid-2003. The exhibit halls will reopen with a state-of-the-art interactive exhibit space, which will include the "Charters of Freedom": the Declaration of Independence, the Constitution, and the Bill of Rights. A traveling version of the celebrated documents will be making an eight-city tour beginning in fall 2001.

At the National Archives in College Park, Maryland, visitors can access millions of still photographs, maps, charts, and architectural and engineering plans; and hundreds of thousands of sound and video recordings. In addition, visitors can view the Nixon presidential materials. Nixon's materials are the third largest collection of any presidential library and include text, audiovisual materials, and the Watergate tapes. The project is not associated with the Nixon Library in California.

In addition to the Nixon Presidential Materials Project and the recent Clinton Presidential Materials Project, the administration of the presidential library system takes place from the NARA offices in College Park. The presidential library system includes libraries for Presidents Hoover, Franklin D. Roosevelt, Truman, Eisenhower, Kennedy, Johnson, Ford, Carter, Reagan, and George W. Bush. Prior to the establishment of the presidential library system, each president and/or his heirs dispersed of their papers as they chose at the end of their administrations. Some earlier presidential collections are in the Library of Congress; some are in private collections or historical societies; and others were lost altogether.

Each presidential library and each of the NARA offices offers a variety of programming for the public from seminars on genealogy to historical presentations to exhibits and conferences. Researchers can find information on preparing for their visit on the NARA website.

NEAREST AIRPORT: Washington, D.C.; Baltimore, Maryland
GENERAL DIRECTIONS: Washington, D.C.—no parking is available at the building but there are commercial lots nearby. Public transportation is a recommended alternative with the Archives/Navy Memorial station on the Yellow or Green line located across Pennsylvania Avenue from the Archives building.

College Park—from I-495 (the Capital Beltway), exit 28B to New Hampshire Avenue south. Turn left on Adelphi Road and watch for Archives II sign on left.

A shuttle bus runs between the Archives I and Archives II buildings Monday through Friday.
NEARBY ATTRACTIONS: Washington Monument, Jefferson Memorial, Lincoln Memorial, Vietnam Veterans Memorial, Smithsonian Institution, White House, Library of Congress, and many more sites in the Washington, D.C., area.

LIBRARY OF CONGRESS

101 Independence Avenue SE, Washington, D.C. 20559
PHONE: 202-707-5000
www.loc.gov
HOURS: Monday to Saturday; closed federal holidays
ADMISSION: no fee
WHEELCHAIR ACCESSIBILITY: yes

With three buildings and a collection of more than 124 million items, the Library of Congress is the United States', and perhaps the world's, greatest cultural institution. In addition to being the official library of the United States government, the

Library of Congress acts as the country's copyright agency and provides public access to a wealth of historical materials.

The library's history is nearly as old as that of the United States itself. In 1800, John Adams signed into law an act of Congress allowing for the establishment of a congressional library. The first books in the collection arrived in 1801 and were stored in the U.S. Capitol; but the collection was lost in the burning of the Capitol by the British in 1814. Thomas Jefferson, who had the country's most extensive library at the time, offered to sell his personal collection to the Library Committee of Congress. The offer was accepted, and Jefferson's collection formed the basis of the rebuilding of the Library of Congress. Disaster struck again in 1851 when a fire in the library destroyed nearly 35,000 of the collection's 55,000 volumes. Since that time the library has grown through acquisitions, donations, and the transfer of collections to the Library of Congress from other governmental collections.

Among the materials available for research by the public are the papers and diaries of twenty-three presidents from the time of Washington to Coolidge. For preservation purposes, materials are made available to researchers on microfilm. These include records from the Continental Congress, Thomas Jefferson's rough draft of the Declaration of Independence, George Washington's first inaugural address, and James Madison's notes on the Federal Convention. Some portions of the presidential papers are contained within the library's Manuscript Division as a result of 1903 legislation requiring the State Department to transfer historical documents to the library. Others are gifts of presidents and heirs: Theodore Roosevelt

Jefferson Building, Library of Congress

was the first president to donate his materials directly to the library in 1917. Abraham Lincoln's son donated his father's papers to the library in 1923, and Woodrow Wilson's wife Edith donated her late husband's personal library in 1946.

In addition to papers and records, the permanent exhibit "American Treasures of the Library of Congress" features on a rotating basis the most significant historical items drawn from all areas of the library's collection. The exhibition, located in the Treasures Gallery on the second floor of the Thomas Jefferson building, always includes presidential items in addition to a wide array of social and cultural objects. Recent display items have included James Polk's presidential diaries, the *New York Herald*'s April 15, 1865, article about Lincoln's assassination, audio recordings of the 1912 Roosevelt/Wilson campaign speeches, and the contents of Abraham Lincoln's pockets on the evening of his assassination.

Main Reading Room, Jefferson Building, Library of Congress

The architecture of the library is of as much significance as its contents. Docent-led tours are available to visitors Monday to Saturday, and these tours focus on the impressive neoclassical architecture, paintings, and murals of the Great Hall of the Thomas Jefferson building.

The Adams and Madison buildings round out the structures of the Library of Congress. In addition to housing administrative offices, the Office of the Librarian, the Copyright Office, the Congressional Research Service, and the Law Library, the James Madison building serves as the national memorial to the fourth president of the United States.

NEAREST AIRPORT: Washington, D.C.; Baltimore, Maryland
GENERAL DIRECTIONS: On First Avenue between Independence Avenue and East Capitol Street; Capitol South is the closest Metro station.
NEARBY ATTRACTIONS: Washington Monument, Jefferson Memorial, Lincoln Memorial, Vietnam Veterans Memorial, Smithsonian Institution, National Archives and Records Administration, White House, and many more sites in the Washington, D.C., area.

APPENDIX

Map Note

The green squares on the maps on the following pages mark the approximate location of the sites. Due to space limitations, some state maps show only that area of the state in which relevant sites are located.

ARKANSAS

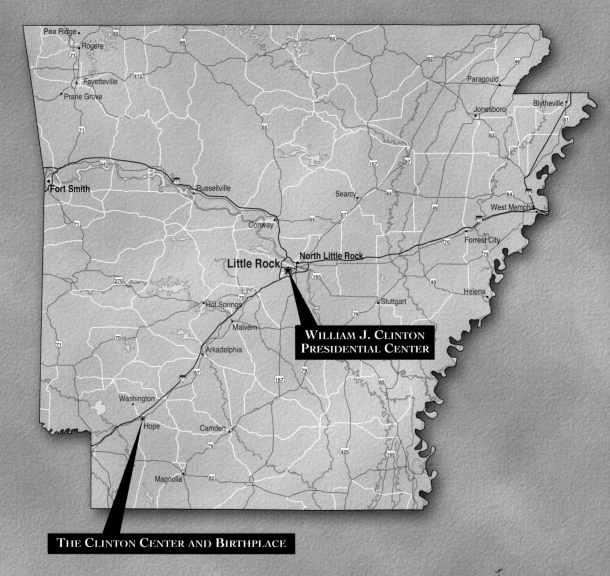

Pea Ridge
Rogers
62
71
65
62
62
49
Paragould
Fayetteville
412
Jonesboro
Blytheville
Prarie Grove
61
71
65
63
65
167
67
64
64
Fort Smith
Russellville
Searcy
West Memphis
64
67
49
71
Conway
64
70
Forrest City
Little Rock
North Little Rock
79
270
165
70
49
Hot Springs
Helena
Malvern
79
Stuttgart
71
Arkadelphia

WILLIAM J. CLINTON PRESIDENTIAL CENTER

67
30
167
79
65
Washington
Hope
Camden
79
425
165
Magnolia
82

THE CLINTON CENTER AND BIRTHPLACE

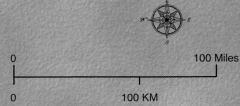

0   100 Miles

0   100 KM

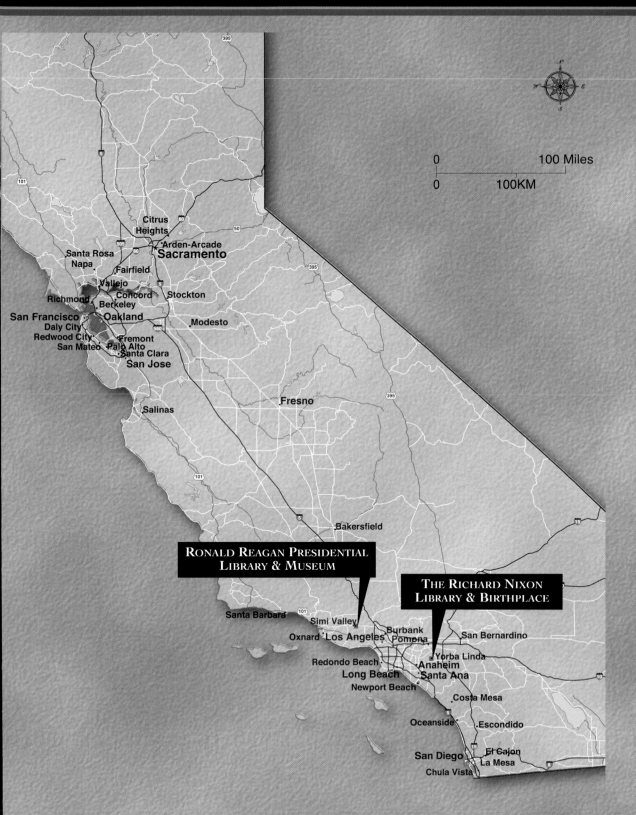

CALIFORNIA

FLORIDA

331
90
231
98
Tallahassee
319
98

10
19
221
90
98
27
129
90
41
19
27
27A
41
75

Olustee
Gainesville

1
17
301
Jacksonville
Fernandina Beach
1
St. Augustine

92
Daytona Beach
441
95

19
98
301
27
Orlando
17
Toll
192
1

19A
92
Clearwater
Tampa
98
St. Petersburg
275
301
17
41
75

441
95
98
1

27
West Palm Beach
441
95

41
75
Toll
Fort Lauderdale
Hialeah
Miami
Homestead
1

HARRY S TRUMAN LITTLE WHITE HOUSE MUSEUM

1
Key West

N
W   E
S

0 ——————————— 100 Miles

0 ——————————— 100 KM

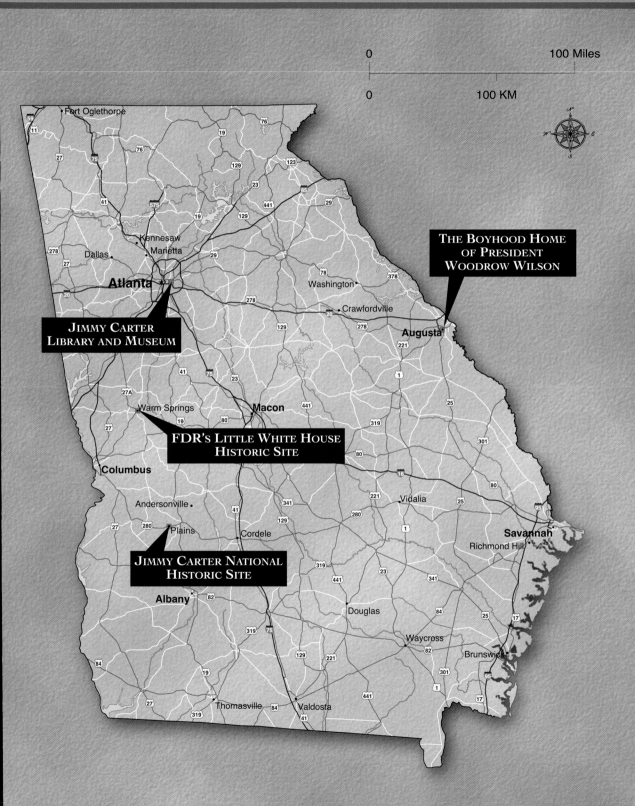

0   100 Miles

0   100 KM

Fort Oglethorpe

76

19

76

129

123

27

75

23

575

85

441

19

129

29

THE BOYHOOD HOME OF PRESIDENT WOODROW WILSON

Kennesaw

Marietta

278

Dallas

29

27

78

378

20

Washington

Atlanta

Crawfordville

278

JIMMY CARTER LIBRARY AND MUSEUM

129

278

Augusta

221

41

75

1

23

27A

25

Warm Springs

19

80

441

Macon

27

319

FDR's LITTLE WHITE HOUSE HISTORIC SITE

80

Columbus

16

80

221

Vidalia

25

Andersonville

341

280

95

27

280

129

1

Savannah

Plains

Cordele

Richmond Hill

JIMMY CARTER NATIONAL HISTORIC SITE

319

23

341

441

Albany

82

Douglas

84

25

17

75

319

Waycross

82

Brunswick

84

129

221

301

95

19

1

17

27

Thomasville

84

Valdosta

441

319

41

ILLINOIS

Galena

Waukegan

RONALD REAGAN
BOYHOOD HOME

U. S. GRANT HOME

Evanston

Elgin

52

Toll

Dixon

88

Aurora

Chicago

Tampico

30

Oak Lawn

34

RONALD REAGAN BIRTHPLACE

80

34

Joliet

6

52

80

74

150

34

55

45

51

Kankakee

57

52

34

150

Eureka

67

Peoria

RONALD REAGAN MUSEUM
AT EUREKA COLLEGE

Canton

24

136

LINCOLN'S NEW SALEM
STATE HISTORIC SITE

55

51

150 74

Lincoln

Danville

24

Champaign

Petersburg

150

Springfield

THE LINCOLN
COLLEGE MUSEUM

36

36

55

70

LINCOLN HOME NATIONAL
HISTORIC SITE

ABRAHAM LINCOLN
PRESIDENTIAL LIBRARY
AND MUSEUM

51

Effingham

70

45

40

57

50

East St. Louis

50

Mount Vernon

64

51

45

0   100 Miles

57

0   100 KM

45

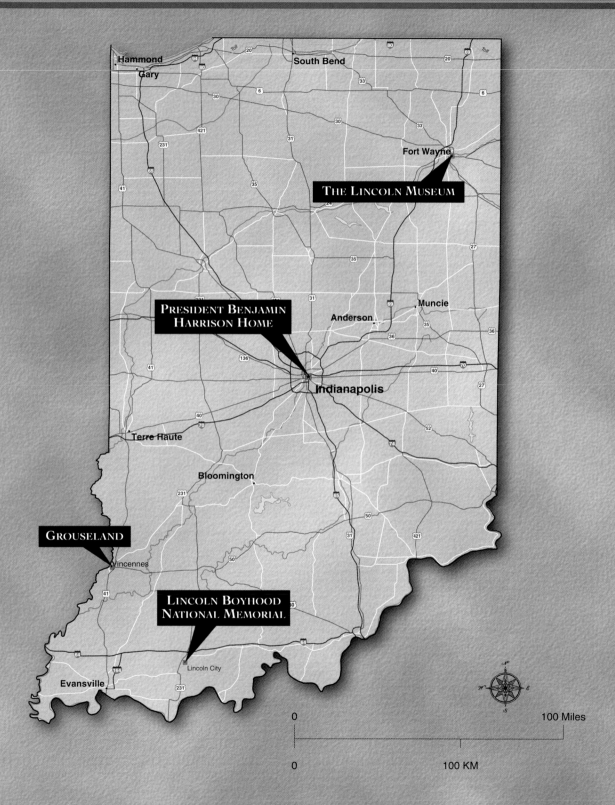

Hammond
Gary
South Bend
Fort Wayne

THE LINCOLN MUSEUM

PRESIDENT BENJAMIN HARRISON HOME

Muncie
Anderson
Indianapolis
Terre Haute
Bloomington

GROUSELAND
Vincennes

LINCOLN BOYHOOD NATIONAL MEMORIAL

Lincoln City
Evansville

0   100 Miles

0   100 KM

Sioux City

Waterloo

Dubuque

Cedar Rapids

Iowa City
West Branch

Davenport

★ Des Moines

Council Bluffs

**HERBERT HOOVER
NATIONAL HISTORIC SITE**

**HERBERT HOOVER
PRESIDENTIAL LIBRARY
& MUSEUM**

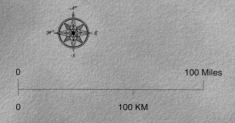

0	100 Miles
0	100 KM

EISENHOWER CENTER

Abilene

Topeka

Kansas City

Lawrence

Wichita

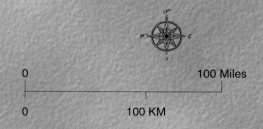

0		100 Miles

0		100 KM

KENTUCKY

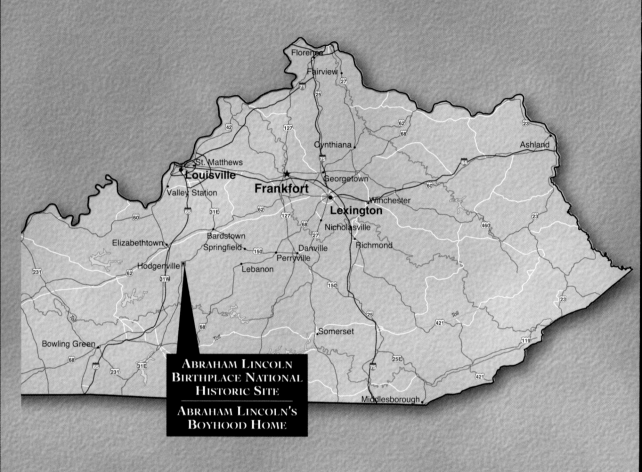

Florence
Fairview
1
25
27

42
127
62
68
23

Cynthiana
75
Ashland

St. Matthews
64
Louisville
Georgetown
60
Frankfort
Winchester
23
Valley Station
65
31E
62
127
Lexington
68
460

60
68
27
Nicholasville
Bardstown
Springfield
150
Danville
Richmond
Elizabethtown
Perryville
231
Hodgenville
62
31W
Lebanon
150

68
150

ABRAHAM LINCOLN
BIRTHPLACE NATIONAL
HISTORIC SITE

ABRAHAM LINCOLN'S
BOYHOOD HOME

Somerset
25
421
Toll

Bowling Green
119
68
65
231
31E
25E
75
421

Middlesborough

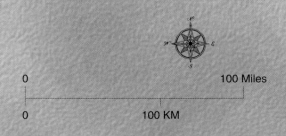

0   100 Miles

0   100 KM

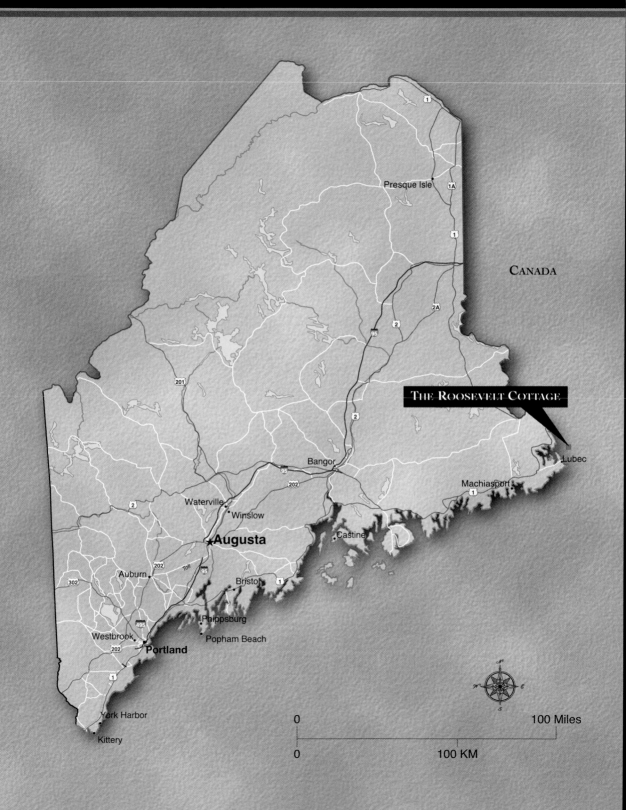

Presque Isle

1A

1

CANADA

2A

2

95

201

THE ROOSEVELT COTTAGE

2

Lubec

Bangor

95

202

Machiasport

1

Waterville

Winslow

2

Castine

★Augusta

Auburn

202

Toll

95

302

Bristol

1

Phippsburg

Westbrook

495

Popham Beach

202

Portland

York Harbor

Kittery

0   100 Miles

0   100 KM

MARYLAND

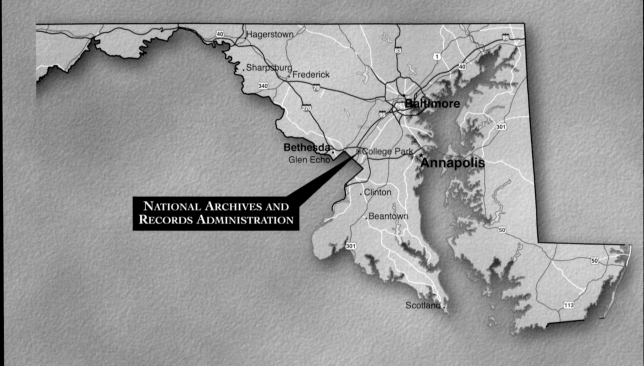

Hagerstown

Sharpsburg .Frederick

Baltimore

Bethesda
Glen Echo
College Park

Annapolis

.Clinton

.Beantown

Scotland.

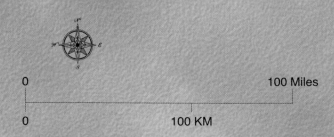

NATIONAL ARCHIVES AND
RECORDS ADMINISTRATION

0   100 Miles

0   100 KM

MASSACHUSETTS

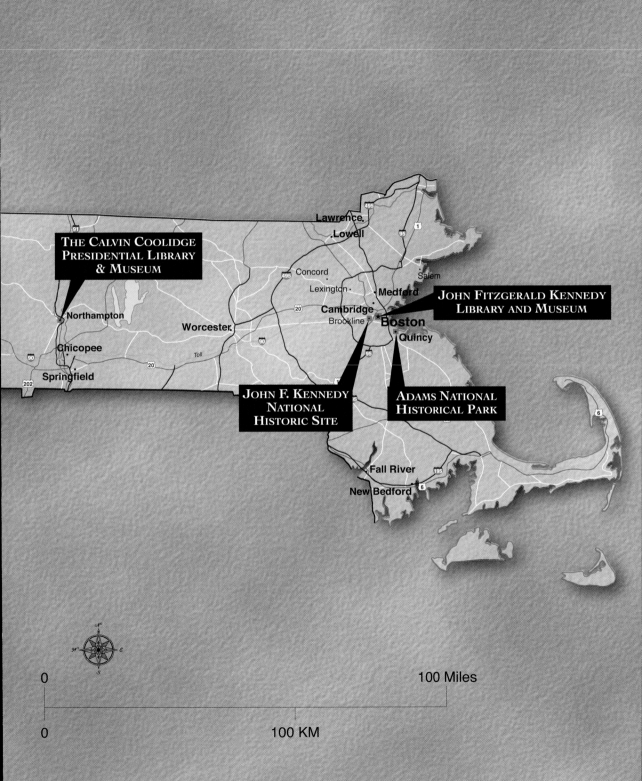

THE CALVIN COOLIDGE
PRESIDENTIAL LIBRARY
& MUSEUM

JOHN FITZGERALD KENNEDY
LIBRARY AND MUSEUM

JOHN F. KENNEDY
NATIONAL
HISTORIC SITE

ADAMS NATIONAL
HISTORICAL PARK

Lawrence.
.Lowell

Concord
.
Lexington .

Medford .

Salem .

Cambridge
Brookline

Boston

Quincy

Northampton

Worcester.

Chicopee

Toll

Springfield

Fall River

New Bedford

0   100 Miles

0   100 KM

MICHIGAN

41

41

141

2

2

41

75

23

2

131

75

31

31

10

23

31

131

27

GERALD R. FORD MUSEUM

95

Saginaw

10

75

Grand Rapids

Flint

GERALD R. FORD LIBRARY

69

Lansing

96

127

Troy

196

Kalamazoo

69

127

Ann Arbor

Detroit
Taylor

94

27

12

275

31

131

12

127

223

23

75

94

12

69

0   100 Miles

0   100 KM

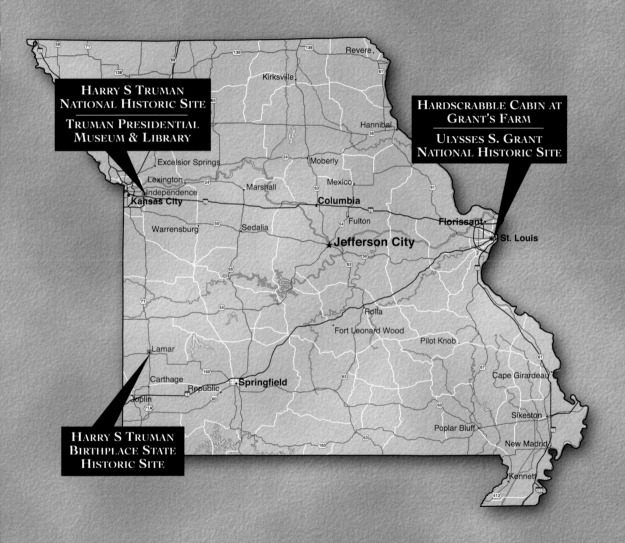

HARRY S TRUMAN
NATIONAL HISTORIC SITE

TRUMAN PRESIDENTIAL
MUSEUM & LIBRARY

HARDSCRABBLE CABIN AT
GRANT'S FARM

ULYSSES S. GRANT
NATIONAL HISTORIC SITE

HARRY S TRUMAN
BIRTHPLACE STATE
HISTORIC SITE

Revere
Kirksville
Hannibal
Excelsior Springs
Lexington
Independence
Kansas City
Marshall
Moberly
Mexico
Columbia
Fulton
Warrensburg
Sedalia
Jefferson City
Florissant
St. Louis
Rolla
Fort Leonard Wood
Pilot Knob
Lamar
Carthage
Republic
Springfield
Cape Girardeau
Joplin
Sikeston
Poplar Bluff
New Madrid
Kennett

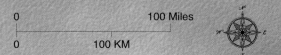

0   100 Miles

0   100 KM

NEW HAMPSHIRE

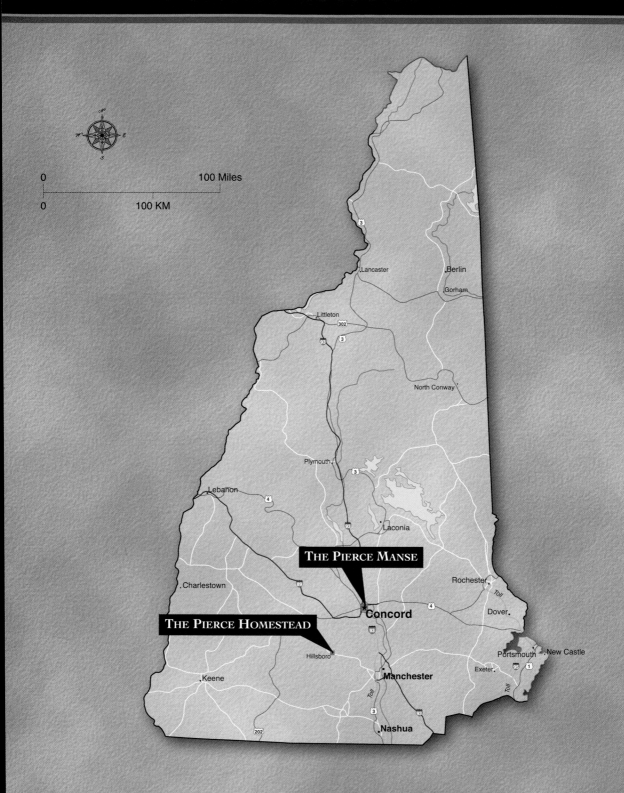

0
100 Miles
0
100 KM

Lancaster

Berlin

Gorham

Littleton
302
3

North Conway

Plymouth
3

Lebanon
4

Laconia

93

THE PIERCE MANSE

Rochester
Toll

Charlestown
89

Concord
4
Dover

THE PIERCE HOMESTEAD

93

Hillsboro

Portsmouth
New Castle

Keene

Manchester
Exeter
95
1

Toll

Toll

3
93

202

Nashua

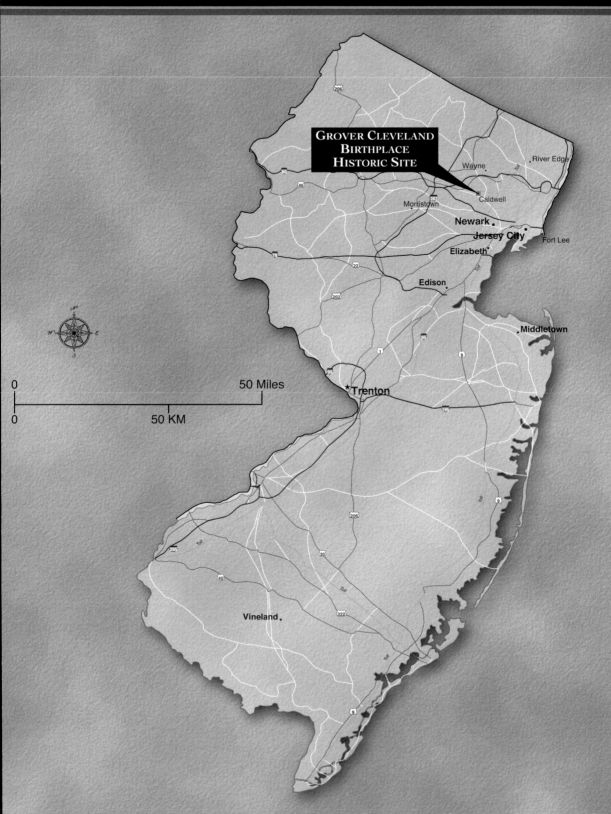

GROVER CLEVELAND
BIRTHPLACE
HISTORIC SITE

River Edge

Wayne

Caldwell

Morristown

Newark

Jersey City

Fort Lee

Elizabeth

Edison

Middletown

0   50 Miles

0   50 KM

Trenton

Vineland

NEW YORK

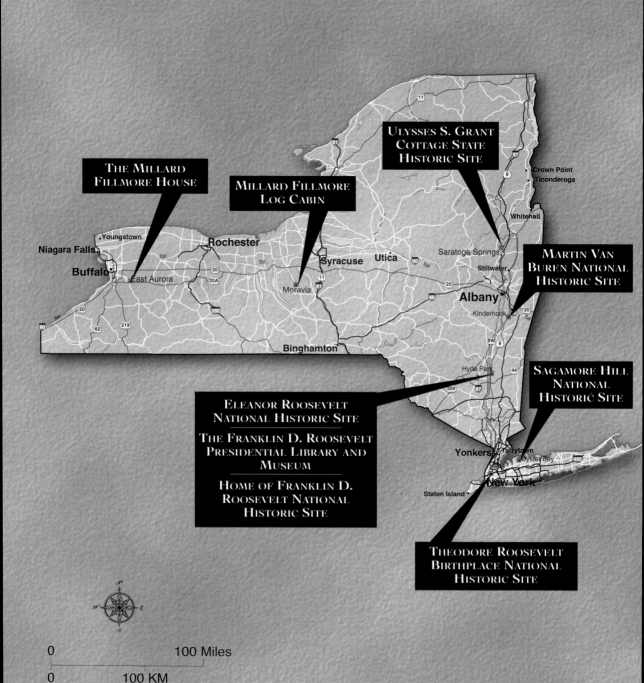

THE MILLARD
FILLMORE HOUSE

MILLARD FILLMORE
LOG CABIN

ULYSSES S. GRANT
COTTAGE STATE
HISTORIC SITE

MARTIN VAN
BUREN NATIONAL
HISTORIC SITE

SAGAMORE HILL
NATIONAL
HISTORIC SITE

ELEANOR ROOSEVELT
NATIONAL HISTORIC SITE

THE FRANKLIN D. ROOSEVELT
PRESIDENTIAL LIBRARY AND
MUSEUM

HOME OF FRANKLIN D.
ROOSEVELT NATIONAL
HISTORIC SITE

THEODORE ROOSEVELT
BIRTHPLACE NATIONAL
HISTORIC SITE

Niagara Falls
Youngstown
Rochester
Buffalo
East Aurora
Syracuse
Utica
Moravia
Saratoga Springs
Stillwater
Crown Point
Ticonderoga
Whitehall
Albany
Kinderhook
Binghamton
Hyde Park
Yonkers
Tarrytown
Oyster Bay
New York
Staten Island

0   100 Miles

0   100 KM

ANDREW JOHNSON BIRTHPLACE

JAMES K. POLK MEMORIAL STATE HISTORIC SITE

Winston-Salem
Greensboro
Hillsborough
Durham
Liberty
Raleigh
Sanford
Charlotte
Pineville
Wadesboro
Fayetteville

0   100 Miles

0   100 KM

OHIO

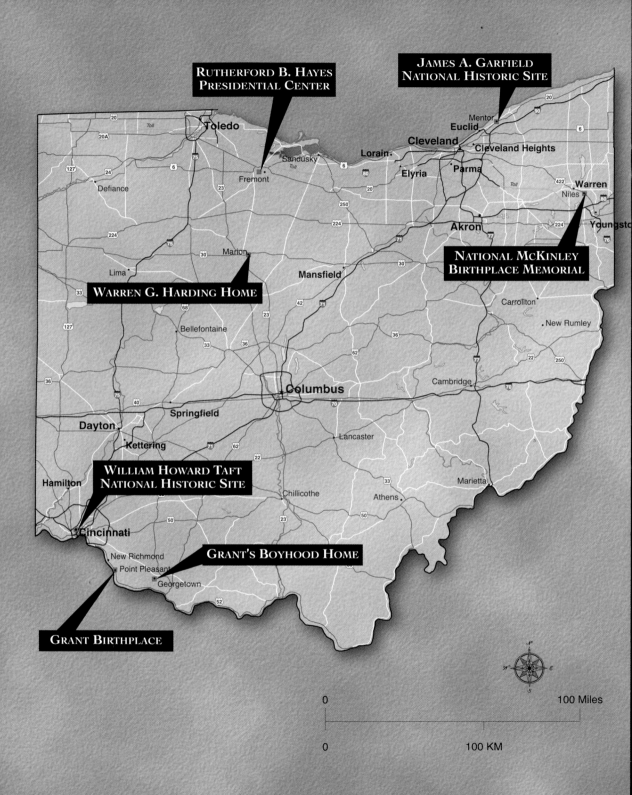

RUTHERFORD B. HAYES
PRESIDENTIAL CENTER

JAMES A. GARFIELD
NATIONAL HISTORIC SITE

Toledo

Mentor
Euclid
Cleveland
Cleveland Heights
Lorain
Sandusky
Parma
Fremont
Elyria
Defiance

Warren
Niles
Youngsto

Marion

Akron

Lima

NATIONAL McKINLEY
BIRTHPLACE MEMORIAL

WARREN G. HARDING HOME

Mansfield

Carrollton

New Rumley

Bellefontaine

Columbus

Cambridge

Springfield

Dayton

Lancaster

Kettering

WILLIAM HOWARD TAFT
NATIONAL HISTORIC SITE

Marietta

Hamilton

Chillicothe

Athens

Cincinnati

New Richmond
Point Pleasant
Georgetown

GRANT'S BOYHOOD HOME

GRANT BIRTHPLACE

0   100 Miles

0   100 KM

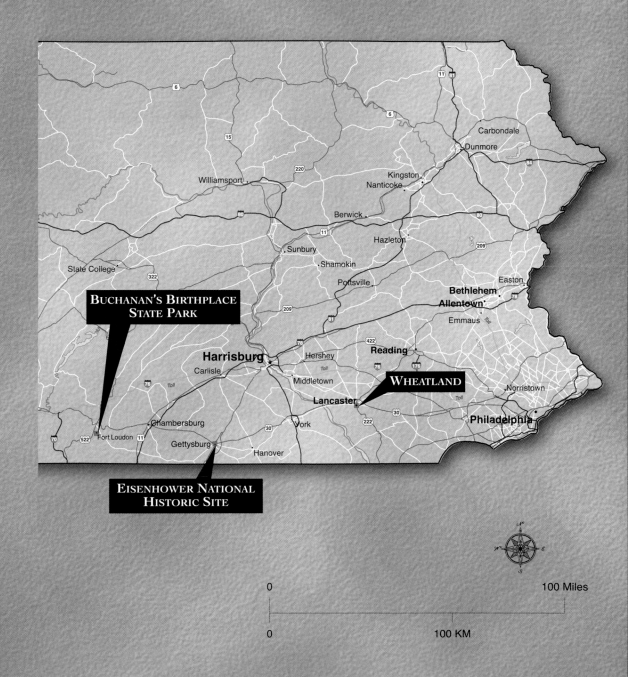

BUCHANAN'S BIRTHPLACE
STATE PARK

WHEATLAND

EISENHOWER NATIONAL
HISTORIC SITE

Carbondale
Dunmore
Kingston
Nanticoke
Williamsport
Berwick
Hazleton
Sunbury
State College
Shamokin
Easton
Pottsville
Bethlehem
Allentown
Emmaus
Reading
Harrisburg
Hershey
Carlisle
Norristown
Middletown
Fort Loudon
Chambersburg
Lancaster
Philadelphia
Gettysburg
York
Hanover

0   100 Miles

0   100 KM

SOUTH CAROLINA

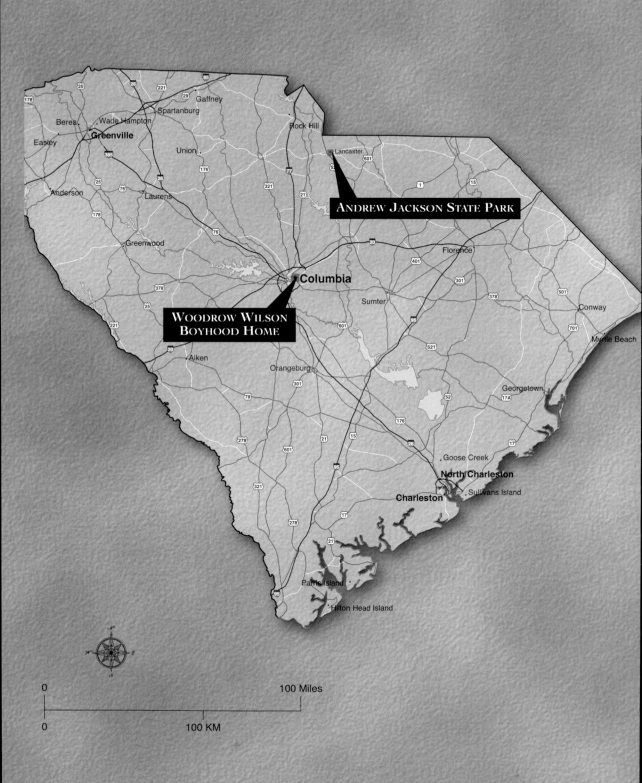

25
26
221
178
29 Gaffney
Spartanburg
Berea
Wade Hampton
Rock Hill
Easley
Greenville
Lancaster
601
Union
176
77
ANDREW JACKSON STATE PARK
385
1
15
25
25
321
21
76
Anderson
Laurens
176
76
Greenwood
85
Florence
Columbia
401
WOODROW WILSON
BOYHOOD HOME
Sumter
378
501
378
Conway
295
601
521
701
221
Myrtle Beach
20
Aiken
Orangeburg
521
Georgetown
301
52
17A
78
176
275
21
15
17
601
26
Goose Creek
95
North Charleston
321
Charleston
Sullivans Island
276
17
21
Parris Island
95
Hilton Head Island

0
100 Miles

0
100 KM

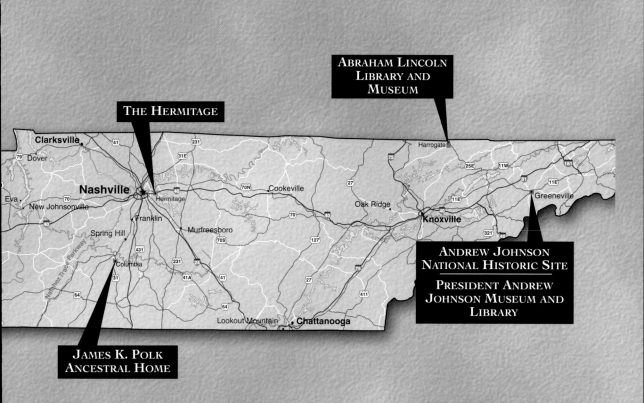

ABRAHAM LINCOLN LIBRARY AND MUSEUM

THE HERMITAGE

Clarksville
41
231
79 Dover
31E
Nashville
70N Cookeville
27
Eva
70
New Johnsonville
Hermitage
Franklin
70
Murfreesboro
Spring Hill
431
705
Columbia
231 24
31
41A 41
64
64
Lookout Mountain
Chattanooga
75
127
27
411
321
40
Harrogate
75
25E 11W
81
31 11E
11E
Oak Ridge
Knoxville
Greeneville

Natchez Trace Parkway

JAMES K. POLK ANCESTRAL HOME

ANDREW JOHNSON NATIONAL HISTORIC SITE

PRESIDENT ANDREW JOHNSON MUSEUM AND LIBRARY

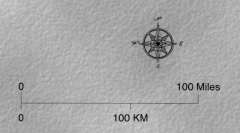

0   100 Miles

0   100 KM

TEXAS

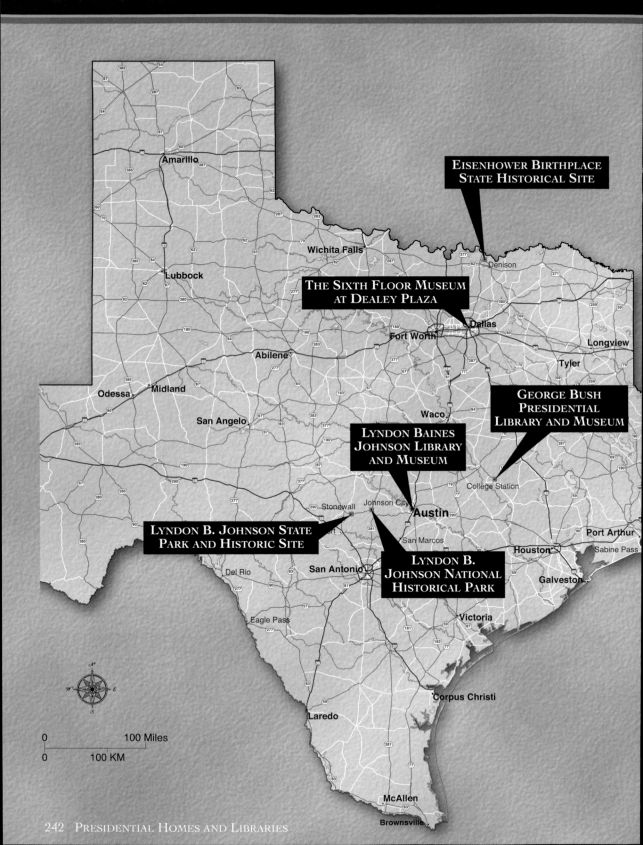

EISENHOWER BIRTHPLACE
STATE HISTORICAL SITE

THE SIXTH FLOOR MUSEUM
AT DEALEY PLAZA

GEORGE BUSH
PRESIDENTIAL
LIBRARY AND MUSEUM

LYNDON BAINES
JOHNSON LIBRARY
AND MUSEUM

LYNDON B. JOHNSON STATE
PARK AND HISTORIC SITE

LYNDON B.
JOHNSON NATIONAL
HISTORICAL PARK

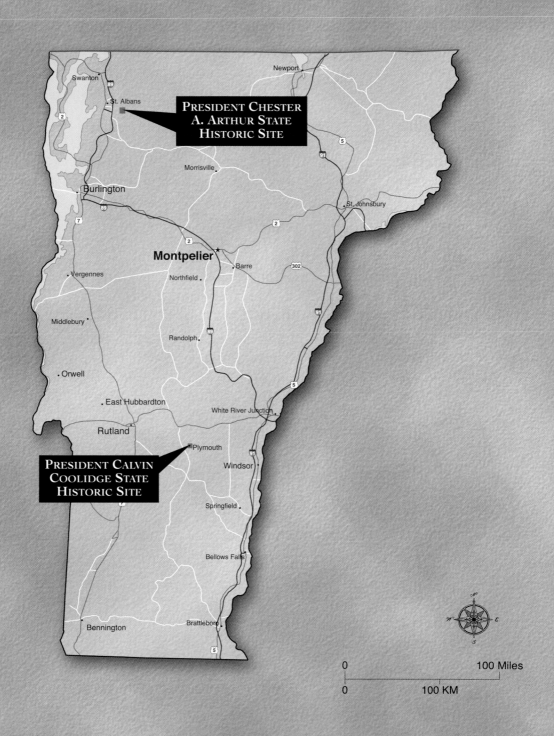

Swanton
89
St. Albans
2
Newport

PRESIDENT CHESTER A. ARTHUR STATE HISTORIC SITE

91
5

Morrisville

Burlington
89
7

St. Johnsbury

2

Montpelier
2
Barre
302

Vergennes
Northfield

91

Middlebury
89

Randolph

Orwell

East Hubbardton
5

White River Junction

Rutland
Plymouth
91
Windsor

PRESIDENT CALVIN COOLIDGE STATE HISTORIC SITE

Springfield

Bellows Falls

Bennington
Brattleboro
5

0   100 Miles
0   100 KM

VIRGINIA

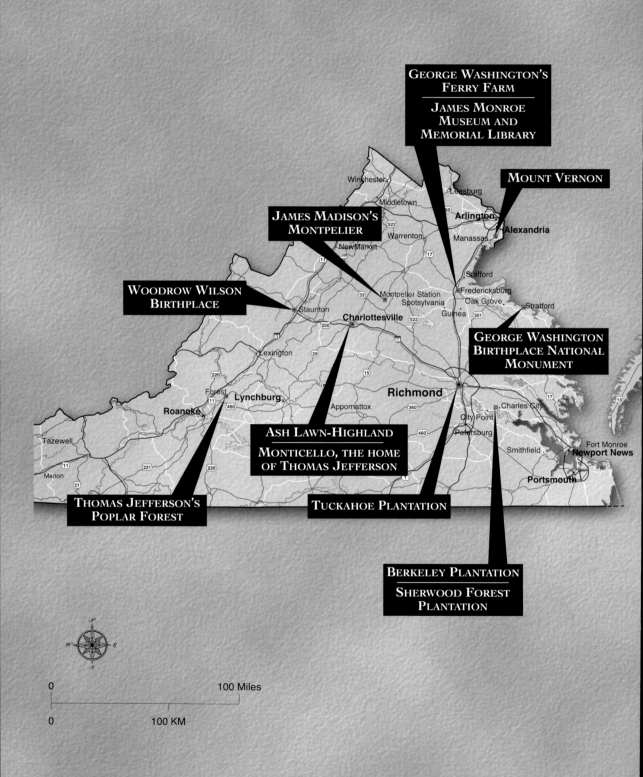

GEORGE WASHINGTON'S FERRY FARM

JAMES MONROE MUSEUM AND MEMORIAL LIBRARY

MOUNT VERNON

JAMES MADISON'S MONTPELIER

WOODROW WILSON BIRTHPLACE

GEORGE WASHINGTON BIRTHPLACE NATIONAL MONUMENT

ASH LAWN-HIGHLAND

MONTICELLO, THE HOME OF THOMAS JEFFERSON

THOMAS JEFFERSON'S POPLAR FOREST

TUCKAHOE PLANTATION

BERKELEY PLANTATION

SHERWOOD FOREST PLANTATION

Winchester
Leesburg
Middletown
522
Arlington
Warrenton
Alexandria
NewMarket
Manassas
11
Stafford
Fredericksburg
33
Montpelier Station
Oak Grove
Spotsylvania
Stratford
250
Staunton
Charlottesville
522
Guinea
301
81
64
Lexington
29
15
220
Forest
Lynchburg
Richmond
17
13
Roanoke
460
Appomattox
360
Charles City
City Point
Tazewell
460
Petersburg
11
Smithfield
Fort Monroe
Marion
221
220
Newport News
21
1
Portsmouth

0   100 Miles

0   100 KM

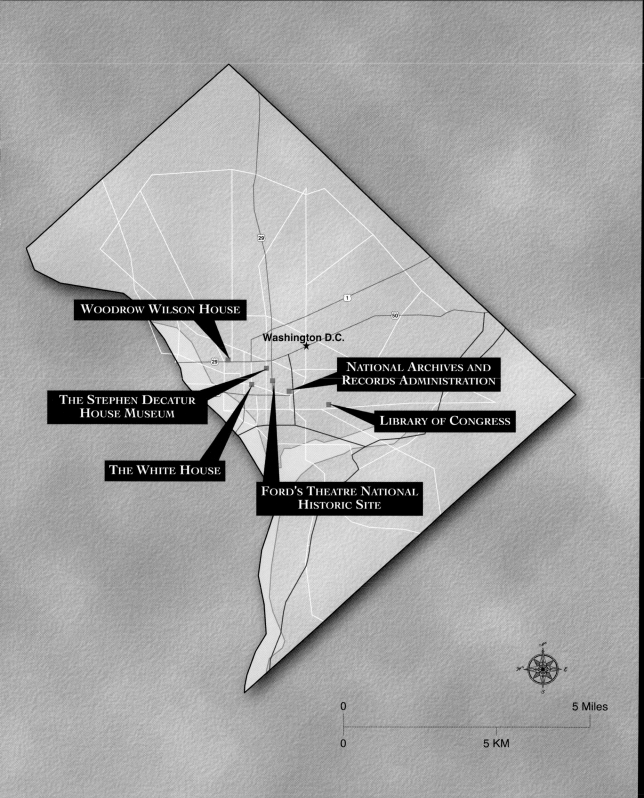

WOODROW WILSON HOUSE

Washington D.C.

NATIONAL ARCHIVES AND
RECORDS ADMINISTRATION

THE STEPHEN DECATUR
HOUSE MUSEUM

LIBRARY OF CONGRESS

THE WHITE HOUSE

FORD'S THEATRE NATIONAL
HISTORIC SITE

0   5 Miles

0   5 KM

PRESIDENTS, VICE PRESIDENTS, AND FIRST LADIES

GEORGE WASHINGTON
1st President 1789–1797

Born February 22, 1732, Westmoreland County, Virginia
Died December 14, 1799, Mount Vernon, Virginia
Vice President: John Adams
First Lady: Martha Dandridge Custis Washington

JOHN ADAMS
2nd President 1797–1801

Born October 30, 1735, Braintree (now Quincy), Massachusetts
Died July 4, 1826, Quincy, Massachusetts
Vice President: Thomas Jefferson
First Lady: Abigail Smith Adams

THOMAS JEFFERSON
3rd President 1801–1809

Born April 13, 1743, Albemarle County, Virginia
Died July 4, 1826, Charlottesville, Virginia
Vice President: Aaron Burr (1801–1804); George Clinton (1804–1809)
First Lady: None
Wife: Martha Wayles Skelton Jefferson, died 1782

JAMES MADISON
4th President 1809–1817

Born March 16, 1751, King George County (now Orange County), Virginia
Died June 28, 1836, Montpelier, Virginia
Vice President: George Clinton (1809–1813); Elbridge Gerry (1813–1817)
First Lady: Dolley Payne Madison

JAMES MONROE
5th President 1817–1825

Born April 28, 1758, Westmoreland County, Virginia
Died July 4, 1831, New York, New York
Vice President: Daniel D. Tompkins
First Lady: Elizabeth Kortright Monroe

JOHN QUINCY ADAMS
6th President 1825–1829

Born July 11, 1767, Braintree (now Quincy), Massachusetts
Died February 23, 1848, Washington, D.C.
Vice President: John C. Calhoun
First Lady: Louisa Johnson Adams

ANDREW JACKSON
7th President 1829–1837

Born March 15, 1767, The Waxhaws, South Carolina
Died June 8, 1845, Nashville, Tennessee
Vice President: John C. Calhoun (1829–1832); Martin Van Buren (1832–1837)
First Lady: None
Wife: Rachel Donelson Robards Jackson, died 1828

MARTIN VAN BUREN   *8th President 1837–1841*

Born December 5, 1782, Kinderhook, New York
Died July 24, 1862, Kinderhook, New York
Vice President: Richard M. Johnson
First Lady: Angelica Van Buren (daughter-in-law)
Wife: Hannah Hoes Van Buren, died 1819

WILLIAM HENRY HARRISON   *9th President 1841*

Born February 9, 1773, Berkeley, Virginia
Died April 4, 1841, Washington, D.C.
Vice President: John Tyler
First Lady: Anna Tuthill Symmes Harrison

JOHN TYLER   *10th President 1841–1845*

Born March 29, 1790, Charles City County, Virginia
Died January 18, 1862, Richmond, Virginia
Vice President: None
First Lady: Letitia Christian Tyler, died 1842
First Lady: Julia Gardiner Tyler, married 1844

JAMES K. POLK   *11th President 1845–1849*

Born November 2, 1795, Mecklenburg County, North Carolina
Died June 15, 1849, Nashville, Tennessee
Vice President: George M. Dallas
First Lady: Sarah Childress Polk

ZACHARY TAYLOR   *12th President 1849–1850*

Born November 24, 1784, Orange County, Virginia
Died July 9, 1850, Washington, D.C.
Vice President: Millard Fillmore
First Lady: Margaret Mackall Smith Taylor

MILLARD FILLMORE   *13th President 1850–1853*

Born January 7, 1800, Cayuga County, New York
Died March 8, 1874, Buffalo, New York
Vice President: None
First Lady: Abigail Powers Fillmore

FRANKLIN PIERCE   *14th President 1853–1857*

Born November 23, 1804, Hillsborough, New Hampshire
Died October 8, 1869, Concord, New Hampshire
Vice President: William R. King (1853), died April 18, 1853
First Lady: Jane Means Appleton Pierce

JAMES BUCHANAN   *15th President 1857–1861*

Born April 23, 1791, Cove Gap, Pennsylvania
Died June 1, 1868, Lancaster, Pennsylvania
Vice President: John C. Breckinridge
First Lady: Harriet Lane (niece)

ABRAHAM LINCOLN   *16th President 1861–1865*

Born February 12, 1809, Hardin County, Kentucky
Died April 15, 1865, Washington, D.C.
Vice President: Hannibal Hamlin (1861–1865); Andrew Johnson (1865)
First Lady: Mary Todd Lincoln

ANDREW JOHNSON   *17th President 1865–1869*

Born December 29, 1808, Raleigh, North Carolina
Died July 31, 1875, Carter County, Tennessee
Vice President: None
First Lady: Eliza McCardle Johnson

ULYSSES S. GRANT   *18th President 1869–1877*

Born April 27, 1822, Point Pleasant, Ohio
Died July 23, 1885, Mount McGregor, New York
Vice President: Schuyler Colfax (1869–1873); Henry Wilson (1873–1875), died 1875
First Lady: Julia Boggs Dent Grant

RUTHERFORD B. HAYES   *19th President 1877–1881*

Born October 4, 1822, Delaware, Ohio
Died January 17, 1893, Fremont, Ohio
Vice President: William A. Wheeler
First Lady: Lucy Webb Hayes

JAMES A. GARFIELD   *20th President 1881*

Born November 19, 1831, Orange Township, Ohio
Died September 19, 1881, Elberon, New Jersey
Vice President: Chester A. Arthur
First Lady: Lucretia Rudolph Garfield

CHESTER A. ARTHUR   *21st President 1881–1885*

Born October 5, 1829, North Fairfield, Vermont
Died November 18, 1886, New York, New York
Vice President: None
First Lady: None
Wife: Ellen "Nell" Lewis Herndon Arthur, died 1880

GROVER CLEVELAND   *22nd President 1885–1889*

Born March 18, 1837, Caldwell, New Jersey
Died June 24, 1908, Princeton, New Jersey
Vice President: Thomas A. Hendricks (1885)
First Lady: Frances Folsom Cleveland

BENJAMIN HARRISON   *23rd President 1889–1893*

Born August 20, 1833, North Bend, Ohio
Died March 13, 1901, Indianapolis, Indiana
Vice President: Levi P. Morton
First Lady: Caroline Scott Harrison

GROVER CLEVELAND   *24th President 1893–1897*

Born March 18, 1837, Caldwell, New Jersey
Died June 24, 1908, Princeton, New Jersey
Vice President: Adlai E. Stevenson
First Lady: Frances Folsom Cleveland

WILLIAM MCKINLEY   *25th President 1897–1901*

Born January 29, 1843, Niles, Ohio
Died September 14, 1901, Buffalo, New York
Vice President: Garret A. Hobart (1897–1901); Theodore Roosevelt (1901)
First Lady: Ida Saxton McKinley

THEODORE ROOSEVELT   *26th President 1901–1909*

Born October 27, 1858, New York, New York
Died January 6, 1919, Oyster Bay, New York
Vice President: Charles W. Fairbanks (1905–1909)
First Lady: Edith Kermit Carow Roosevelt

WILLIAM HOWARD TAFT   *27th President 1909–1913*

Born September 15, 1857, Cincinnati, Ohio
Died March 8, 1930, Washington, D.C.
Vice President: James S. Sherman
First Lady: Helen "Nellie" Herron Taft

WOODROW WILSON   *28th President 1913–1921*

Born December 28, 1856, Staunton, Virginia
Died February 3, 1924, Washington, D.C.
Vice President: Thomas R. Marshall
First Lady: Ellen Louise Axson Wilson, died 1914
First Lady: Edith Bolling Galt Wilson, married 1915

WARREN G. HARDING   *29th President 1921–1923*

Born November 2, 1865, Bloomington Grove, Ohio
Died August 2, 1923, San Francisco, California
Vice President: Calvin Coolidge
First Lady: Florence Kling Harding

CALVIN COOLIDGE   *30th President 1923–1929*

Born July 4, 1872, Plymouth Notch, Vermont
Died January 5, 1933, Northampton, Massachusetts
Vice President: Charles G. Dawes (1925–1929)
First Lady: Grace Goodue Coolidge

HERBERT HOOVER   *31st President 1929–1933*

Born August 10, 1874, West Branch, Iowa
Died October 20, 1964, New York, New York
Vice President: Charles Curtis
First Lady: Lou Henry Hoover

FRANKLIN DELANO ROOSEVELT *32nd President 1933–1945*

Born January 30, 1882, Hyde Park, New York
Died April 12, 1945, Warm Springs, Georgia
Vice President: John Nance Garner (1933–1941); Henry Wallace (1941–1945);
Harry S Truman (1945)
First Lady: Eleanor Roosevelt

HARRY S TRUMAN *33rd President 1945–1953*

Born May 8, 1884, Lamar, Missouri
Died December 26, 1972, Kansas City, Missouri
Vice President: Alben W. Barkley (1949–1953)
First Lady: Elizabeth "Bess" Virginia Wallace Truman

DWIGHT D. EISENHOWER *34th President 1953–1961*

Born October 14, 1890, Denison, Texas
Died March 28, 1969, Washington, D.C.
Vice President: Richard M. Nixon
First Lady: Marie "Mamie" Geneva Doud Eisenhower

JOHN F. KENNEDY *35th President 1961–1963*

Born May 29, 1917, Brookline, Massachusetts
Died November 22, 1963, Dallas, Texas
Vice President: Lyndon Baines Johnson
First Lady: Jacqueline Lee Bouvier Kennedy

LYNDON B. JOHNSON *36th President 1963–1969*

Born August 27, 1908, Johnson City, Texas
Died January 22, 1973, San Antonio, Texas
Vice President: Hubert Horatio Humphrey (1964–1969)
First Lady: Claudia "Lady Bird" Alta Taylor Johnson

RICHARD M. NIXON *37th President 1969–1974*

Born January 9, 1913, Yorba Linda, California
Died April 22, 1994, New York, New York
Vice President: Spiro T. Agnew (1968–1973); Gerald R. Ford (1973–1974)
First Lady: Thelma Catherine "Pat" Ryan Nixon

GERALD R. FORD *38th President 1974–1977*

Born July 14, 1913, Omaha, Nebraska
Vice President: Nelson A. Rockefeller (1974–1977)
First Lady: Elizabeth Ann "Betty" Bloomer Ford

JIMMY CARTER *39th President 1977–1981*

Born October 1, 1924, Plains, Georgia
Vice President: Walter F. Mondale
First Lady: Eleanor Rosalynn Smith Carter

RONALD REAGAN
40th President 1981–1989

Born February 6, 1911, Tampico, Illinois
Vice President: George H. W. Bush
First Lady: Nancy Davis Reagan

GEORGE H. W. BUSH
41st President 1989–1993

Born June 12, 1924, Milton, Massachusetts
Vice President: J. Danforth Quayle
First Lady: Barbara Pierce Bush

WILLIAM JEFFERSON CLINTON
42nd President 1993–2001

Born August 19, 1946, Hope, Arkansas
Vice President: Albert Gore
First Lady: Hillary Rodham Clinton

GEORGE W. BUSH
43rd President 2001–

Born July 6, 1946, New Haven, Connecticut
Vice President: Richard Cheney
First Lady: Laura Welch Bush

SITE INDEX

GEOGRAPHICAL INDEX

INDEX

PHOTO CREDITS

Pages 9, 11, 12, 13, Mount Vernon Ladies' Association; page 14, Stan George/National Park Service; page 16, Dan Fitzpatrick/George Washington's Fredericksburg Foundation; page 17, Superstock; page 19, 20, Adams National Historical Park/National Park Service/Department of the Interior; page 21, White House Historical Association—portrait by Rembrandt Peale; page 23, Monticello/Thomas Jefferson Foundation, Inc.; page 25, Les Schafer/Thomas Jefferson's Poplar Forest; page 27, Superstock; page 29, Superstock; page 30, Michael Remorenko/James Madison's Montpelier; page 31, Superstock; page 33 (top), Phillip Beaurline/Ash Lawn-Highland, (bottom), C. Harrison Conroy Co./Ash Lawn-Highland; page 34, City of Fredericksburg; page 35, Superstock; page 37, Alan D. Briere/Superstock; page 39, 41, 42, The Hermitage; page 44, Getty Images; page 46, Martin Van Buren National Historic Site; page 47, John Harrington/Decatur House; page 48, H. Armstrong Roberts; page 50, Berkeley Plantation; page 51, Grouseland Foundation, Inc.; page 52 Getty Images; page 54, Greg Hadley/Sherwood Forest Plantation; page 56, Superstock; page 58, James K. Polk Memorial; page 59, James K. Polk Ancestral Home, Columbia, Tennessee; page 60, Getty Images; page 62, Getty Images; page 65, Jeff Gnass Photography; page 66, Superstock; page 68, Hillsborough Historical Society; page 69, The Pierce Brigade; page 70, Superstock; page 72, James Buchanan Foundation; page 74, Superstock; page 76, Abraham Lincoln Birthplace National Historic Site; page 77, Kentucky Department of Travel; page 78, Lincoln Boyhood National Memorial/National Park Service; page 79, 80, Lincoln Home National Historic Site/National Park Service; page 81, 82 (top), Illinois Historic Preservation Agency; page 82 (bottom), Lincoln College Museum; page 83, Abraham Lincoln Library and Museum; page 84, 85, The Lincoln Museum, Fort Wayne, Indiana; page 86, Carol M. Highsmith/Parks and History Association; page 88, Superstock; page 91, Tusculum College Department of Museum Program and Studies; page 92, Mordecai Historic Park; page 93, H. Armstrong Roberts; page 95, Ulysses S. Grant National Historic Site/National Park Service; page 97, 98, U.S. Grant Home; page 99, Friends of the Ulysses S. Grant Cottage, Inc.; page 101, Superstock; page 103, 104, Rutherford B. Hayes Presidential Center; page 105, Superstock; page 108, Getty Images; page 110, Vermont Division for Historic Preservation; page 111, Getty Images; page 114, Superstock; page 116, 117, President Benjamin Harrison Home; page 118, Getty Images; page 120, McKinley Memorial Library; page 121, Superstock; page 124, Superstock; page 125, 127, William H. Taft National Historic Site/National Park Service; page 128, Getty Images; page 130, 131, Tommy Thompson/Woodrow Wilson Birthplace; page 132, Erick Montgomery/Historic Augusta, Inc.; page 133, Bill Barley & Assoc., Inc.; page 134, Woodrow Wilson House; page 135, Getty Images; page 138, Vermont Division for Historic Preservation—portrait by Herman Hanatschek; page 140, Johnson's Photography; page 142, Harris and Ewing/Herbert Hoover Presidential Museum; page 144, 145, Herbert Hoover National Historic Site/National Park Service; page 146, Herbert Hoover Library; page 147, Superstock; page 149, Superstock; page 151 (top), Roosevelt Campobello International Park; page 151 (bottom), Michael Wood/Roosevelt Campobello International Park; page 152, Superstock; page 154, Georgia Department of Natural Resources; page 156, Superstock; page 158, B. Hoduski/Harry S Truman National Historic Site; page 159, Jeff Wade/National Park Service; page 160 (top), Truman Presidential Library & Museum; page 160 (bottom), Harry S Truman Birthplace State Historic Site; page 161, Historic Tours of America; page 162, Superstock; page 164, 165, Dwight D. Eisenhower Library; page 166, Eisenhower National Historic Site; page 167, Eisenhower Birthplace State Historical Site; page 168, Superstock; page 170, Superstock; page 171, H. Armstrong Roberts; page 173, Bret St. Clair/The Sixth Floor Museum at Dealey Plaza; page 174, Superstock; page 176, Lyndon B. Johnson National Historical Park/National Park Service; page 179, Lyndon Baines Johnson Library and Museum; page 180, Getty Images; page 182, 183, Richard Nixon Library; page 184, Getty Images; page 187, International Stock; page 188, White House Historical Association—portrait by Herbert E. Abrams; page 190, Jeff Gnass Photography; page 192, Jimmy Carter Library and Museum; page 193, Getty Images/American Stock Photos; page 195, 196, The Reagan Foundation; page 197, Lloyd McElhiney/Ronald Reagan Birthplace; page 198, Reagan Boyhood Home; page 199, Eureka College, College Relations; page 200, Getty Images; page 202, 203, George Bush Presidential Library and Museum; page 204, Superstock; page 207, Wanda Powell/Bill Clinton Birthplace Foundation; page 208, George W. Bush Campaign Headquarters; page 210, Superstock; page 212, H. Armstrong Roberts; page 214, Washington, D.C., Convention & Visitors Bureau; page 216, Carol M. Highsmith/Parks and History Association; page 217, Washington, D.C., Convention & Visitors Bureau.